RIGHT ON
THE EDGE
OF CRAZY

On Tour With

RIGHT ON

the U.S. Downhill

THE EDGE

Ski Team

OF CRAZY

Mike Wilson ==

TIMES 𝕿 BOOKS

RANDOM HOUSE

Library of Congress Cataloging-in-Publication Data
Wilson, Mike.
   Right on the edge of crazy : on tour with the U.S. downhill ski
team / Mike Wilson.
       p.   cm.
   ISBN 0-8129-2144-5
   1. United States Ski Team. I. Title.
GV854.4.W55 1993
796.93—dc20   92-50503

Manufactured in the United States of America
9 8 7 6 5 4 3 2
FIRST EDITION

For my father,

who taught me

to ski

Contents

Contents

RIGHT ON
THE EDGE
OF CRAZY

1

Whoops

Val d'Isère, France. A cool, sunny morning in December 1990.

Bill Hudson, racer number forty-six, lunged out of the starting shack, pushed himself frantically downhill with his ski poles and settled into a tuck, poles wrapped around him, fists forward to deflect the wind. This was it, the event he had been waiting for, the first World Cup downhill race of the new season. Before him stretched the narrow race course, bordered by bright red gates sprouting from the snow like tulips. Hudson's long, heavy downhill skis clattered as he gained speed. Soon he was doing fifty, sixty, then seventy miles an hour, nothing but his skin-tight suit between him and the snow. But not even seventy was fast enough, not for him. It was time to go for it. Time, as he and his teammates liked to say, to "punch it."

Punch it, yes, but stay in control. That was important. As he speeded down the hill, the racer had two words in his mind: Controlled aggression. His coach, Bill Egan, had coined the term. For Hudson, being aggressive was easy. His approach to downhill ski racing—his approach to everything—was simply to go like hell. He had never seen a hill steep enough, a jump big enough, a turn sharp enough, to scare him. Once, in Kitzbühel, Austria, one of his skis fell off just as he shot off the crest of a huge jump. He flew more than one hundred feet, landed on one foot, and managed to ski to a stop. The TV people broadcast the feat all over Europe that night. Punch it? He always punched it.

But in downhill, you couldn't just point your skis down the mountain and expect to finish standing up. You had to shoot like a bullet through the air, land smoothly, stay in your tuck, time your turns perfectly, *think*. You couldn't win a downhill race if you didn't think. Well, Bill Hudson was thinking now. Controlled aggression, he told himself. Controlled aggression.

Hudson skied well on the top half of the course. He had never felt so confident. He felt as if his skis were extensions of his feet, as if he had been born wearing them. And these skis weren't even his! Hudson had borrowed them from Patrick Ortlieb, an Austrian racer who, like Bill, was sponsored by Head skis. Ortlieb was skiing well and Bill thought the skis might be partly responsible. Bill's boots were too small for the bindings, so he had screwed a piece of hard plastic onto the heels to make them fit. Jury-rigging your boots was risky—if the plastic came loose in a turn, Hudson was a goner—but he didn't care about that now. He was flying. Had been all week. Hudson's world ranking was in the forties, so he might have been expected to finish in the forties in this race. But in training runs earlier in the week, he had finished eighth and seventeenth. The training runs didn't count for anything, but Hudson knew he could do just as well, if not better, today. I can beat these guys, he told himself. Controlled aggression, that's all I need. And he was right. Hudson would not know it until much later, when he checked the time sheets, but as he began the last twenty seconds of the two-minute run, he was in eleventh place. He was having one of his best races ever.

He soared off the tunnel jump, landed, and turned left, the edge of his right ski gripping the ice, his left leg skimming along beneath him. The hill fell away quickly as he entered the section known as the compression, a deep, wide hole followed by a jump. Skiing through a compression—lots of downhill courses had them—was something like bouncing on a trampoline: You plummeted downward, used your knees as shock absorbers at the bottom, and then sprang out, weightless. The trick was to come out without going too high in the air. When the racers landed, they had to make a left turn, then a quick right; their momentum in the second turn carried them out to a long, padded fence. This was at seventy miles an hour. Some guys got close enough to the fence to touch their elbows to it. Others got closer than that. Earlier that day, Italian racer Pietro Vitalini had caught his ski tip in the plastic sheets that covered the padded fence. His feet were ripped from his bindings and he was sent spinning down the course, a human helicopter rotor. When he stopped twirling, he got up and walked away. Lucky guy. People who screwed up in the compression usually didn't walk away.

As he dropped into the bottom of the hole, Hudson said to himself, Find the right line. If he was going to make a smooth turn after the compression, he had to be heading in the right direction when he came out of it. Too far in one direction and he'd lose time. Too far in the other and he'd cream the fence. Find the line, he told himself, find the line. His aim was perfect when he came out of the hole, but there was a problem: He was six feet in the air when he wanted to be on the ground.

Hudson had been so intent on finding the right line that he hadn't even tried to stay low off the jump. You could say he just kind of forgot. This was bad. Some of the other racers had zipped through here without putting so much as an inch between the snow and the bottoms of their skis. But not Bill Hudson. He was soaring through the air like some kind of freaked-out bird, his knees bent and his arms flapping and his eyes the size of manhole covers. As he soared, the young man in the green skin-tight racing suit said something to himself, something any athlete in this situation might have said.

Bill Hudson, six feet high and racing toward disaster, said: Whoops.

Hudson was twenty-four years old that winter. He was a member of the United States Ski Team. Lots of people assumed the men and women of the U.S. Ski Team competed only once every four years, in the Olympics, but that wasn't so. They raced in World Cup events all winter, every winter. The World Cup circuit, also known as the White Circus, was to ski racing what the PGA Tour was to professional golf: Each week, the athletes went to a new place, practiced for a while, competed, and then moved on. Skiing on the World Cup tour was Bill Hudson's life, his career.

To understand him, you have to understand skiing. Hudson was not a slalom racer. In slalom, the skier dances through a tight series of gates, cha cha cha, pushing them aside as he goes. Top speed is about twenty-five miles an hour. If he falls, maybe he blows out his knee. More likely, he stands up, dusts himself off, and goes home. No big deal. Hudson wasn't a giant slalom specialist, either. Giant slalom is a longer version of slalom. The people who compete in it are marvelous athletes, great athletes, but a GS specialist isn't going to approach the speed of a sports car on the interstate highway. Slalom and giant slalom are known in the ski world as the technical events. Competing in them is considered fun, healthy, reasonably safe. Normal.

Bill Hudson was not normal. He was a downhiller.

Downhill is fast, sexy, perilous. Downhill racers go like hell from the top of the mountain to the bottom, sometimes at eighty miles an hour, frequently out of control. They think nothing of going off a jump and flying one hundred and fifty feet, or of making sharp, high-speed turns on solid ice. When they crash—they call it crashing, not falling, and if you have ever seen a crash you know why—they often get hurt so badly that they have to be zipped to the hospital in a helicopter. People have died in downhill races. But Bill Hudson never thought about dying (or getting paralyzed, or breaking his legs, or cracking his skull), because thinking about it might get in the way of a good time. And to Bill, downhill racing was indeed a good time, the most fun he could possibly have.

Bill and his teammates competed in the so-called speed events—the downhill and the super giant slalom, or super G, a longer, much faster version of the giant slalom. They couldn't understand why everybody didn't. The American speed-event skiers (there were four to eight of them on the tour at any given time) saw the technical events the way jet fighter pilots see riding tricycles. They were pretty hard on the technical skiers: When they talked about slalom and giant slalom specialists, they often used words like "ovaries." They were half-kidding—some of the American downhillers enjoyed the technical events, and they all had close friends on the technical team—but they were also half-serious. The downhillers regarded themselves as real men, studs, the fighter pilots of the ski world. AJ Kitt went so far as to paint this saying, well known among racers, on his crash helmet: "Sl and GS are events. DH is a cult." The downhillers knew the cult could hurt them, but they tried not to think about that.

It wasn't that Hudson and his teammates did not care about their own safety. They did. But probably they did not care as much as other people do. Imagine a lunatic driver who pushes his rustbucket Chevy to one hundred fifteen miles an hour on a narrow country road and then cackles, "Let's see what this baby will really do." Well, the downhillers thought that way about their bodies. *Let's see what this baby will really do.*

Some people, having seen the sharp teeth of danger, turn away and never look back. Bill Hudson did the opposite. Every time he had an accident that didn't kill him, he took it as evidence—not proof, just evidence—that an accident couldn't kill him. He then proceeded to have another one just to make sure he was right. His adventures, both on skis and off, were legend. Once, he bungee-jumped off a railroad trestle in the middle of the night—tied a big rubber band to his foot and jumped off a bridge several hundred feet high. When he stopped boinging around and was hoisted back onto the bridge, he pronounced the experience "OK." Another time, he borrowed another racer's parasail—a cross between a parachute and a hang-glider—and, unburdened by any knowledge of how to use it, nearly slammed into the side of a barn. He later crash-landed in the street, wearing skis.

His teammates couldn't decide which one of his ski stories they liked best. Some preferred the one about the time Bill skied off a race course and into a twenty-foot-deep crevice (he had to be hauled out on the end of a rope), while others liked to tell about the day he skied off a cliff in Alaska (he ended up sort of wrapped around a tree). By the winter of 1990 it was hard to get Bill to tell these stories anymore, partly because he was tired of telling them, and partly because he understood that when somebody did it for him, he came off as much more of a mythical hero. Yes, Bill and his teammates did unsafe things because they honestly liked to, but also because they had images to maintain. They were role models for kids who hoped to grow up to be reckless.

Their concern for their images was apparent in a feature story an American television crew had done just before the World Cup race in Val d'Isère that December. The segment, broadcast all over America, referred to four of the skiers—Hudson, AJ Kitt, Tommy Moe, and Jeff Olson—as "America's Young Guns." The athletes were shown hanging around the streets of Park City, Utah, the home of the U.S. Ski Team, hooking their thumbs in the pockets of their jeans, wearing mirror sunglasses, and sneering like flyboys. Jeff Olson was quoted as saying, "We do everything to extremes. We work hard, we play hard, we train hard, and we ski hard."

And, as Bill Hudson would demonstrate in Val d'Isère, they also fell hard.

Whoops.

Hudson was in the air now, his arms flapping and his heart thudding. He made a clean landing, but by the time he touched snow he was much farther down the hill than he wanted to be. To get through this section he would have to make a couple of quick turns, first left and then right, like stepping out of a speeding car and doing a tap dance. He made the left turn all right, but when he shifted his weight to make the right turn his skis came out from under him and he fell, whack, on his side. That was the last thing Hudson would remember—skidding along on his side, toward the tall, orange, padded fence. His skis hit the fence first. Then his legs, upper body, and head whiplashed into it too. He slid limply a few yards down the hill and came to a stop lying on his side, unconscious.

At the top of the hill, Coach Bill Egan heard a scratchy voice through his radio. It belonged to Ueli Luthi, the Swiss-born head coach of the American men's team. He had been standing on the side of the course, near the compression, when Hudson fell. Now he was skiing to where Hudson lay.

"Hang on," Luthi said, "Huddy's down."

Egan never knew what those words meant. He always stayed at the top of the course during races so he could give his athletes a rubdown and a final word of encouragement before they took off. Ten seconds into the course, the racers skied out of sight for good. So when someone fell, all Egan ever heard was a crackling voice saying, "He's down." Did that mean the guy had tipped over and skidded to a stop? Or had he punched a hole in a snow fence and vanished into the woods? Egan was especially concerned this time because it was Hudson who had fallen. Egan liked all of his racers—he called them "the kids," his kids—but he and Hudson had always been particularly close. Egan clomped a few yards up the hill and grabbed his skis just in case he was needed at the bottom. He kept listening for Luthi's voice, but he heard nothing. He could only wait.

Dr. Courtney Brown, a back specialist from Lakewood, Colorado, was near the top of the course when Hudson fell. The U.S. Ski Team paid to have a doctor with the downhillers at every race, and this was Brown's turn in the rotation. Brown, who had been tending to downhill racers for eighteen years, was standing near a jump only twenty seconds into the course. He'd had a race doctor's adage in mind when he positioned himself there: Always ski down to trouble. The doctors never wanted to be below the site of a crash because then they would have to walk uphill or take a lift to get to the injured racer. That would take too long. Just after Hudson fell, a couple of coaches standing nearby shouted, "Courtney, go!" Brown stepped into his skis and glided quickly and expertly down the course, carrying a small bag with a stethoscope and an airway. Oh, shit, he thought. I hope he's not too bad.

By the time Brown reached the bottom, Hudson was sitting up, mumbling to Ueli Luthi and some guys from the ski patrol. The racer, still wearing his helmet, was bleeding from small cuts in his lips. Brown looked into his eyes; the pupils were equal, a good sign. Bill said his left knee hurt him, and he thought he had done something to his shoulder. But mostly he seemed concerned about his teeth. He kept putting his fingers to his front teeth and saying, "Are my teeth all right? How are my teeth?" Bill's teeth were important to him. They were full and white and perfectly straight; he flossed them every day, sometimes in the team van as it rolled toward some new destination. The smile was the focal point of a decidedly handsome face, a face so memorable that the ski team media guide described Bill as having "matinee idol looks." (His teammates saw the description, of course, and made sure he never lived it down.) In truth, it was a fair description. Hudson had blue eyes and broad shoulders and a narrow, aristocratic nose and, of course, very nice teeth. He was, all in all, the kind of man women notice, the kind of man women talk about in a way that makes other men sullen and quiet. So yes, he valued his teeth quite a bit, but at that moment Courtney Brown got the impression that he was asking about them not out of vanity, but because he had just whacked his noggin and was trying, in a kooky, half-conscious way, to make conversation.

The doctor, the coach, and the ski patrol people tried to lead him off the course, but Bill wanted to walk back up the hill, toward the compression. It didn't make sense. Maybe he wanted to climb up and give the jump another go. Who could tell? Brown was tugging him sideways across the hill and Hudson kept pointing up the slope saying, "Let's go up there."

Finally, the doctor coaxed him into a ski patrol sled. The sled was equipped with a long, narrow beanbag that supported Bill's body as he lay. As the patrolman skied him down the hill, Bill kept lifting his head and saying, "What about my teeth, Courtney? Are my teeth all right?"

"Keep your head down. Relax," the doctor said. He was afraid Bill would stir and tip over the sled, and then Courtney would have to contend with a second series of injuries.

The whole scene reminded Courtney Brown of an experience he had had years earlier. It was 1976, weeks before the Winter Olympics in Innsbruck, Austria, and he was tending to the Canadian and American downhill teams at a race in Wengen, Switzerland. (By 1990, the North American teams always had their own doctors with them, but in those days they shared one.) Brown was standing near the top of the course when he got word that a talented Canadian racer named Dave Irwin had flown off a jump, landed hard, lost control, gone off the course, tumbled over a railroad track, and stopped in a field of downy, waist-deep snow. The doctor arrived to find Irwin unconscious, his face a road map of shallow cuts and his tongue extending backward down his throat. When the chopper arrived, Brown and the ski patrol guys hoisted the limp racer through the side door—only to discover that the helicopter wasn't big enough for the stretcher. No matter how they positioned the thing inside, they couldn't close the door. After a moment of fidgeting, Brown decided he couldn't wait any longer. Irwin was a mess; he had to get him to the hospital. Brown and the ski patrolmen climbed inside and, with the door still open, turned to the pilot and gave the thumbs-up sign.

The chopper was more than one thousand feet above the jagged, icy Swiss Alps when Irwin woke up. He came to abruptly, as if reacting to the sound of a loud alarm clock only he could hear. Without warning he sat bolt upright, an expression on his face that said, "What? Where?" Brown had no time to explain. Irwin's sudden movement upset the chopper's balance—made it tip to one side the way a rowboat does when someone leans out to net a fish. When the chopper tipped, Irwin's stretcher, a classy model with well-lubricated wheels, began to roll toward the open door. Brown gasped. His patient, a badly injured young man, a fellow he was supposed to be helping, was about to catch the ultimate air. Brown, sitting near the open door, desperately stuck out a leg. The stretcher kept rolling. At the last instant, just as Dave Irwin was about to go weightless for the last time, Brown managed to jam his ski boot between the wheel of the stretcher and the helicopter strut. Suddenly, the stretcher stopped moving, and Irwin was saved.

Now, in Val d'Isère in 1990, Brown had another patient with a knot on his head, another kid who wouldn't lie still in the stretcher. Brown, never a ski racer himself, really admired these kids, but God, they could do a number on themselves. Bill Hudson had, it seemed. At the bottom of the hill, the doctor slid the young man's groaning, immobilized body into the back of an ambulance for the ride into town.

At the doctor's office, Brown cut through Hudson's racing suit and examined his knee. The medial collateral ligament was loose, but not terribly so. An X-ray confirmed that the ligament was still fairly strong. Brown could say tentatively that Hudson would not need surgery, but the ski team doctor in Vail, Colorado, would have to make the final decision. Nor was Bill's skull fractured, as Brown had feared it might be. Brown diagnosed the injury as a serious concussion, and prescribed rest and small amounts of fluid. He sent Bill to bed with a big bucket, in case he felt like vomiting.

Before he left, the doctor gave Bill one last order: Stay off skis for a while. The two downhill races the next weekend in Val Gardena, Italy, were definitely out. The one in Garmisch, Germany, in early January probably was out, too. And the Hahnenkamm race in Kitzbühel, Austria, the oldest and most dangerous of the World Cup downhills, might not be such a good idea either. The truth was, Brown didn't know when Bill would race again. The young man had just endured a serious head injury; recovering was all that mattered.

That might have been how the doctor saw it, but Hudson saw it differently. As far as he was concerned, the most important thing—the only thing—was to race again. Racing was everything to him. He did it for kicks, did it for a living, did it in his dreams. Hudson, who started racing as soon as he could balance himself on a pair of skis, came from a skiing family. His mother, Sally Neidlinger Hudson, was an Olympic ski racer in 1952, and both of his older brothers had been racers (one was an All-America at the University of Colorado). But nobody in his family, not even his mother, had sacrificed as much for the sport as Bill had. He had left Dartmouth College after one year so he could join the U.S. Ski Team. He was an intelligent kid, smart enough to know he would only get one chance to compete with some of the greatest athletes on skis, so he took it. And he never regretted it, not for a second. He loved the speed and the danger. Skiing made him what he was—tough, glamorous, strong, a rebel against gravity. He had never won much; indeed, few people knew who Bill Hudson was. But he was sure that someday they would. To a young man anything seems possible, and Bill was a particularly brave and determined young man.

Or at least he had been. In the darkness of this creaky old Val d'Isère hospital, he didn't feel so optimistic. An hour before, he was a strapping young athlete flirting with greatness, an international matinee idol ski stud. Now he was just a scared kid with a volcanic headache and a barf bucket next to his mattress. No longer a tamer of the slopes, he lay hurt in the dark, thousands of miles from home, a lonely, moaning American in a country where, it seemed to him, nobody much cared about Americans. Bill Hudson had always tried not to doubt himself, but he was doubting himself now. What if I need surgery? he asked himself. Will I ever ski again? And if I do, will I ever ski as well as I did before? He tried to imagine life without ski racing, but he couldn't. Just couldn't. When he looked into the future he saw . . . nothing. The future was supposed to be ski racing, the World Cup circuit, the Olympics. Yes, the 1992 Olympics, here in Val d'Isère. Hudson was going to cruise into this town in February 1992, and he was going to prove something. He was going to ski brilliantly, the best he had ever skied. That had been the plan, anyway. Now it all seemed in doubt. Bill's whole life seemed in doubt.

The athlete was still lying in bed when his coach walked into the room. The moment Hudson saw Bill Egan, he began to cry. He never cried, never, but seeing his coach, his good friend, was too much. It was, he felt, all gone. The career, the Olympics, the dream, gone. Bill was gushing now, bawling into his hands. Egan moved toward him, a knot swelling in his throat.

The coach put his arms around the young man and held him as he wept.

2

Euro-Fever

The American men's downhill team did well in the World Cup race in Val d'Isère, France, in December 1990—if you didn't count the guy in the hospital. Two of Bill Hudson's teammates, Tommy Moe and Kyle Rasmussen, tied for fifteenth place that day. The last time two Americans had finished in the top fifteen in a World Cup downhill was February 1987, when Doug Lewis and Jeff Olson had finished seventh and fourteenth, respectively, in Furano, Japan. Now, after years of frustration, the Americans were competitive again in downhill. The results at Val d'Isère seemed to prove that they could ski with the best in the world, and they felt great about it. Sure, today fifteenth was their best finish. But maybe in the next race somebody would be tenth, or even fifth. Anything seemed possible.

Of course, the folks back home weren't going to pay any attention until the downhill team began to win a lot of races, and that wasn't about to happen. As hard as it was for Americans to accept, the U.S. was not a significant power in alpine ski racing. The Americans weren't as lowly as, say, the Chilean twins Nils and Dieter Linneberg, who rarely finished any higher than fiftieth, and who looked so much like the *Mad* magazine underworld characters that the American downhillers called them "Spy vs. Spy." But the American racers didn't get much more respect than the Chileans did. The real powers in racing were, and always had been, the Europeans—or, as the Americans called them, the Euros—especially the Swiss and the Austrians. The greatest racer of the 1980s, and maybe of all time, was Pirmin Zurbriggen, a Swiss, and the best overall racer on the World Cup circuit at the time Bill Hudson was crashing in Val d'Isère was Marc Girardelli, an Austrian who skied for Luxembourg. Franz Klammer, who dazzled the world with his downhill win in the 1976 Olympics (ABC Sports replayed the run dozens of times that winter), was Austrian, too. In talking about the greats, many people also mentioned a Swede, Ingemar Stenmark, and a Frenchman, Jean-Claude Killy. The American twins Phil and Steve Mahre, technical specialists who combined to win three Olympic medals in slalom in the 1980s, were also highly regarded. But everyone agreed the Euros were the best—not only in the downhill, but in alpine ski racing in general.

People in the ski world spent a lot of time arguing about why this was so, but almost everyone agreed on a couple of points. First, the Euros were at a big advantage because most World Cup races were held in Europe. The downhill ski racing season began each December with races in Val d'Isère, in Val Gardena, Italy, and, if there was time, in some other European ski resort. After the Christmas break, the circuit moved to Garmisch, Germany, Kitzbühel, Austria, and then, in late January, to Wengen, Switzerland. After a break for the Olympics or the Alpine World Championships, the downhill tour moved to North America for races in Aspen, Colorado, and someplace in Canada (the site changed almost every year). The season usually ended in March with a downhill in Scandinavia or Japan. For the Euros, then, almost every game was a home game. They trained on the European courses all the time; indeed, many of the racers grew up in the villages where the races were held. When they competed, they could be sure that thousands of their countrymen and countrywomen would be standing alongside the course, yodeling and getting drunk on schnapps or *Glühwein*. They knew, too, that the races would be televised live across Europe, and that the ski press would do its best to make them more famous and beloved than they already were. And if, during the racing season, they got homesick, they could hop on the autobahn and zip home for some bratwurst or linguine or whatever.

The Yanks were much less comfortable. When American tourists thought of Europe, they thought of lovely old buildings, fine wines, beautiful, rustic country, and strange and delightful currencies and languages. But for the American ski racers, who were not, after all, on vacation, Europe meant rickety old ski lifts, impossible mountain roads, and millions of smelly, pushy people, all of whom seemed, ugh, to smoke. The first thing the Americans got in Europe was a bad case of jet lag; it got worse from there. They often had to work out in hotel hallways because the ski team couldn't afford to take them to a fitness center. They had to wear their T-shirts and socks for three or four days because they couldn't get anybody to do their laundry for a reasonable price. They had to go without many other things that made them feel at home—American TV, magazines, English-language movies, bacon and eggs, French toast (they couldn't find it in France), peanut butter, American women, Heinz ketchup. Sometimes days went by before they learned the score of a big college or pro football game. They even had to sleep side by side in narrow double beds. (It felt strange at first, but after a while they got used to it.) They did like some things about Europe, especially Italian food, Austrian firecrackers, down comforters, the wood carvings on some of the buildings, high-speed driving, and the Alps. But as downhiller Steve Porino once said, the thing the racers definitely liked best about Europe was leaving it.

The Euros dominated ski racing for another, more significant reason: They cared more about the sport than the Americans did. In the United States, kids grew up playing a lot of sports. In the summer they wanted to be Nolan Ryan. In the fall they wanted to be Joe Montana. In the winter and spring, Michael Jordan. Very, very few wanted to be Marc Girardelli, or for that matter even knew who Marc Girardelli was. In European ski country, on the other hand, just about every kid hoped to be Girardelli.

Of course, American kids knew they could make a lot more money playing basketball or baseball than they could ski racing. In 1990, the World Cup tour was just beginning to award prize money, and it wasn't much—only a few thousand dollars to the winner of a race. Still, by endorsing products, some ski racers made a substantial living. They endorsed skis, boots, bindings, goggles, sunglasses, gloves, ski poles, ski resorts, and even some products that had nothing to do with skiing (a couple of racers had a deal with Rolex, the watch company). A few

Americans, including downhiller AJ Kitt, earned more than $100,000. The best-known racers in the world, people like Girardelli and Italy's Alberto Tomba, were paid hundreds of thousands of dollars a year for using, or saying they liked, certain things.

The one sure way an American ski racer could get really rich was to win an Olympic medal, preferably a gold one. And that was damned hard to do. Only one American man had ever won a medal in an Olympic downhill. His name was Bill Johnson, and he had won the gold in 1984, in what was then Sarajevo, Yugoslavia. Johnson had grown up near Bend, Oregon, skiing like a lunatic and getting drunk with his buddies. At sixteen he was arrested for swiping a car, but the judge let him off easy: He sent him to a ski racing academy. During the 1980 Olympics in Lake Placid, New York, when he was still unknown, he finagled an opportunity to take some practice runs on the downhill course. He skied so well that he was invited to join the U.S. Ski Team. In 1984 he found a slick pair of skis and won a race in Wengen, Switzerland, his first World Cup victory. Soon after, he predicted that he would win the Olympic gold medal. The Euros didn't like that at all. Johnson was so disliked on the circuit that Franz Klammer, the great Austrian downhiller, one of the greatest figures in the history of ski racing, referred to him as *Nasenbohrer*, or nose picker. But the nosepicker could ski: He went out and won the downhill, and before he knew it he was jetting into Los Angeles for a guest spot on the Carson show. Hollywood later turned the story into a TV movie, *The Bill Johnson Story*. Johnson was still living off his fame years later, as the resident famous person at Crested Butte ski resort in Colorado.

Bill Hudson and his teammates also dreamed of Olympic medals, and of cushy jobs when they retired. And yet some would never even get to the Olympic games. Of the eight men on the American team, only four would be chosen to race in the 1992 Olympic downhill in Albertville, France. In January 1992, the competition for those four spots would be ferocious. But that didn't matter just now. In December 1990, the American guys were still trying to figure out how to win World Cup races. The World Cup was what mattered. If they couldn't succeed in the White Circus, the downhillers would have to learn to live with themselves— well, not as losers, but as mortals. Regular guys. Which to them was the same thing as being losers.

*   *   *

Picture the top of a mountain. The peak is Mt. Mansfield, home of Stowe, one of the largest ski resorts in Vermont. It is sometime in the mid-1970s, and AJ Kitt, on vacation with his parents, has just coasted off the chair lift. AJ, six or seven years old, follows his dad, Ross, to the entrance of a run called Starr.

The resort has erected a large snow fence at the top of the hill, leaving only a small opening for people to ski onto the trail. Young AJ skis to the opening in the fence, stops, and looks down. What he sees is one of the steepest, nastiest ski runs in North America, a seemingly vertical white pitch studded with big, pointy moguls. If you fall on this slope, you won't stop bouncing and sliding until you get to the bottom, and somebody behind you will have to collect your poles and goggles and hat and carry them down to you. As AJ gazes into that white hole, that icy canyon, his father, an expert skier, stands next to him, wondering what he will do. AJ is a wild kid. Sometimes, when Ross Kitt rides his motorcycle, the boy sits in front of him on the seat and cries, "Faster, Daddy! Faster!" But the father really does not know what AJ will do now.

And then the little boy makes his choice. AJ Kitt, future racing star, future member of the U.S. Crazy-Ass Get-Out-of-My-Way Downhill Maniac Team, plants both poles in the snow and pushes himself . . . backward. He wants no part of Starr.

AJ Kitt always prided himself on thinking things through. He had as much nerve as the next downhiller, but unlike some other racers, he never took unnecessary risks. He was not the best athlete among the American downhillers, but he was easily the best racer. If you asked coach Bill Egan why it was so, he didn't say anything, but instead pointed to his head. AJ was smart.

The name on his birth certificate was Alva Ross Kitt IV, but he was never called Alva. His father, who went by the name Ross, once said, "We wanted him to have his own moniker. But you can't name a kid Alva Ross Kitt IV and call him David." So Ross and Nancy Kitt settled on AJ, without periods. The name didn't stand for anything; the Kitts just liked the sound of it. Nobody ever wanted to believe that. When AJ did well in a race, a reporter invariably would ask him what AJ stood for.

Kitt would always reply, "Nothin'."

"Nothin'?"

And AJ would say again, "Nothin'." And so on.

Kitt's teammates usually called him Alva (just to get on his nerves) or Al. If you asked them what AJ stood for, they had any number of witty answers. Sometimes they said "Alpine Jet," but only when they were feeling charitable. At other times they said the initials stood for "Albino Jamaican": AJ had skin the color of an eggshell and stiff, loopy brown hair that he kept trimmed close to the scalp. (His father had long since gone bald; it appeared that AJ was going to follow him.) Sometimes the other downhillers said AJ stood for "Arrogant Jerk." It was mostly a joke—the other guys liked AJ. He had a good sense of humor and a funny, high-pitched laugh; he was scrupulously honest and fair; he would always invite his teammates into his room when he was watching a movie on video (it wasn't unusual to walk into AJ's hotel room and find five or six athletes sprawled on the beds and on the floor, engrossed in a film); he respected people's privacy (a good quality to have when you're part of a traveling team); and he was a lot of fun to have a beer with. As AJ put it, "The fact that we're able to live together and still be good friends and not kill each other, I think, shows that we're close." And yet his teammates did not give him the name Arrogant Jerk for nothing. Reggie Crist, a young racer from Sun Valley, Idaho, recalled that he disliked AJ when he first met him; Kitt seemed to swagger instead of walk, brag instead of talk. Reggie remembered thinking, This guy's an asshole. He thinks he's the best guy out here and nobody can touch him. Only after he had known AJ for a while did Reggie change his mind about him. Other athletes noticed that, in team meetings, AJ was always the first to speak up when there was a controversy. Nobody had named him the team captain; he just assumed the role. AJ was aware that some people thought he was arrogant, but he preferred to think of himself as confident, sure that what he was doing was right for him.

An only child, he learned to ski when he was two years old. On weekends his parents served on the ski patrol at Frost Ridge, a gentle slope that adults could ski from top to bottom in less than a minute. (A rope tow was the only lift.) Soon the Kitts began spending weekends at Swain Ski Center, which was grand compared to Frost Ridge, but not compared to the mountains AJ would ski later. (Swain had a vertical drop of six hundred fifty feet. The Lauberhorn downhill course in Wengen, Switzerland, which as an adult AJ would complete in two minutes and thirty seconds, sometimes topping eighty miles an hour, had a vertical drop of three thousand, four hundred feet). AJ loved Swain. He and his pals bombed down the hill time after time, laughing, shrieking, and doing tricks in the air. They kept this up until the lifts closed. Sometimes Ross and Nancy would stop in a bar on the way home and their exhausted son would sleep on the pool table, if nobody was playing.

AJ joined Swain's junior racing program when he was still in grade school. Practices were held on Friday night (the slopes were lighted) and Saturday morning. Races were held on Sunday. Ski racing became part of AJ's childhood routine. He also enjoyed freestyle competition—mogul skiing and aerials—and he knew someday he would have to decide what kind of skier he wanted to be. That day came when he was about ten years old, when he was competing against two other kids for a chance to go to a regional freestyle meet. He danced happily down the hill, the tips of his skis jumping like a conductor's baton, but when he hit the last bump he made a bad mistake. He tumbled forward out of his skis, did a flip, and crossed the finish line on his face. He got up bawling, but the judges gave him a high score: They thought he had planned the whole thing. His prize was a trophy with a hot dog on top. But he passed up the regional meet; he wanted to be a racer.

Once, his father grabbed him before the start of a race and asked him a question.

"What are you going to do in the first turn?"

"I don't know," AJ said.

"Didn't you look at the course?"

"Yeah."

"How do you expect to do well if you don't study the course?"

AJ didn't have a clue.

His father said, "You've got fast feet. But there are a million people out there with fast feet. The people who win races are the ones with fast brains." From then on, AJ skied with his brains. By the time he entered junior high school, he was an accomplished racer.

About that time, AJ informed his parents that he planned to leave home soon to enroll in a ski academy—a high school for ski racers. He had outgrown the local junior racing programs; he needed more sophisticated coaching and felt he could get it only at a racing school. Nancy Kitt was stunned. She had always admired her son's independent streak, but this was too much.

"You're not leaving home at thirteen," she said.

"Yes I am," AJ said.

"Out of the question," Nancy said.

AJ entered the Mountain House School in Lake Placid, New York, when he was thirteen years old. He stayed for the winter term—the ski season—and then returned to his local high school to finish his freshman year. His skiing improved at the racing academy, but his grades suffered. At the beginning of his junior year he enrolled at the Green Mountain Valley School in Waitsfield, Vermont, which had an excellent academic reputation.

It was there that AJ became a downhiller. As a junior racer, he had competed only in slalom and giant slalom; downhill wasn't offered to kids. And at the Mountain House School, he had quit downhill in frustration because the races kept getting snowed out. "I told the coaches, 'I hate this. This is stupid,'" he would say later. But in his senior year at the Green Mountain Valley School, AJ got his hands on a pair of five-year-old Rossignol downhill skis that changed his attitude, and his life. Skis are funny. Seemingly identical pairs of skis have distinct characteristics and, some ski technicians believe, their own free will. A company can manufacture two pairs of downhill skis in exactly the same way, using precisely the same materials, and for reasons nobody fully understands, one pair will go fast and the other won't. Perhaps the most famous pair of skis in the history of racing were the ones Bill Johnson used to win the Olympic gold medal in Sarajevo. Years after his victory, he still kept them in his garage. They were fast, all right. Some cynical people argued that the skis, made by Atomic, had more to do with Johnson's victory than Johnson did. But everyone agreed they had magic in them. AJ's Rossignols did too. AJ, who, because of his cocky attitude, was known among some of his schoolmates as Big Head, won all but one of the downhills he entered in his senior year. He also finished fourth in the junior national championships, beating a lot of people on the U.S. Ski Team.

After graduation, AJ was accepted at the University of Colorado, his parents' alma mater, but he didn't go. Instead, he entered a postgraduate racing program designed by Kirk Dwyer, his coach at the Green Mountain Valley School. For a year, AJ and several other young men competed in races in Europe and North America. Halfway through that season, AJ skied in what he considered his first "real" downhill—a race at Nakiska, Alberta, Canada. The race was part of what was known as the Nor-Am tour, a minor-league version of the World Cup circuit. (Nor-Am was short for North American Trophy Series. Its equivalent in Europe was called the Europa Cup tour.) The Nakiska course was far steeper and scarier than anything he had skied in prep school. Leaving the starting gate was "like skiing down an elevator shaft," he said.

But AJ, who finished in the middle of the pack, was not cowed; he enjoyed the challenge. Sure, the course was dangerous. But it was also fun. The more big, scary courses he skied, the more he liked downhill. "It was like getting in a Lamborghini and doing whatever you wanted on the road—with the approval of the police. What more could you ask for?" he said. He spent his entire postgraduate year skiing on the gray Rossignols. But that spring, during a race in Alaska, he skied over a bare spot in the snow and wrecked them. "It was like having a horse that carried you around for years and years, and then all of a sudden it breaks its leg, and that's it: It's dead," he said. He removed the bindings and then sawed the skis in half "so no one else could ever have them."

AJ was named to the U.S. Ski Team's downhill training group in 1987. He spent most of his first season racing in Nor-Am and Europa Cup events. Then, in January 1988, he and some other young racers, including Kyle Rasmussen and Tommy Moe, went to Europe to compete on the World Cup tour. Things went well: AJ finished twelfth in a downhill in Leukerbad, Switzerland, and, voilà, got himself named to the 1988 Olympic team. He was nineteen years old. AJ became an Olympian mostly by process of elimination. Bill Johnson was so busy being famous that he had never got back into shape, and veteran racer Mike Brown was hurt (well, he felt he could race but the coaches didn't). AJ felt overwhelmed only once in Calgary. It was during the opening ceremonies, when it seemed the whole planet was looking at him. Wow, he thought. This really is a big deal. The downhill was contested at Nakiska, the scary course with the elevator-shaft start. In a field of fifty,

AJ finished twenty-sixth, the best finish by an American. Jeff Olson was twenty-eighth and U.S. Ski Team veteran Doug Lewis was thirty-second. Bill Hudson missed a gate near the top of the course and was disqualified. AJ was satisfied with the way he skied. The point, in Calgary, was not to win a medal, but to get Olympic experience, and he had done that. Things had gone about the way he thought they would.

AJ's independent streak was just as evident on the ski team as it had been when he was thirteen years old. He did things his way, period. While Jeff Olson worked out until his body turned to stone, AJ lifted just enough weights and pedaled just enough miles to get into competitive shape. His physique wasn't as impressive as Jeff's, but he didn't care. He wanted to have the strongest will, not the strongest legs. (As Bill Egan put it, "He's not addicted to exercise.") And when Egan told his racers to take five more runs and work on their turns, AJ sometimes headed for the lodge. Seeing this, the other guys would shake their heads, look at each other, and say, "O.P." It stood for "Own Program." AJ Kitt had his own program.

AJ's third season on the team was a good example. In December 1989, he assessed his racing technique and found himself wanting. Yes, he was a superb glider—someone whose aerodynamic tuck and instinctive feel for the snow made him fast in the flats. But he was not very good at maneuvering his skis. If he was to become a great downhiller, he had to do better in the turns. So when the rest of the downhill team flew to Europe for the start of the World Cup season, AJ stayed in North America to compete in, of all things, Nor-Am slalom and giant slalom races. He was going to be a technical weenie! The decision caused a stir. Most guys on the team clamored to get to the World Cup circuit, the famous White Circus; why would AJ purposely demote himself to the minor leagues? But AJ knew what he was doing. He skied well that December, lowering his world ranking in slalom and giant slalom considerably. And for the first time in his life, he really understood how to ski. "I began to feel what my skis were doing in conjunction with my feet and my legs, and I began to understand what different movements did to the ski. The whole experience just made me really confident," he said.

When he got to Europe in January 1990 he was a better skier, and therefore a better racer. The first race was on a tricky course in Schladming, Austria. AJ had raced there only once, and in four runs, including training runs, he had wiped out three times, snapping a pair of skis, hyperextending one knee, stretching ligaments in the other, and separating his shoulder. This time he finished thirty-first. It wasn't great, but it was better than hospitalization. Later that month, in Kitzbühel, Austria, Bill Egan watched AJ make a long, sweeping turn in a section called the Seidlalm and thought, That kid can ski as well as anyone in the world. AJ finished thirty-first—he made some mistakes Bill didn't see—but again, he learned from the experience.

His breakthrough race came in Cortina d'Ampezzo, Italy, in February. He finished fifteenth in a couple of training runs and went into the race sensing that if he stayed calm, he would do well. While he waited for his turn to ski, AJ went into a restaurant at the top of the hill. Inside, people were watching the race on television. AJ usually didn't pay any attention to what the other guys were doing. He couldn't control the way they skied, only the way he did. But that day something caught his eye. He happened to pass the TV set while Italian racer Kristian Ghedina was making his run. (AJ would later say that moment was "destiny or whatever.") He noticed that Ghedina leaned forward in his boots just slightly as he skied over a small bump, or "roller." To AJ, that tiny movement, imperceptible to most of the people watching in the restaurant, was a revelation. By pressing forward, the Italian had picked up speed and propelled himself into the next section. Ghedina went on to win the race, his first World Cup victory. AJ couldn't wait to apply the technique during his run. He started forty-sixth and skied smoothly down to the small bump in the course. Then, as Ghedina had done, he adjusted his weight forward and shot down the hill. AJ skied under the finish banner and turned his skis sideways to stop.

The crowd shrieked. Oh, great, he thought. I've just finished my run and they're already giving the trophy to the winner. AJ thought the crowd was cheering for someone else. But that wasn't it at all. He looked at the clock and found he had finished fourth, a hundredth of a second behind third-place finisher Daniel Mahrer of Switzerland.

"I got a warm fuzzy. I was psyched. It was like, I've done it. I'm there," AJ said.

The downhillers flew to Are, Sweden, that March for the last two

World Cup downhills of the season. AJ was still skiing well: He finished third in one of the training runs. The night before the race, he went to Bill Egan and told him he felt anxious.

"I've got a really good shot at winning this race tomorrow. What do I do?" AJ said.

Bill said, "Don't do anything different. Don't let yourself get nervous. Don't overthink it."

AJ skied well on the top part of the course, which began with a steep pitch, a couple of quick turns, and three jumps. But then the course got choppy—the earlier racers had chewed it up—and AJ got into trouble. One of the ruts threw him off his line and he never really got back on it. He finished twenty-ninth, not what he had in mind. The next day, in the second downhill, that section was just as rutted (it had rained all morning), but AJ adjusted his line and skied through it cleanly. He flew off the finish jump, landed, skied under the banner, and found himself facing a thirty-by-thirty-foot puddle. AJ thought, OK, if I try to stop in the water I'm going to eat shit. So he glided over the puddle like a water-skier and made a fast stop, spraying the crowd with slush. "They didn't care. They were already wet," he said.

In Are, the scoreboard showed the racers' times but not where they had placed. After a few minutes someone told him, "You're sixth." It was his second-best finish ever. A moment later, a Swedish racer named Niklas Henning told AJ, "Congratulations. You're in the first seed." In ski racing, being in the first seed meant you were ranked in the top fifteen in the world in a given event. Before each race, the names of the top guys were placed in a hat and a starting order was drawn. Everyone else skied according to his world ranking. The main advantage to being in the first seed was that you always got to ski on a clean, unrutted course. But for AJ, making the first seed meant more than that: It meant that all his plans had worked out, that he had been right all along.

"You've got to be confident in yourself to be a good person and to be good at whatever you want to do," he said after the season. "I'm confident now. I'm confident as hell. I know I can do well. I'm not wondering. You know, there's no question there anymore. It's just a matter of time and a matter of hard work."

AJ cruised into Val d'Isère in December 1990 thinking he could win the race, and his training runs showed he was right. But when he pushed out of the start on race day, a fierce wind swept up the hill and slowed him down. He finished forty-fifth, more than two seconds behind the winner, Leonhard Stock of Austria. He was, in his own words, "really pissed," but he didn't let it get to him. Letting it get to him wasn't part of the program.

One of AJ's teammates also had a rough week in Val d'Isère. During one training run, Jeff Olson did something it was likely no one else had ever done on a downhill course. As he approached a jump his skis drifted apart just slightly. The inside edge of his left ski snagged in the snow, jerking his leg behind him—it was as if someone had lassoed his ski boot as he passed—and turning him around one hundred and eighty degrees. Jeff went off the jump at sixty miles an hour, backward.

"I thought I was just going to eat living shit into the side of the mountain," he said later.

But he didn't. Having spun halfway around, he decided, in an instant, to keep spinning. He twisted his upper body to the left and his skis followed, twirling beneath him. When he landed he was facing downhill again, so what the heck, he kept skiing. He made his way back onto the course after missing only one gate. It was a miracle, an incredible athletic feat. Jeff, whose nickname was "Olie," became a legend among the coaches and racers who saw it on videotape. Olie, what a madman. What a crazy fucking nut.

The maneuver also messed up his head. If a horse throws you, they say, you're supposed to scramble right back into the saddle so the fear won't get to you. Well, when this young gun got back on his horse, he was a different cowboy. He moved stiffly, woodenly, as if being forced to ski at gunpoint. He finished in the back of the pack in that race, almost four seconds behind the winner. Well, fine, he told himself. I'll do better next time. And then he went to Val Gardena, Italy, and skied even worse: He failed to complete one race and finished five seconds out in the other. He couldn't believe the problem was serious; there was something wrong with his technique, that was all. He couldn't accept that his mind might be the source of his troubles. He could correct a technical problem. But how was he supposed to conquer fear?

Jeff Olson was born in Missoula, Montana, but his family moved to

Bozeman when he was a year old. His father, Jack, who specialized in working with the deaf, was a speech professor at Montana State University, and his mother, Val, was an elementary school speech therapist. Jeff, the oldest of three children, was raised in a churchgoing family; he was an acolyte and his father sang in the choir. Jeff also enjoyed skiing: the Bridger Bowl ski area was only fifteen miles from his home. One day, his father took him to sign up for the junior racing program. Kids could race on Saturday and Sunday, or only on Saturday. Jack Olson forgot all about church (Jeff described him as sort of an absentminded professor) and enrolled his son in the two-day program. When they got home Val Olson "flipped out," Jeff recalled years later. But when she saw how badly her son wanted to become a good racer, she agreed to let him skip church from then on.

He would do anything to win, and it took a toll on his body. Jeff sustained his first serious injuries when he was thirteen years old, at a race in Crystal Mountain, Washington. While tucking toward the finish line, he stuck his head between his knees to get some extra speed. He caught an edge, fell, and slammed into the timing shack. (He didn't quite make it across the finish line.) He broke his leg, arm, thumb, and nose, and spent the next month in a wheelchair. It was the first in what would become a long series of bone-cracking spills.

When he didn't crash, Jeff usually did well. By the time he was a sophomore in high school he had won everything there was to win in Montana. So in his junior year he moved to Vermont to attend the Green Mountain Valley School (this was a couple of years before AJ enrolled). The pivotal moment in his prep school racing career came during a slalom race in his senior year. Jeff's entire racing future hung on that race: Those who skied well would qualify to compete on the Nor-Am racing circuit, and those who excelled in the Nor-Ams would then be invited to a U.S. Ski Team training camp.

Jeff fell in the first run of the slalom. Normally that would have disqualified him from competing in the second run, but in this race that rule was waived. Jeff, not known as a great technical skier, skied way over his head in the second run, finishing fifth. He qualified for the Nor-Am races, where he did well enough to get invited to the ski team camp at Mt. Bachelor, Oregon, in the spring of 1986.

The pressure was on again at Mt. Bachelor. The U.S. Ski Team had invited thirty young racers to the camp; only eight would be named to the National Training Group. Jeff thought he had a chance to make the team. But then, during super G training, he accidentally touched one of his fists to the snow while making a turn. He was going so fast—speeds in super G reached fifty miles an hour or more—that his hand shattered the moment it touched the hardpack. It took six screws and several long pieces of wire to put the bones back together. (Years later, Jeff still had the hardware in his hand; he planned to have it removed when he retired from racing.) Well, that's that, Jeff thought. I'm not going to make the team now. He went back to Bozeman and made plans to attend Montana State, which had offered him a ski racing scholarship. What he did not know was that the ski team coaches had been impressed with him. A couple of weeks before Jeff was to begin college, Ueli Luthi called and said, "We're going to Switzerland at the end of September and we want you to come." Jeff, the ninth man chosen for what was supposed to be an eight-man team, was thrilled. His hand would be healed by late September. College could wait. When Jeff got to the airport in Boston, the meeting point for the flight to Zurich, the other guys on the team said, "What are you doing here, Olson?" Later, they ragged him by calling him "Free Agent." So what? All that mattered was that he was there.

Jeff crashed in his first Europa Cup downhill training run. He was making a roundhouse turn when his ski got caught in some soft snow and began tracking in the wrong direction. He got his skis back together, but not in time to save himself. He ended up straying off the course—and flying off a fifteen-foot-high cliff. Fortunately he came down in thick powder and did nothing worse than wrench his knee.

In 1987, Jeff began to establish himself as the up-and-coming star of the downhill team. He finished fourth in the national downhill championship race early in the year and fourteenth in a World Cup downhill in Furano, Japan in December. He won the national downhill title in 1988 and again in 1989. As far as the downhill coaches were concerned, Jeff Olson was The Future. Then he started piling up the doctor bills again. While free-skiing during the Christmas break in 1989, he fell on a rock and badly bruised his hip. The next month, in Kitzbühel, Austria, he crashed and broke his collarbone; he later aggravated the injury while (the coaches couldn't believe this) playing softball. At last things started to go his way again: He bought a condominium in Park City, Utah; became engaged to marry a former U.S. Ski Team member (the wedding was scheduled for June 1991); and won the giant slalom title at the Pan Am Games in Las Leñas, Argentina. He was a happy guy. When he headed to Val d'Isère, France, in December 1990, he was sure he would have his best year ever. And then he went off that jump backward and got thoroughly and enduringly confused.

Things might have been easier for Jeff that December if he had had the emotional support of his teammates, but he didn't. Jeff was bright, well-spoken, and friendly, but he also was intensely, almost obsessively competitive, the kind of guy who liked to be first at breakfast, first in the weight room (he was an amazing physical specimen, one hundred ninety-five pounds of canvas and steel—his teammates called him "Arnold," as in Schwarzenegger), first in the lift line, first in the team van, first everywhere. Jeff acknowledged that he was always competing, but said he meant no harm by it. Still, the other downhillers didn't like it. Jeff and Bill Hudson had a particularly contentious relationship, in part because they had joined the ski team at the same time and were always vying for the same spots on the Nor-Am, Europa Cup, and World Cup circuits. Besides, Bill was a pretty hard-driving character himself. AJ liked to describe the relationship by saying, "It's a wicked sibling rivalry, except they're not brothers." Bad things seemed to happen when Jeff and Bill were in a competitive situation. Once, they got into such a bad argument in the finish at Kitzbühel that they nearly started swinging. And after a Nor-Am race early in 1990, Jeff said something uncalled-for and Bill shot back, "Jeff, I hate your fucking guts." The other downhillers rarely had run-ins with Jeff, but they weren't necessarily warm to him either. This didn't help Olson much. A person in his mental condition could have used some encouragement—a clap on the back, maybe some helpful advice—but he didn't get any. When you're several thousand miles from home and you feel as if your career is crumbling, it's nice to feel like one of the guys. Jeff's teammates didn't make him feel like one of the guys.

The downhill team traveled around Europe that December in three rented vehicles—a cargo van to carry the skis and the luggage, a Volkswagen bus, and a sporty little car called a Passat. Jim Tracy, Bill Egan's assistant, usually drove the cargo van, while the racers rode in the slow, clunky VW bus, a tin can with windows. Egan drove the Passat. (Head coach Ueli Luthi usually had his own car to commute between downhill races and technical events.) The downhillers often griped about the VW bus: The heater didn't work very well; the tires didn't hold the road; and worst of all, the thing didn't go fast enough. So before the two downhill races in Val Gardena, Egan offered a deal: If, in either race, three guys finished in the top twenty, two in the top fifteen, or one in the top ten, he would let the athletes drive the Passat to the next race, a Europa Cup super G in nearby Alba di Canazei. Now, that was incentive.

In the first downhill, AJ Kitt finished fifteenth and Tommy Moe thirteenth. The Passat was theirs. Just for good measure, AJ came in ninth in the second race; Tommy was thirteenth again. Kyle Rasmussen was sixteenth, a fraction of a second out of the top fifteen. The racers, graduates of the "So What? It's a Rental" School of Driving, zoomed off to Alba di Canazei in the Passat, with AJ behind the wheel. (They arrived safely in spite of the way he drove.) But having a fast set of wheels was only part of the racers' satisfaction. The real excitement came from knowing they were doing well. A few months earlier, it had seemed no American downhiller would ever break into the top fifteen in a World Cup race, and now several guys had done it. Earlier that season, former Olympic slalom skier Phil Mahre had been quoted as saying the American racers were a bunch of lazy, spoiled kids who weren't willing to work hard for results. Spoiled? Lazy? The remark had really pissed off the downhillers. Where did he get off? On second thought, they didn't put much stock in Phil Mahre's opinion, especially his opinion of speed skiers.

What did he know? He was a technical weenie.

3

The Gods
They Were

The downhillers flew into Zurich, Switzerland, on New Year's Day, 1991, brimming with hope. Bill Hudson, who had recovered quickly from his accident in Val d'Isère, couldn't wait to test his injured knee. Tommy Moe and Kyle Rasmussen hoped to improve on their good results in December, and AJ Kitt was thinking not just of doing well, but of winning races. (Jeff Olson had stayed in Utah to compete in some Nor-Am super G races.) For the guys arriving in Europe, the dawning of 1991 made all things seem possible. At the airport, the racers picked up, sigh, a VW van and drove east across Switzerland into the southernmost part of Germany. The first downhill race of the year would be held in the twin Bavarian villages of Garmisch and Partenkirchen, just north of the Austrian border.

But the drive into town gave the athletes a gray, sinking feeling. All around them, umbrellas sprouted like colorful mushrooms. Inside the van, they could hear the windshield wipers squeak against the glass. It was raining in Garmisch-Partenkirchen.

Poor, sweet, miserable Garmisch. For years, the Garmisch downhill, called the Kandahar, had been an important stop on the World Cup circuit. Among the past winners were the Austrian hero Karl Schranz, Swiss star Roland Collombin, and Olympic downhill champions Franz Klammer and Pirmin Zurbriggen. But those great days were long gone. In the summer of 1987, the summer after Zurbriggen set the new course record of 1:50.33, Garmisch spent one hundred fifty thousand deutsche marks to redesign the course and build bleachers in the finish area. Soon, the community thought, with characteristic German pride, the world will see what a great thing we have done. That summer turned to autumn, and autumn turned to . . . autumn again. Winter, the guest of honor, never came. Snow fell in some parts of Europe, but not in low-lying Garmisch. The organizers had no choice but to cancel the race.

That was only the beginning. Each year after that, the people of Garmisch got ready for the big event. They named an organizing committee, printed posters, hauled in a big electronic scoreboard, arranged to house and feed the athletes and coaches and technicians, engaged sponsors, notified the press of the date and time of the race, and otherwise got into a tizzy. But the village never got enough precipitation to hold a decent snowball fight, much less a race. Each year, the event, scheduled for the first week of January, was canceled before Christmas. By 1990, maybe the driest, grimmest year of all, there were some young racers on the circuit who had scarcely heard of Garmisch, which tended to detract from its reputation as a historic event. Even Berni Huber, Germany's best young racer, knew about the course "just from hearsay," a 1991 press release said.

It was all very upsetting to the locals. Garmisch, the site of the 1936 Winter Olympics, was the only village in Germany that was scheduled to hold a World Cup race between 1988 and 1990. The repeated cancellations denied people an opportunity to display their national pride, which was not something Germans, as a group, took well. The village was getting an inferiority complex.

But in 1991, there was hope. In the weeks before the race, snow fell thickly on Garmisch, as it had on Val d'Isère, Val Gardena, and the rest of the European mountains. For the first time, Garmisch also had snow-making machines (a press release called them "artificial snow devices"). The desperate resort had paid four million, five hundred thousand marks for the snow cannons, which began shooting ice onto the mountainside in early December. To describe the community's feelings about the previous three years, the Garmisch press people used phrases like "fruitless waiting" and "frustrating," but there would be no more of that.

"After three years," a press release said, "Germany's downhill racers can finally experience the feeling again to race down in front of a home crowd in their own country. The hard slog has come to an end—Garmisch-Partenkirchen belongs to the World Cup circuit once again."

Well, maybe. By the time the U.S. Ski Team van pulled up to the Hotel Mercure, the rain had already begun to poke holes in the snowbanks in the center of town. On the lower part of the mountain, grass showed through the gleaming sheet of snow, and the evergreen branches, having shed their fluffy burden, sprang to life. By the next afternoon, some slopes were completely bare.

This, at least in recent years, was typical European weather, and though the American athletes were always disappointed when races were canceled, they had learned that sitting around was part of the job. There was nothing for them to do that dreary Tuesday night but check into the Hotel Mercure and wait. Moving into a hotel was always an ordeal for the downhillers. Each racer traveled with one or two enormous bags of clothing, a briefcase or backpack full of important papers (passports, airplane tickets, address books, letters from girlfriends, pictures of friends and family), and two or three bags of skis, each weighing one hundred pounds or more. When they arrived in Garmisch, the racers lugged the clothing bags and backpacks into the lobby and left them in a pile four feet high. Then they went to the front desk and got their room assignments, which had been made by the Garmisch organizing committee. After dumping their things in their rooms, the downhillers carried the ski bags to a room on the second floor. The hotel had set aside its breakfast hall for use as a ski room—the place where the technicians would wax and sharpen the skis before each training run and race. Finally, the racers helped Jim Tracy carry several heavy boxes of video equipment into the building. After dinner, everyone went to bed and thought snowy thoughts.

It didn't work. Wednesday's training run was canceled because of rain. The downhillers went free-skiing in the morning, but the conditions were poor. After lunch, Bill Egan drove them to the U.S. Army base in Garmisch to stretch and play basketball. As long as they had to wait, Bill figured, they might as well keep loose.

Each evening after the team arrived, Ueli Luthi, the coach with overall responsibility for the men's downhill and technical teams, walked about a mile into downtown Garmisch for the nightly coaches' meeting. Even with the on-again, off-again sprinkling of rain it was a pleasant walk. In the center of the village was a church whose bell, a big one with a low voice, sounded on the hour. Nearby was the *apotheke,* or drugstore. Like any ski town, Garmisch had numerous boutiques that appealed to visitors with a lot of time and even more money. (In Garmisch, it was easier to find a fur-lined designer ski parka or a silver serving tray than a loaf of bread.) The village also had McDonald's and Pizza Hut restaurants, neither of which contributed much to the Old World ambience. Garmisch, surely a pretty place any time of the year, was even prettier around Christmas, when the villagers strung white lights across the narrow main streets. Their light mingled with the glow from Luthi's cigarette as he made his way downtown.

Ueli (pronounced "Oo-lee") was forty-two years old, but at first glance he looked much older: He was shiny-bald on top, and the puffs of hair on the back and the sides were old-man white. Some people on the ski team liked to make newcomers guess Ueli's age just because it was always fun to see how wrong they would be. But Ueli did not act like an old man. His laugh was an insane whinny and he always had a wild look in his lively blue eyes. He liked to round corners in his rental car on two wheels (Bill Egan, who hoped to die old, refused to ride with him) and enjoyed sitting at the hotel bar until the early morning, drinking schnapps and telling jokes. He was the sort of guy who could drink a lot and never exhibit a change in personality. Ueli was raised near Wengen, Switzerland, but lived in Mammoth, California, and considered himself an American. He had lots of traits that many people considered typically Swiss: He was punctual; he was stubborn; he paid close attention to detail (he was always making notes for himself in a little notebook); when he said he would take care of something he took care of it; and he did not warm up to people quickly, but when he finally did befriend them the friendship was permanent. Though Ueli had been working for the U.S. Ski Team on and off since 1982, he still didn't have complete control of the American idiom. For example, instead of saying, "Let's talk," Ueli would translate directly from the Swiss German: "We make a meeting." And if he saw a racer crash, he might tell about it later by saying, "One of a sudden, he bits the dust." Once, Ueli complained that he could "only be in one place at the same time," and Bill Egan laughed so hard he couldn't breathe. Ueli always said the same thing when someone laughed at him: "Fock you." Bill made fun of Ueli, but he also respected him. Ueli's whole life was the ski team; no one worked harder to make sure the downhillers and technical racers had a chance to do well.

Part of that job was standing up for the team at the nightly coaches' meeting. The mood of Wednesday night's meeting in Garmisch was dark. The race organizers sat forlornly at a long table in the front of the room. At 5:30 they began the business of choosing a starting order for the next day's training run. Numbers were drawn from a hat and the names of the racers in the first seed arranged on a bulletin board. But few of the coaches present believed there would be a training run. Outside it was wet and warm, and the forecast was not good. The organizers didn't seem to believe anyone would be training in the morning either. If you had had to choose a word to describe what they all seemed to feel, it would have been a German word: angst. Everyone on the committee seemed to consider it his personal responsibility to bring off the World Cup races, to restore the community's pride. Now it seemed they might not be able to do it. When the meeting ended, they all tromped outside and walked or drove home in the teasing rain.

The next morning, Thursday, the organizers announced that the training run had indeed been canceled. The announcement was written in the most cheerful language possible. The Kandahar downhill course "is in excellent condition," it said. But it added that it wouldn't be a good idea to actually ski on it.

"Due to the warm weather, we want to preserve the course," the announcement said. "The teams can now train free on the Zugspitze."

The ski area at Garmisch consisted of two craggy mountain peaks. The Alpspitze, where the Kandahar downhill was held, was at two thousand six hundred meters in elevation. It had the most lifts and the largest number of trails. On the lower part of the Alpspitze the snow was turning to water and causing all the problems. But this wasn't so on the Zugspitze, the Alpspitze's big brother. At nearly three thousand meters, it had received snow when parts of the Alpspitze were getting rain. By Thursday, the only good skiing in Garmisch was on the Zugspitze.

When the lift stopped at the top of the peak, the athletes felt they had alighted on a different world. The Zugspitze formed a half bowl of sugar, and all the sun in Germany seemed to be shining on it. The snow was so shiny white that you had to squint against the glare, so soft and thick that it went *flomp* when the athletes dropped their skis on it. It took only a moment for the downhillers to click into the bindings and fasten their boot buckles. Everything so far that week—the boredom of travel, the waiting, the tiny European beds—had made them feel confined, closed in. But now the snow and the sunshine made them free. There were two ways down the hill. One was a wide, gentle slope covered in well-packed snow. The other was a steep pitch with no ski tracks on it. Bill Hudson, who led the way, naturally chose the near-vertical pitch, and skied it effortlessly. His teammates followed. Tommy Moe skied from top to bottom in a tuck, making turns the shape of parentheses.

The slopes were crowded. Virtually every national ski team was there. (After one run, Tommy rode the T-bar to the top and saw Swiss downhiller Peter Müller chatting with a woman. "There's Peter, working the chicks again," he said.) And after the word spread about the Zugspitze's new powder, many recreational skiers arrived there, too. The downhillers did not ski the way the vacationers did. The recreational skiers cruised for thirty seconds, forty-five if they were really into it, then stopped to catch their breath and chat and enjoy the scenery. The downhillers, on the other hand, tossed aside the T-bar at the top of the hill, battened down their buckles, and pointed their skis at the valley. They passed as a blur, *fwoosh, fwoosh,* using the vacationers as downhill gates. They never paused to catch their breath the way the average skiers did, because it never got away from them in the first place. And they never looked at the scenery, the silver mountains and the blueberry sky, because they were enjoying themselves so much, and because in their minds they *were* the scenery.

That evening, Bill Hudson, dressed in jeans and sandals, sat in a wooden chair in the ski room and modified his helmet, a hard purple shell with a Bell sticker on the side. He began by drilling holes in the earflaps. Then he used screws to attach a plastic chin protector, much like the ones that motocross racers wear. The extra protection would help in a crash.

Bill Hudson was born in Los Angeles in 1966. When he was three years old his parents divorced and he moved to Squaw Valley with his mother and two older brothers. (His father died when Bill was nineteen.) Sally Hudson, who worked as a ski instructor at Squaw, had three rules for teaching children how to ski. First, carry their skis and poles from the car to the hill; she saw no reason to make kids struggle with equipment. Second, pick them up when they fall down. And third, never tell them what to do; just let them have fun. Bill started having fun right away. As a little boy, he often took naps going up the chair lift; his mother constantly had to buy new gloves because Bill sucked the thumbs off them. Racing was still a big part of Sally Hudson's life—her friends were former ski racers and she spent a lot of time raising money for the U.S. Ski Team—so naturally it became part of Bill's too. He grew up racing the way some kids grow up playing Little League baseball or church league basketball. The Squaw Valley Ski Team, which over the years produced several U.S. Ski Team members, competed all around the Lake Tahoe basin. Bill didn't win every race he entered, but he won a lot of them. He attended a couple of U.S. Ski Team camps when he was in high school but didn't make the team. When he finished high school in 1985, Bill, an A student, enrolled at Dartmouth, where Sally Hudson's father had once been dean. He returned to Squaw Valley after his first year with every intention of going back to school.

He was on vacation with a girlfriend in Santa Barbara, California, that spring when he heard about a ski team qualifying camp at Mt. Bachelor, Oregon—the same camp Jeff Olson was about to attend. Bill zipped up to Squaw Valley, dropped off his girlfriend, and picked up a few pairs of skis. Then he headed to Oregon and skied his way onto the team. For a year he specialized in the technical events. Then Theo Nadig, who coached the speed events at the time, asked him to give downhill a try. The team had several good slalom and giant slalom skiers, but few good downhillers; Nadig thought Hudson had potential. After a couple of races, Bill discovered that downhill suited his personality. He was intense, hard-driving, a little nuts; he didn't want to ski down the mountain so much as fling himself off the top of it. That was evident during the

1988 Olympic downhill in Calgary—he skied wildly and missed a gate near the top of the course. In 1989, after gaining some experience on the Nor-Am and Europa Cup circuits, Bill finished thirteenth in a World Cup downhill in Kitzbühel, Austria.

He had entered the 1990 World Cup season thinking he would soon ski his way into the first seed. And then he had bonked his head and tweaked his knee and wound up in the hospital. After the race in Val d'Isère, the team had spent a night in Mols, Switzerland, on its way to Italy. The owner of the hotel there had videotaped the European TV coverage of the race, and the Americans had watched it when they arrived. The tape had provided a clear view of Bill's head smacking against the snow, and of his limp body sliding into the fence. The sight had made Bill feel sick to his stomach; he hadn't realized how awful the crash had been, how ragged he had looked. The next day, Bill had boarded a plane for Denver. From there he had taken a van to Vail, where U.S. Ski Team surgeon Richard Steadman had determined that his knee injury was indeed minor. Within a few days Bill had begun working out, and by Christmas he had started skiing again.

Now, in Garmisch, he had a lot on his mind. Tomorrow, weather permitting, Bill would make his first downhill run since his spill at Val d'Isère. He was concerned, first, about his knee. Would it hold up? Dr. Steadman had fitted him with a brace, and it had supported him well on the Zugspitze. How it would work in a high-speed turn was another question. Downhillers probably worried more about their knees than they did about any other joint, and rightly so. Hudson knew it wouldn't take much to turn his minor injury into a major one.

And yet he tried not to dwell on disaster. The idea now—the trick, really—was to avoid thinking about the only thing it seemed natural to think about. But Hudson felt certain he could do it. In Val d'Isère, he had made a silly mistake: he hadn't prepared for the jump at the end of the compression. How could he have been so careless? That's what it was, carelessness. Not the inherent danger of the sport, and certainly not a defect in him. Carelessness. He could run that course ten times and never make that mistake again. He wouldn't do the same thing here, at Garmisch. He might be a little hesitant in the first run, sure. But scared? No, not scared.

* * *

Ueli Luthi got out of bed early Friday morning and drove to the mountain to meet the other coaches and the race jury. About 7:30 A.M., he radioed back to the hotel with his report: It had not rained on the Alpspitze. Training was on.

The racers ate a quick breakfast, grabbed some bananas and oranges for the road, and headed for the hill. To reach the start of the course, they packed into one of Garmisch's tiny old cable cars and rode part of the way up the Alpspitze. From there, they cruised down to a chair lift, which carried them, two by two, to the little wooden starting shack at the top of the course.

Course inspection is always a solemn ritual, but that morning it was especially so. Most of the Americans had never seen this track, and though it was by no means the most challenging on the circuit, it wasn't easy. They wanted to know it as well as they could before they left the gate. Inspection simply meant looking at the course. It was against the rules, in inspection, to actually run gates the way you would during the race, but some outlaw racers did it anyway. The Austrians were so well known for breaking this rule that this particular form of cheating was known as "Austrian inspection." Bill Hudson was disqualified from the downhill at the American national championships one year for doing an Austrian inspection. He wasn't about to let that happen here. He and his teammates made their way deliberately down the hill. They stood in the starting gate and surveyed the first couple of turns. Then they slid from gate to gate, stopping often to observe the condition of the snow. When they reached a jump, they paused on its crest, looking down the hill and then back up. Then they stepped, herringbone style, back up the hill to look at the approach to the jump one more time. The whole inspection took at least thirty minutes.

The Kandahar downhill began with two easy turns, then a steep drop and a long, sweeping right turn. The next difficult section was the Troglhang, which required the racer to make several fast, tight turns in a row. Soon the skier reached a jump that would send him fifteen feet into the air and more than one hundred feet down the hill. Here, the average speed would be perhaps seventy miles an hour. It would reach seventy-five or even eighty in the section called Hölle, which was German for Hell. To get out of hell, skiers would have to make a sudden, and quite terrifying, right turn. Prayer was said to help. The course culminated in another steep section, a teeth-shaking left turn, a long flat, and then one last jump before the finish.

Even by World Cup standards, this was a big jump. The race organizers had built it to add excitement at the finish, and it was sure to do that. The bump was so large, and the landing so steep, that on his approach the racer would see nothing but slate gray sky. Only upon leaving the ground would he get his first glimpse of the finish banner.

Bill Hudson could scarcely believe the size of the jump. The Americans loved getting air, loved the feeling they got when their stomachs flew up and knocked against their hearts. The best thing about being a downhill racer was that you got to spend time aloft, the snow a white blur beneath you. Well, the racers were going to get some serious air here. Near the end of inspection, Bill stopped on the top of the jump and looked down at the finish banner, which hung about fifteen feet above the snow. He said, "Are we supposed to go under it or over it?"

The first forerunner left the gate just before noon. Forerunners were young men, usually local club racers, who skied down the course ahead of the regular competitors. Their job was to smooth out the track so the big names could go fast. They performed this service for no reward save for the thrill. Their times were not recorded—they were not official competitors—and their names usually were not announced on the loudspeaker. Sometimes, one of the forerunners wore a tiny camera in his helmet so TV viewers could see the course as the racers saw it.

The forerunners also served another, more subtle, purpose—they showed how hard downhill really was. Forerunning a downhill race was a form of human sacrifice. Though they were all expert skiers, few forerunners were prepared for the rigors of a World Cup course. Most of them clattered down the course looking terrified, bodies stiff and eyes bulging, like scared middle-aged men on roller skates. Seeing them, you had to admire the real racers, the guys who would come soon. Some forerunners never showed up in the finish. Indeed, the first racer to ski down the Kandahar course that Friday, a man named Monath, crashed into the fence a few hundred yards before the finish. Then he picked himself up, shook his head, and skied away with a headache and a good story. The training run was on.

In any downhill, the forerunners were followed by the snow seeds. Before each race, six snow seeds were drawn at random from the bottom fifteen percent of the field. Their job, like that of the forerunners, was to smooth the track. Racers ranked in the sixties and seventies considered it great luck to be chosen as a snow seed because it meant you would make a run before the track got rutted and coarse, but after the forerunners had partly smoothed it over. Besides, if bad weather came, the guys in the sixties and seventies might never get to race. Being a snow seed guaranteed you at least an attempt.

The first that day was Jason Gasparoni of San Marino, number ninety-two. He was ranked ahead of only one racer—another San Marinan. Evidently there were few hills in San Marino to prepare Gasparoni for the fast terror of the Kandahar, because halfway down he lost control after hitting a jump and, as the fighter pilots say, augured in. Soon, everyone on the course could hear the thwack-thwack-thwack of the helicopter that hovered up from the valley to hoist this broken sack of bones. The Garmisch press machine later provided a list of the injuries: fracture of the shoulder blade (the press release didn't say which shoulder), the fourth dorsal vertebra (or maybe it wasn't broken; the doctors weren't sure), and the right splint bone (whatever that was). The press release noted helpfully that Gasparoni sustained the injuries "due to a skiing mistake."

Shortly after noon, the racers in the first seed—the top fifteen—were ready to go. By then, a crowd of several hundred had gathered in the finish area. Training runs didn't count for anything, but Europeans enjoyed seeing their racing heroes anyway. The event had the atmosphere of an American high school football game. The air was thin and cold; people laughed and drank and ate picnic lunches; a loudspeaker played happy music. A few dozen hearty people trudged up the hill to watch the run from the last turn, the one where the first forerunner had crashed. In the next two and a half hours, ninety-three racers would make that turn, or try to.

AJ Kitt wore number three. To the spectators, all downhillers looked about the same when they skied, except for the color of their suits. But AJ always did a couple of things that distinguished him from the rest.

Right before he reached a jump he spread his arms wide, like a falcon showing off its wings. As soon as he went airborne he suddenly returned his arms to his side to keep from flying too far. When he did this, he aimed an index finger at the snow as if to point out the place where he would land. AJ looked different from his competitors in Garmisch in other ways too: He stood upright in the turns and didn't hold a low tuck in the flats. Some people may have thought he was scared (frightened racers stood up in the turns to lower their speed), but that wasn't the case. AJ was skiing the way he always did in the first training run—slowly, gently, completely in control. AJ was Mr. Deliberate. He liked to think of the first run as a fast inspection, a way of introducing himself to the course. Hello, course. I'm AJ, and I'm going to have my way with you. Only in the second and third training runs would he begin to turn on the speed. On race day he would really go for it. It was all part the plan, part of AJ's Own Program. For now he just moseyed down the slope, if doing seventy miles an hour could be considered moseying.

But a good downhill course allowed you only so much control before it asserted itself. The Kandahar downhill worked its will on AJ in the last turn, the left turn leading to the finish straightaway. He needed to lean on his right ski as he turned, but at the last second he got into a rut and found himself on his left. Instead of turning he was speeding toward the snow fence—the section of fence with the forerunner's head print still in it. AJ would have hit it much harder than the forerunner had, but he managed to shift his weight to the right ski and make the turn. Later, someone mentioned that he had looked like he was in some trouble there.

"No shit," AJ said.

Tommy Moe, wearing number forty-four, was the next American to go. At age twenty, Tommy was almost exactly half boy and half man. It even showed in his looks. He had the body of a man, and a rugged one at that. He stood six feet tall in ski boots and had a thick neck and broad sloping shoulders, shoulders built for work. His thighs were as solid and round as marble pillars, his stomach as hard and flat as a drafting table. He was, overall, sort of blocky and angular, which, though he probably was no stronger than the other downhillers, made him look stronger. This was a grown-up physique.

The rest of him, though, was all boy. He smiled in the sudden, unrehearsed way that little boys do, and he laughed like a delighted kid. His hair was thin and sandy-blond, the color you get after playing for hours in the sun. His youth also became apparent when he spoke. Tommy had a funny, sometimes nonsensical way of expressing himself. When someone farted in the team van, for example, Tommy was likely to say, "Oh, man—air biscuit." He referred to the bits of wax he picked from his ear as "moon rocks." His downhill skis were "long dongs." There were many more examples. When discussing his summer plans, he might say, "I'm definitely going kayaking in Idaho maybe," or, "I go mountain biking a lot sometimes." You always had a pretty good idea what he meant, but you wouldn't want to be called to testify about it. Also, when Tommy agreed with you he never said, "I agree," or "You're right." He always said, "No doubt." Tommy said one other thing that gave away his youth: He called almost everybody "man"—including his girlfriend. Because of these qualities, and because he had made a lot of money at a young age, some of his teammates called Tommy the Golden Child.

But he wasn't always golden. Tommy Moe was born in Missoula, Montana. His parents divorced when he was two years old, and he and the other children were split up: Tommy and his brother went to live with their father, and his sister went with her mom. When their father's second marriage broke up and he moved to Alaska, Tommy and his brother stayed in Montana with their grandmother. Little Tommy was too much for her. By the time he was thirteen he was a good skier and a better troublemaker. That year he was asked to model clothing at a fund-raiser for his ski club. During changes of clothes he and a friend drank all the liquor they could find and got plastered. When a woman on the board of directors drove Tommy home, he thanked her by puking on the floor of the car.

"She was bummed out," Tommy said later. No doubt.

Tommy started smoking marijuana about that time. He enjoyed pot and he enjoyed ski racing, so eventually he combined the two. Once, he and some other kids took a bag of pot with them to a ski race. Smoking dope took the edge off things, which was nice, but it also made Tommy careless. One of the other kids discovered the stash and turned him in. He tried to lie his way out of it, but he wasn't too convincing, because the coaches called his grandmother and told her to take him home. After that Tommy was no longer permitted to compete in his ski region, which included Northern Idaho and Montana.

When Tom Moe, Sr., heard what had happened, he decided to bring Tommy to Alaska to live with him. Soon after he arrived, Tommy competed in a series of races near his new home. He crashed in every race. He was so miserable that he considered giving up the sport. What was the use? It just got him in trouble or gave him bruises. But at the last minute he decided to give it one more try. Later that year, at the Junior Olympics, Tommy won just about everything. About that time people began to see that Tommy Moe could be very, very good.

Meanwhile, he was still out to prove that he could be bad. Tommy spent most of his ninth-grade year in a cloud of marijuana smoke. He generally started the day by getting stoned with his buddies outside the school building. Then he would breeze into class, smelling like a brushfire and squinting through bloodshot eyes. He'd giggle through a couple of classes and then get high again at lunch. After school he and his pals would play some hacky sack—years later, Tommy still took a sack with him on the road—and get even more stoned. Lots of people smoke a little dope when they're kids; so what? But Tommy Moe was doing much more than that. He was making a life of it.

Ski racing was about the only other thing he cared about. In February 1986, just before his sixteenth birthday, he was given the opportunity to go to the U.S. Alpine Championships at Colorado's Copper Mountain. He was thrilled. Never mind that he had never heard of the U.S. Alpine Championships and didn't know what they were. Tommy, always short of money at that time, was elated just to be able to travel to a ski race. It turned out to be his big break, the thing that would begin to change him from troublemaker to Golden Child. In the downhill he started near the back of a crowded field and finished sixth. The U.S. Ski Team coaches were watching. Who was this prodigy? Later that year he won the downhill, super G, and giant slalom titles at the Junior Olympics and got himself named to the ski team.

What a break! Tommy clearly was a talented athlete; a break like this could change his whole life. But making the ski team was no reason to quit partying. In the spring of 1986 he went to a ski team camp in Alyeska, Alaska. One night he stopped in the woods to smoke a bowl and was spotted by a coach named Lex Patten, who blew the whistle. Tommy was put on probation. One more mistake and his ski team career would be over.

Tom Moe, Sr., had just returned home from two weeks of backbreaking work when he got the news of Tommy's foul-up. The news was a poor welcome home. Tom Moe was in the business of erecting steel buildings—airplane hangars, garages, storage shacks. He did well at it, but it was grueling work. He decided to serve Tommy a slice of reality. That summer he and his son boarded a plane and flew for five hours to grim, remote Dutch Harbor in the Aleutian Island chain. It was there that Tom Senior put his boy to work. Tommy's job was to build the wooden forms into which other workers poured the cement for foundations. Once the foundation was set, the crew would build a frame of red iron and then tack on the sheet-metal walls. It was like playing with an erector set.

Except, Tommy Moe would say years later, it wasn't any fun. He worked sixteen to eighteen hours a day for two months. He got out of bed when the sun rose at 4 A.M., worked, ate lunch, worked some more, ate dinner, and went back to work until sunset. Meanwhile, Tommy's new friends on the ski team were at a training camp in South America, catching air and mangling the Spanish language. Tom Moe, Sr., did not really want his son to grow up to work with plywood and sheet metal. He was just making a point. Whenever Tommy seemed really miserable, his dad would say something cheerful like, "What would you rather be doing right now—skiing in Argentina or working down here, sweating your ass off?"

"It was just kind of mental torture," Tommy remembered. "It was like, this sucks, man. It was bad news. It was rough labor, man. Rough. So it humbled me up pretty fast."

Sufficiently humbled up, Tommy went to the World Junior Championships in Hemsedal, Norway, in 1987 and finished second in the downhill and fourth in the giant slalom. That was when a lot of people started thinking of Little Tommy Moe (that's what they called him) as a future star. Some of those people sold skis and skiing gear. Tommy was still in his teens when Dynastar, the French ski manufacturer, signed him to an endorsement deal. Kerma ski poles soon signed him up, too. Later, Park City ski area offered him a headgear deal: For several thousand dollars a year, Tommy agreed to ski with the Park City emblem on his helmet. Heck, why not? The deals put Tommy on Easy Street, or at least what a teenager would have considered Easy Street.

By the winter of 1991, Tommy was still golden, but he was no longer a child. Now there was pressure on him. He had skied in his first World Cup downhill at sixteen, in Garmisch (he had taken time off from high school and hacky sack to compete), and he had been racing on the World Cup circuit on and off ever since. Even so, his accomplishments as a junior wouldn't carry him forever. Pretty soon the sponsors would expect results. A lot of people, including Tommy, felt it was time he started winning, or at least coming close. His thirteenth-place finishes in December 1990 were terrific, marvelous, his best ever. But if Tommy meant for this season to be a success, he had to do better than that. And Garmisch was his first chance.

Jim Tracy, stationed at the last turn, was concerned about how far the racers were flying off the finish jump. Just before Tommy's run, Tracy radioed up to the start and said, "Just make a good move, OK, off the jump." Making a move meant scrunching up your body just before you reached the takeoff point so you wouldn't fly too far. When AJ spread his wings like a falcon, he was making a move.

Tommy said yeah, fine, he'd make a big move. But then he didn't. He flew off the finish jump as if he'd been sprung from a catapult. Sometimes, when a racer gets out of kilter going off a jump, you think, hey, maybe he'll catch his balance in time to land on his feet and not his neck. But when Tommy hit the finish jump at Garmisch, the people lining the course—there were quite a few—knew he was going to pack it in, as the racers put it. He was leaning back way too far to save himself. As he sailed through the air, Tommy Moe said to himself: "Whoa, I'm going to land on my ass, man." The fun-loving race organizers had spray-painted bright red numerals in the snow to indicate the distance the racers flew off the finish jump. Tommy made his impact on the thirty-meter mark.

Jim Tracy, standing way up the hill, watched Tommy go out of control, then saw him disappear on the other side of the jump. Only when Tommy stood, picked up his bright green downhill skis, and waddled off the course did Tracy radio to the other coaches that he seemed to be all right.

Right on the Edge of Crazy

Bill Hudson got ready to go twenty minutes later. He wore a tight green racing suit with a spider-web design on the legs. The right lower leg was made of purple material bearing three white letters: USA. A knee brace bulged beneath the left leg of the suit. The brace looked bulky, but it didn't feel heavy. Bill stood in the starting gate and wiggled his knee side to side, then back and forth. It felt fine. Soon he blasted out of the starting shack and headed for the first gate. The first couple of turns were easy. As Bill approached the big right turn at the bottom of the hill, he thought, OK, here we go. This is the test. Here, he would have to put all his weight on the left leg. If the knee was going to give out, this was where it would happen. Bill gritted his teeth as he entered the turn. He set the edge of his ski and . . . the knee held perfectly. It was as good as new! Bill was ecstatic. In the next ten seconds he was required to make several more sharp turns on the left leg. No problem. He felt great. A little rusty, but great. He was a ski racer again. When he launched off that crazy finish jump his arms flew behind him and his ski poles touched together, click. He saw Tommy Moe's butt print as he skied under the banner.

For Reggie Crist, in his fourth year on the ski team, the meaningless practice race might as well have been the Olympic downhill. He was that nervous. This would be his first World Cup race in three years, his chance to compete with the big boys, and he didn't want to screw up. Reggie had skied his way onto the World Cup downhill team by winning a couple of Nor-Am races in December. Now he wanted to perform like a World Cup racer, to prove that his success meant something. Besides, the harrowing downhill race in Kitzbühel was next week, and though he didn't want to think about that yet, Reggie knew Ueli Luthi and Bill Egan wouldn't let him go if he didn't ski well here. It was a lot of pressure.

But damn, he felt lousy. He hadn't eaten enough that morning, so as he stretched his muscles in the starting area his stomach gurgled and growled like a mean old dog. It seemed his turn to ski would never come. All around him racers stretched their hamstrings, tested the straps on their helmets, and ran in place to keep warm. Television cameras followed some of the better-known racers as they prepared. A small crowd lined the snow fence near the top of the course and tried to see their favorites up close. Every couple of minutes, Reggie saw an athlete slide into the darkness of the starting shack. Moments later, he would hear the slap of skis as they hit the snow, followed by the encouraging shouts of the coaches and fans. Reggie felt envious. He wished he just could click into his bindings and go for it, but he couldn't. Waiting your turn, and staying calm while you waited, was part of ski racing. When you were starting fifty-ninth, as Reggie was that day, you waited a long time.

Reggie Crist was born in 1968 in Okinawa, where his father, Roger, was serving as a lawyer in the Marine Corps. The oldest of three children, Reggie spent the first part of his childhood near Palo Alto, California. The family home had a steep driveway. When Reggie was a little boy he liked to build jumps out of plywood and fly off them in his Big Wheel, a low-riding tricycle. His mother, Diane, took the jumping as a sign that he liked speed and danger. Reggie attended elementary school at the extremely progressive Peninsula School in Menlo Park, whose philosophy was to let kids learn what they wanted when they wanted. The place had no desks; students were urged to go outside and experience the world. That was great for some kids, but not for Reggie; he didn't learn much, and as a result he grew withdrawn and unhappy. That changed in the late 1970s, when the Crists moved to Sun Valley, Idaho, and Reggie discovered ski racing. He began to win races and his self-esteem improved. "That was where he got his strokes," Diane Crist said.

Reggie's father, the lawyer, was a thinking person; he generally tried to solve problems with reason. His mother was a feeling person; she read Tarot cards and meditated every day to connect with her higher self. When Reggie was grown, she attended the Jung Institute in Zurich and became a psychologist. Reggie was mostly like his dad, but he didn't rely entirely on reason: Because of superstition, he never put his hands through the straps of his ski poles until after he was in the starting gate. Reggie recalled that his parents always did their best to treat him and the other children with respect and trust, and it paid off: He remained close to both parents and felt he could tell them anything. Sometimes, all that trust backfired. At thirteen, Reggie announced that he wanted to try marijuana. His mother, a product of the sixties, said he could smoke it if he wanted to, but added that she'd feel better if he did it at home, not on some street corner. Not long after that, Diane Crist opened the door to Reggie's bedroom and found herself in a cloud of smoke.

Right on the Edge of Crazy

Every kid in the neighborhood was in there with Reggie, getting stoned. Diane, ever honest, told her son, "I'm not comfortable with this. I'm really sorry. I've never been a parent before." That was OK with Reggie, who was more interested in skiing than smoking anyway.

The complaint about Reggie as a downhiller was that he was too passive. He had the ability to do well, but in the coaches' opinion, he didn't go for it, didn't punch it. He was too laid-back. Well, if he was mellow on the slopes it was probably because he was mellow off the slopes. If you met Reggie and had to guess which sport he excelled in, you would have guessed surfing, not skiing. His teeth and hair were a brilliant white; he was soft-spoken and easygoing; and he moved in the slow, loose-limbed style favored by people who spend a lot of time at the beach. (To walk, he just leaned forward until his feet had no choice but to start shuffling along.) Reggie, who did enjoy surfing, was aware of his cool reputation. He was trying to change, trying to be more like . . . well, like AJ Kitt. Now, there was somebody who was never accused of being laid-back. AJ may have been an Arrogant Jerk, but he was fast, and that was what counted. Reggie was trying to work up that kind of useful arrogance now, in Garmisch. It wasn't easy. He had raced in only two World Cup downhills in his life, and both had been in North America, on relatively easy courses. This was his first European World Cup race, his first real test. He wanted to be cocky, but the truth was he really didn't know if he belonged here.

Finally, the Soviet racer starting fifty-eighth lunged out of the starting house and Reggie moved in. His own start was smooth enough. He made the first two turns easily, and then glided in his tuck through the sweeping right. About thirty seconds in he began making mistakes. As he moved around one gate, he raised his hands for balance, the way a goose flaps its wings when it lands in the water. It cost him precious tenths. He had a hard time finding his line again after that. The last big left turn, the one where Jim Tracy was standing, treated him especially badly. As he entered the turn he encountered a patch of "death cookies"—big chunks of ice that formed on the course after forty or fifty racers whizzed by. Skiing over death cookies was like riding a bicycle into a patch of sand: you might make it through and you might not. Reggie made it through, but not by much. He lost his edge and, with it, a lot of his speed. He finished, if not in first place, then at least in one piece.

"You're always a little intimidated your first run," he said afterward. "You think, God, are these guys really that much better? But probably not. And you just keep telling yourself that.

"This is where I'm starting my World Cup career, right now. Five seconds out in my first run. And you know, I'm hoping to just keep moving up from there. I don't want to be five seconds out again, so we'll see how it goes. I mean, when I ran my very first World Cup I was ten seconds out. I cut that in half today. If I can cut it in half again tomorrow I'll be happy.

"It's amazing how much of this is mental. Everybody's in good shape. Everybody knows how to ski. Everybody has good equipment. When it really boils down to it, it's who wants it the most, and who's the most confident on his skis. That's why I say every run for me is really a confidence builder. I'm going to ski tomorrow with a lot more confidence.

"Those bumps, there's really nothing to them."

As expected, the race organizers canceled the training run scheduled for that afternoon, saying they needed to preserve the course. The racers, who got the news while they were eating lunch at the hotel, were disappointed. They had come to know this hill only in passing, so racing tomorrow would feel odd, unfamiliar, like dancing with a stranger.

Late that afternoon the coaches and athletes gathered in a lobby on the second floor of the hotel for a team meeting. The meeting, a nightly ritual for the downhillers, unfolded the same way every night. Ueli Luthi, just back from the coaches' meeting, would pass out the numbered racing bibs and announce the schedule for the next day. Then he would give his impressions of the day's training run. Next, Bill Egan would say a few words about the course and give a brief inspirational speech. If the athletes had any questions or comments, they could raise them when Egan was done. They usually didn't. On this night, Kyle and AJ sat in overstuffed chairs. The rest of the racers sat or sprawled on the floor. Ueli and Bill stood side by side near the wall.

"If there is a race tomorrow, take it serious," Ueli said. "Warm up. Make sure you are warmed up. One more time, a really thorough inspection. It may be Mickey Mouse or there may be bad weather; you can find a hundred things what it is, eh? But somebody, somebody will get something out of it, and I hope it's you guys. It's the guys who take it serious, get ready, and go for it."

Bill spoke more slowly, with long pauses between sentences. He had a natural sense of drama.

"Yeah, there's a lot of distractions," he said. "Don't let them distract you. You guys skied well today. I saw some good technique and that's the most important thing. Just give it your best shot tomorrow. I don't expect anything. It's not like I expect you to win or I expect you to do shitty or anything like that. You shouldn't really, either.

"It would be nice to have more training runs. It would be nice for everybody to have more training runs. We're in the same boat they are. You guys ski as well as anybody that's there. So just go out there and be confident. Make a good inspection, decide where your line's going to be, and then go for it. If you don't hit it, it's not that big a deal. Let's have a hell of an effort out there tomorrow."

Before the meeting could end, AJ Kitt brought up the matter of the Passat. The racers wanted it, AJ said. Egan made a proposal. This time he made the deal tougher. The kids could drive the car to Kitzbühel if, in tomorrow's downhill, the team placed one racer in the top five, two in the top ten, three in the top fifteen, or four in the top twenty.

Fine, AJ said. He had the final word at the meeting.

"Think Passat, guys."

Surprise, surprise. The night before the downhill, it snowed on Garmisch. Moist, thick, white, lovely. Also unwanted. Racers everywhere have an ironic saying: If you want snow, hold a downhill.

At sunrise, fog surrounded the base of the mountain like the apron around a Christmas tree. All along the course, German army men used shovels to push away the new snow. These men wore close haircuts, green backpacks, green jackets, and ugly government-issue skis that seemed designed to make them look oafish and old-fashioned. But thanks to their work, the jury was able to announce, early in the day, that the race would be run as scheduled.

The Americans, eating breakfast at the hotel, greeted this news with silence. Nor did they talk much in the van on the way to the hill. For them, this was an almost religious occasion. They were doing what many athletes do just before the race, or the game—summoning strength, collecting courage. Downhill skiing, like all athletic challenges, was at least partly about faith. For some racers on the circuit, it was faith in God. For the Americans in Garmisch, none of whom was especially religious, the race would require other kinds of faith—faith in their athleticism, in their mental acuity, and in the experience and wisdom they had acquired as athletes. For the course workers and the technicians and the coaches, going onto the mountain was a job—an enjoyable one, but still a job. For the racers, floating through the morning mist in the cable car was a spiritual journey, an ascension. At the top, they would pray to God, or just have faith in the gods they were.

The decoration in the finish area of the Kandahar downhill illustrated, in full color, the idea that there were few places in the world where you could go without someone trying to sell you a product. Every square inch of the finish corral bore an advertisement for something. Agfa film. S. Oliver jeanswear. Volvo. Warsteiner beer. Did people feel compelled, having seen these signs painted on canvas, to buy the products? Somebody thought so.

At the top of the hill, the first racers were beginning to stretch their muscles. The fog that had shrouded the moutain early in the morning now rose like puffs of cigarette smoke into the sky. It was turning into a clear day. An army man guarded the entrance to the starting area. Outside the gates, fans on skis stood and watched the racers get ready. AJ Kitt paid no attention. He spoke to no one, but only nodded at some of the other racers. Today, AJ wore number seven. The American coaches would watch the forerunners, the snow seeds, and the first three or four racers. Then they would get on their walkie-talkies and give a course report to Bill Egan and AJ. If one of the early racers had found a fast line through one of the turns, AJ would hear about it.

The moment before a race was one of the few times that American downhill racers could truly say they were pampered. The coaches and ski technicians treated them like thoroughbreds; they all seemed eager to get their hands on the athlete, to take part somehow in the thrill the racer alone would experience. As AJ lined up behind Hannes Zehentner, a German racer, Rossignol ski technician Edi Waldburger adjusted AJ's goggles strap and fixed it in place in the back of his helmet. The racer was then sent on, assembly-line style, to Bill Egan, who massaged his lean, hard thighs, pounded his back, and worked his upper arms the way a pizza maker shapes dough. Rubbing down his athletes, his kids, seemed to soothe Egan as much as it did them. AJ lifted his skis off the snow and Edi wiped the bottoms. Then he glided into the starting house, where a man from a goggles company spritzed and wiped his lenses. Hannes Zehentner exploded out of the gate and AJ moved in.

AJ jiggled in the starting house, a lit firecracker. He wiggled his hands, twisted his neck, stomped his skis, *bang bang bang*. Egan stood behind him, saying nothing. You didn't have to coach AJ, not much. Seconds passed. AJ dug his poles into the snow and looked straight ahead. The timing device sounded a series of tones, and on the fifth tone he lurched forward, thrusting his upper body out of the gate, his legs following as if towed by a rope. In a few seconds he disappeared. Bill Egan padded out of the starting house and said into his radio, "AJ on course." Several hundred yards below, Ueli Luthi looked uphill and waited for his star athlete to appear.

As he made the first couple of turns, AJ could hear two voices in his head. One of them told him obvious things: *OK, get on your left ski . . . stay low . . . set up for the next turn . . . you can do it . . .* and so on. This was a helpful, encouraging voice, the voice of a coach. The other voice was different, harsh. This voice said, *You're in trouble, kid. . . . You're dead tired from jet lag and you don't know a thing about this course.* All of which was true. AJ was exhausted, and he could not possibly ski effectively on just one training run. He was not prepared for the Kandahar course.

Within thirty seconds it was over. AJ skied too straight toward one of the gates, made a sharp turn around it, but still ended up too low on the hill to get around the next gate. After he missed it, he stood upright and skied casually the rest of the way down the hill. Jim Tracy radioed to Egan that AJ was through, he had skied out. AJ also glided past Horst Weber, a German-born American ski coach who was traveling with the team. AJ looked relaxed, at ease, but inside he was pissed. He never skied out. Never. It wasn't in his plan. He might ski badly, but not finish? No way. It was humiliating. And now he had to cruise through the finish standing up, like some weenie tourist on his last run of the day. It would have been better, in a way, if he had crashed. Everybody would have admired him for surviving, if he had survived. As it was, people all over the world would see his mistake on TV and think, Huh?

In the finish, after he stepped out of his bindings, AJ grabbed a radio and called up to Egan.

"Tell those guys to get on their skis and hit it hard," he said.

"OK," Egan said.

Egan did not ask AJ why he had not finished. You didn't do that to somebody who was as disappointed as he knew AJ was. Egan could ask his questions later, at dinner, when AJ was in a mood to answer them. For now, he would leave the poor guy alone.

Just then, a voice came over the radio. Horst Weber's voice.

"AJ," he said. "What happened?"

In the finish, something remarkable was happening.

Racers were looking up at the scoreboard and finding that they had exactly the same time as other racers. Daniel Mahrer, the veteran Swiss racer, was alone in first place with a time of 155.01. Atle Skaardal and Hannes Zehentner were tied for second at 155.07. Helmut Höflehner and Lasse Arnesen were next at 155.09. Berni Huber and Rob Boyd followed at 155.13. It wouldn't have been unusual for a single pair of racers to negotiate the 3,455-meter course in exactly the same time. But this bordered on spooky. Some people in the finish thought there must be something wrong with the timing equipment, but that wasn't it. The results merely proved how competitive the World Cup circuit really was. At the end of the day, only twenty-two hundredths of a second would separate the first finisher from the tenth.

Fifteen minutes after AJ left the starting gate, Tommy Moe began putting on his skis at the top of the hill. He was assisted, as he always was, by Mike Decesaro, the Dynastar ski technician. Decesaro, whose job was to tune Tommy's skis before each race, was like a father to Tommy, but then, practically everybody was like a father to Tommy.

Tommy sidestepped downhill to the entrance of the starting house, where Egan awaited. The coach pounded him on the back and said, "Come on, now." The racer coughed, the tones sounded, and he was gone. Tommy skied so well in the first few turns—the only ones Egan could see—that the coach exulted, "Tommy just creamed the top. I mean, he just creamed the top. I think he's, like, the fastest guy."

What Egan did not know was that the fastest guy was feeling a little shaky. Physically, Tommy had recovered nicely from his crash in the training run. His ass was sore and his thumbs felt like little wooden dowels nailed to his hands, but pain wasn't unusual. In downhill, something always hurt. Mentally, though, Tommy was not exactly in the pink. The difference in his mental state from Friday to Saturday was this simple: When he left the gate on Friday, he was not thinking about crashing, and when he left it on Saturday, he was. To put it another way, on race day he was thinking about *not crashing*, which meant he was not thinking about skiing. Among downhillers, thinking about not crashing was the most common form of mental illness, aside from general lunacy and chronically impaired judgment. Thinking about not crashing made you ski badly (see Olson, Jeff). What it did even more than that was make you crash.

Tommy Moe had another reason, besides the soreness in his behind, to worry about disaster. Just before he skied to the starting area, he had stopped in the lodge to watch the first several racers on TV. He had noticed that Switzerland's Franz Heinzer had nearly packed it in in the last turn, the one that had claimed the forerunner the day before. It had scared Tommy, made him jumpy. So now, as he clattered and whizzed into that last turn, Tommy stood up—not straight up, but up far enough to catch the wind in his chest. He made the turn easily, got back in his tuck, and popped off the finish jump, landing safely on his feet. His time was 156.45, a little more than a second behind the leader. If he had not stood up in that turn, he might have been among the leaders. As it was, he was twenty-first.

Fear never made you faster.

"Go, big guy! Go go go go!" Bill Egan shouted as racer number forty-three headed down the hill. Then he said into the radio, "OK, Kyle's on course."

Kyle Rasmussen was a country kid, and looked it. His most memorable features were his eyes, two round blue ice cubes set over a thin, pointed nose and square jaw. He was only twenty-two years old that winter, but the eyes, along with the quickly thinning hair, made him look older, and tougher. When you talked to Kyle, it wasn't unusual to get back, instead of words, a sort of popsicle stare, a look that made a lot of people keep babbling against their will. Kyle had the demeanor of James Coburn, without the sense of danger. If you were casting a Western you'd cast Kyle as the sleek, dusty sheriff who shoulders open the doors of the saloon and, when the noise dies down and everyone's attention is his, nods.

He grew up in Bear Valley, California, a resort area about two and a half hours from San Francisco. The place was founded in part by his grandfather; Kyle was proud to say he was the first baby born to a resident of the village. His father managed Mt. Reba, the little ski area there, and his mother worked in the front office and, some years later, took over the gift shop. For Kyle and his three brothers—two older, one younger—Bear Valley was a safe and remote place to grow up. In winter the three hundred residents rode snowmobiles everywhere because the village didn't plow the roads. Kyle began skiing mostly because everybody in the village skied. Tuesdays and Thursdays, the twenty-seven students at Bear Valley School—a single room that housed grades kindergarten through eight—got out at 12:30 and went skiing. By the time he was eight years old Kyle thought nothing of skiing off a cliff and falling thirty feet to a powdery landing. When he thought about it years later, he supposed it must have been the cliff jumping that turned him into a downhiller. (He didn't give any thought, apparently, to what made him want to jump off the cliffs in the first place.) When he was still in high school he went to Aspen, Colorado, to train with other racers. He was named to the U.S. Ski Team by skiing well at a qualifying camp at Mt. Bachelor, Oregon—the same camp at which Bill Hudson and Jeff Olson qualified for the team.

In the offseason, Kyle worked on his grandfather's cattle ranch and, if he had a spare moment, fished or hunted. In the spring, when the rivers flowed warm and the fish were hungry and aggressive, he fished for bass and trout. On opening weekend he and some buddies always went to Bridgeport, California, to fish the East Walker River and party. They would fish all day, then build a big bonfire, eat what they caught, drink themselves hazy, and bunk down in the beds of their pickups. For a long time Kyle liked to go steelhead fishing when the season opened on January 1, but after a while his racing schedule wouldn't allow it.

He had spent most of the warm months of 1990 hunting for deer, first with a bow, because the bow-hunting season opened first, and then with a rifle. He usually hunted alone because he concentrated better that way. Rasmussen went into the woods not just to kill something, but to test himself. "Outsmarting nature," he called it. One night while bow-hunting, he happened on four big bucks in a meadow. The deer—sleek, limber, suspicious—didn't smell him because the wind was blowing toward him, and besides, he had scrubbed his entire body and skipped a meal to reduce his scent. For several minutes he watched. He was not close enough to try a shot, so he got down on his belly and inched over the twigs and rocks, his bow and quiver slung on his back. It took him ninety minutes to get within thirty yards of them. As he closed in the bucks became still, as if they sensed something but didn't know what it was. Slowly, quietly, Kyle sat up and drew an arrow from his quiver. Across the meadow, one of the bucks stood in profile to him; the animal looked just like the target Kyle had at home. The pounding of his heart made it hard to keep the bow level. He thought, Oh, I've got this thing nailed. He drew the string slowly and evenly, but when he released his grip his arm twisted and the shot flew off line. The arrow hit the buck in the hindquarters. The animal shook the arrow and ran off.

Later in the season Kyle killed a big buck, a four-pointer, with his rifle. Kyle ate everything he killed or caught, so he immediately began to drag the deer home. It was one hundred degrees out and sunny, and he had no water. By moving the animal forty feet he cranked up his heart rate to one hundred eighty beats a minute. After three hours of dragging, he left the dead buck in the woods and went home. He showered, ate, napped, and then went back and dragged some more. His back hurt and his leg muscles burned, but he liked that. He told himself, Boy, this is going to pay off when I go to Kitzbühel this year. He got the deer home before dark.

Kyle was the only married man on the downhill team, including coaches. He and his high school sweetheart, Linda, had eloped to Reno on December 22, 1989, not long after Linda, quite without meaning to, had become pregnant. (As Bill Hudson might have said: Whoops.) Oh, well, the couple figured, we'd always talked about getting married anyway. Kyle and Linda's son Anthony had been born in the spring of 1990. Kyle took along pictures of the boy whenever he left home.

Having a son made Kyle think about life in new ways. While his teammates thought mostly about how to go faster or how to meet more exotic women or what kind of portable CD player to buy, Kyle worried about how he would take care of his family. His ski sponsor, Head, paid him only a few thousand dollars a year. He could earn bonuses by finishing near the top in World Cup races, which was easy to say and hard to do. As it was, his wife and son lived in Linda's father's house because Kyle couldn't afford to get them a place of their own. He knew he couldn't rely on family forever, and more and more he wondered if he should give up the selfish, vagabond racing life. Soon he might not have a choice: Kyle had a congenital back defect that sometimes made it painful for him to ski. Maybe, he thought, I should give up racing and go into the family ranching business. He referred to leading such a life as "being normal."

But he wasn't ready to do that, not yet. Kyle liked being an athlete, liked the regular schedule of road trips and workouts and races. When he stayed home for long stretches he got restless, and he found himself doing things like taking the cover off his boat for no reason and rolling the trailer a few feet to make sure the tires weren't flat and driving out on his grandpa's ranch to look at the cattle. You don't have to stand and look at a cow too long, apparently, before it occurs to you that you don't have enough to do. The other reason Kyle didn't quit racing, the reason he always got around to when he thought about it, was that it was fun, more fun than he could have doing anything else, even fishing and hunting. He had not always felt that way. When he first went to Europe to compete in Europa Cup events, he couldn't believe how fast the guys went. Seventy, eighty miles an hour, speeds he never attained in the United States because the courses were so much easier. It was terrible. He wasn't skiing well in the first place, and his fear made him ski even worse. Every morning he woke up sick because he knew he had to click on his skis and tremble down some big ugly hill. But after a while he got used to it, and when he did he wasn't scared anymore, or at least not as scared as he had been. The idea, in downhill, wasn't to be fearless. The idea was not to let fear kill you.

It was all Kyle could do, in Garmisch, to get to the bottom alive. His run began to go wrong seconds after Bill Egan shouted "Go go go go!" In the second turn, he leaned a little too far inside and slipped, slowing himself down just slightly. It was an unusual mistake for Kyle, who was a fine technical skier. Having made the error, Kyle felt he had to work hard to make up time. In the middle of the course, he didn't ski so much as fly down the hill. He was out of control, the driver of a runaway truck. He flew so far off the Eishang jump that he would later say it was as high as he had ever gotten on skis. The weight of the landing drove his rear end into the ground; Kyle said it was "just like squatting four hundred, five hundred pounds." His right leg shot out to one side, but he quickly summoned it back, a cossack performing his difficult dance.

The effort of the landing, along with the normal strain of a two-minute downhill race, turned Kyle's leg muscles to noodles. As he emerged from Hell and approached the last turn, his skis inexplicably split apart and he found himself nearly on his rear end again. But again, he managed to right himself. As he tucked toward the finish, he said to himself, "I'm tired."

He stayed low off the finish jump, gliding over the snow like a gull swooping over water. He landed smoothly, too. As all the racers did, Kyle slid under the finish banner in a tuck. Unlike the others, he found that he could not stand up again. He was too exhausted. So he lay down on the ice, hoping to skid to a stop. Kyle was doing about seventy miles an hour when he came through the finish, and when he lay down he had the sensation of actually picking up speed. His slick, tight-fitting downhill suit did nothing to slow him down, and he was purposely trying to hold his skis off the snow so he wouldn't catch an edge and snap an ankle.

Kyle was headed straight for the fence at the far end of the finish area. Even lying down, he could see the orange padding rushing at him. Uh-oh, he thought, I'm going to hit this sucker hard. The collision made a crunching noise, like a huge limb snapping off a tree. The racer collided with a part of the fence that happened to carry a canvas banner for Agfa film; the force of the collision crinkled the banner like scrap paper. The people standing nearby scattered. Kyle hit the fence so hard that he drove it back three feet, into yet another fence. Everything around him seemed speeded up, like a film played in fast motion. He sensed several things at once, none of them clearly: the sound of a child crying; the cold snow against his body; a dull pain in his left leg; the drumbeat of his heart.

Almost as soon as he stopped, Kyle sprang to his feet (his skis having released on impact) and surveyed his body. Head? No problem. Arms, hands, upper body? Check. Thighs, knees, lower legs, feet? Got 'em. His whole body tingled with fear and excitement; only his left leg seemed seriously screwed up. Around him, people were asking him questions. Are you all right? Can you walk? Yeah, he could walk. But what was that pain in his leg?

Kyle looked down. At his feet was a thick wooden stake about three feet long. Shit, he thought. That explains it. The stake had been used as a support for the snow fence. Kyle's left shinbone had sheared it off at the base.

Bill Hudson finished in thirty-fourth place. When Bill Egan saw Hudson's time on the chalkboard near the starting house, he said, "That's damned good. We'll take that. That's good." For a guy recovering from head trauma and wearing a hardware-store contraption on his knee, it was.

Reggie Crist, the last American to start, did not finish within two and a half seconds of the winner, as he had hoped he would, but he came close. He finished fifty-seventh, about three and a half seconds out, an improvement of more than a second over the day before. Still, his run could not be called a thing of beauty. Like Kyle, Reggie tipped over in the finish and skidded into the fence (he missed the Agfa film sign, but hit the advertisement for S. Oliver jeans). As if that weren't humiliation enough, the sports network ESPN, broadcasting the race, misspelled his name on the screen. To the folks back home he was not Crist, but Christ, a promotion he hardly felt he deserved.

By the time Switzerland's Daniel Mahrer climbed onto the victory stand, the American racers were back at the Hotel Mercure, eating lunch. After the meal, they went to their rooms to shower and relax. All, that is, except one.

AJ Kitt took the van and went skiing. He wanted to work on his turns.

Kyle Rasmussen's leg hurt him so much after lunch that he went into Garmisch to have it X-rayed. The doctor told him his shinbone appeared to have a lengthwise crack in it.

Kyle thought of Linda and Anthony back in California. Earlier that winter, Kyle had written Anthony's name on a piece of white tape and stuck it to his helmet, so the world could know the name of his son.

"Anthony's the only headgear sponsor you have to pay for," Kyle liked to say. But now, having the kid's name on the helmet seemed sad. Kyle needed money to support the family, and he couldn't do it stomping around in a cast. He had to ski, and ski well, to earn bonuses from his sponsors. He even had dreams of winning a medal at the Alpine World Championships next month in Saalbach, Austria. He couldn't have a broken leg. Just couldn't. The doctor took another X-ray. This time, the leg didn't appear to be broken at all. You're fine, the doctor told him. Just stay off the leg for a couple of days and you'll be all right. Whew, Kyle thought, that was close.

That night, Kyle limped into the team meeting and lowered himself into a chair. Ueli Luthi pointed to the racer's leg and said, "How is it?"

Clearly, it was killing him. "Not bad," Kyle said.

"OK," the coach said. "And how is Moe?"

"No problem," Moe said.

"Anybody else hurt or injured?"

"Just our egos," AJ Kitt said.

Well, that was easy to see. As they sat in the hotel lobby, the downhillers looked glum, like Little Leaguers who had lost the championship game by twenty-three runs. The Americans had come to Europe expecting to do well, and instead they had missed gates and whacked fences and generally looked like a bunch of klutzes. Sure, Tommy Moe had come in twenty-first, and a year ago he might have been satisfied with that. But before Garmisch he had finished in the top fifteen in four consecutive World Cup races, and he was getting kind of used to it. Finishing in the twenties wasn't going to cut it anymore.

Bill Egan seemed annoyed, too. As the kids sprawled in the lobby, he stood, as always, with his hands in his pockets and the corners of his mouth turned downward.

"There were some pleasant things that happened today," he said, mentioning in particular Tommy's first couple of turns, and the parts of the run during which Kyle was upright. "But in order to be in the top fifteen, in order to ski the way you guys can ski, you don't ski good. You have to ski, you know, great. You have to ski as well as the best, the very best skiers in the world. And I guess that's great.

"You know, we can't afford to have three out of five of our top skiers falling in the finish. Now, why we fell in the finish, I don't know," he said. From the way he used the word "we," you'd think he, too, had flashed across the ice and crumpled the Agfa film sign. "Maybe we went through the finish and found it was unbelievably slick. Maybe we let up mentally there. Well, we just can't do that.

"What I'm trying to get to is, we've got to kick our intensity level up just a little bit more. We've got four weeks coming up right now, and they are the meat of the season. Where we're going right now is the big time. I mean, this is it. This is the heaviest race schedule we're going to have. And that's what we've been training for all year, to be really great right now. So we want to put it together now."

Today's downhill, Egan concluded, was a "shitty experience. I wasn't looking forward to today, either. But from now on, let's make sure we do what we can do. OK? Just kick it up. I'm just asking for a month. After that we'll kick it down. But for the next month, we're going to *go*."

4

The Hahnenkamm

Bill Hudson and Reggie Crist drove the American team's van from Garmisch, Germany, to Kitzbühel, Austria, on Monday afternoon. At the border, they flashed their passports and drove through. Bill, who was behind the wheel, followed the autobahn for a while, and turned onto a two-lane road that twisted up one side of a mountain and down the other. Then the road flattened out and led the racers to Kitzbühel. Soon the athletes could see the lower part of the race course—a narrow white pitch bordered on both sides by snow fences. The nets looked, to them, like long orange ribbons flowing toward the finish. This was it. The race known as the Hahnenkamm, or cock's comb.

Bill was excited. This was his kind of course—steep, fast, fear-making. It took nerve to ski this course, and Bill had plenty. In 1990 he had finished thirteenth here, his best World Cup finish ever. He expected to do even better this year. If he was ever going to win a major race, he believed this would be the one.

Reggie, who had never raced in Kitzbühel but had thought about it all his life, was full of questions.

"Do you know where the hotel is?"

"No. We'll have to ask at the race office," Bill said.

"Where's that?"

"Probably the same place it was last year."

Bill and Reggie got along all right, but they weren't great friends. They were too busy competing to be really close. Bill was only two years older than Reggie, but he often talked to him as if he were a green, goofy kid. Bill had no doubt that he was a better racer than Reggie was. Reggie could sense how Bill felt, but he didn't let it bother him. Sure, Hudson had more World Cup experience than he did, and he had skied brilliantly at times. But really, he was no Franz Klammer. Reggie wasn't all that impressed by him.

Still, Bill had an advantage over Reggie at the moment: He had skied in Kitzbühel and Reggie hadn't. As Reggie gazed out the window at the course, Bill said, "So, Reg, does it make you nervous?"

Reggie shot him a look that said: Shut up.

But yes, as a matter of fact, it did. The Hahnenkamm made Reggie as nervous as hell.

It had that effect on a lot of people. The Hahnenkamm had a reputation as the most treacherous downhill course in the world. Everyone, no matter how rugged or experienced or foolish, feared it. Tommy Moe certainly did. He had never competed in the Hahnenkamm, but he had come close. A year earlier, he and his teammates were loading their gear into the van for the drive to Kitzbühel when Tommy suddenly announced that he had changed his mind; he was not going. He was adamant about it. With that, he moved his things to another car and drove to a smaller, safer race. But Tommy could not avoid Kitzbühel forever. This year, he had vowed to ski the course even if it killed him.

The race, set on a slope called the Streif, was first run in 1930, when skiers wore baggy clothing and competed on heavy wooden planks a lot like barrel staves. The first winner, Georg Berger of Kitzbühel, finished in 12:28.6. Over the next six decades, athletes improved dramatically and equipment rocketed into the space age, but the Hahnenkamm course stayed more or less the same. So the racers of the 1990s were skiing the course about five times as fast as it was meant to be skied, with the same small room for error. It was easy to see why bad things happened to people who made mistakes at Kitzbühel.

Guys who made it to the bottom of the Streif standing up talked about it the way a person might talk about nearly driving his car off a cliff or nearly stumbling in front of a subway car. You haven't seen gratitude until you've seen the bright, shining face of a young guy who has just finished the race at Kitzbühel. Andy Mill, an American downhiller in the 1970s and early 1980s, put it this way: "When you go into the starting gate, your eyeballs are open and your ass is tight. And when you go through the finish gate, your eyes close in relief and your ass relaxes. It's just unbelievable."

The starting hut was a sturdy old shack about the size of a double-wide trailer. The beginning of the course was so steep that the racers often exaggerated that they had to peer between their skis just to see the first gate. And they weren't exaggerating much. Five seconds into the run the racers sailed off of a jump called the Mausefalle, German for mousetrap. The name was appropriate: Like mice inching toward cheese, the racers might have been better off leaving the Mausefalle alone. Going off this jump made the earth disappear beneath your feet. The pitch leading to it was steep, but the landing was steeper. Imagine sitting on a bicycle on the top of your house. Now, point the front wheel of the bike down the slope and pump as fast as you can off the edge of the roof. Imagine doing that ten times as fast and you'll know how it felt to go off the Mausefalle.

How far did the racers fly? Some people said a hundred feet. Others said one hundred yards. (The Mausefalle was like a Babe Ruth home run—people tended to exaggerate about it.) In any event, it was farther than most people would want to fly at sixty or so miles an hour, off-balance, on skis.

After a left turn and a roundhouse right, the racers confronted the Steilhang, or steep drop. That it was. To Andy Mill, negotiating the Steilhang was comparable to skiing over the top of a basketball—it kept getting steeper, and you couldn't see what was around the bend. A snow fence ran down the left side of the slope, and no matter how well you skied, your momentum pressed you right up against the fence. A lot of guys had heard their boot buckles clicking against that fence; it was a terrible sound, the sound of the warden taping electrodes to your head.

Many people had crashed in the Steilhang. Jeff Olson once went head-first into the fence, and lived to boast about it. But Brian Stemmle of Canada had the crash most people talked about. In 1989, Stemmle, carrying a lot of speed, caught the tip of his ski in the netting. Instead of bouncing off the fence, he somehow ended up spinning around on top of it. His internal injuries were so severe that for several days the doctors feared he would die. When he lived, they said he would never ski again, and might never walk. So it was a pretty dramatic moment in fall 1990 when Stemmle, having missed an entire year of skiing, won the Pan Am Games downhill in Las Leñas, Argentina. Later that year, he finished tenth in Val d'Isère and fifteenth in Val Gardena. But it would have been awkward for him to be in Kitzbühel for the Hahnenkamm in 1991: He was suing the race organizers.

Once past the Steilhang, the racers followed a long, narrow road for nearly a minute. Relatively speaking, this was the easy part of the course. Then they flew off of the Hausberg jump, sailing perhaps a hundred feet before their skis touched snow. Next, the racers made a left turn through a compression, where they had the sensation of skiing through the bottom of a teacup. After that was the part of the course known as the traverse, a frightfully steep slope with ridges in its side. Instead of skiing straight down, the racers had to ski across it. To get a sense of how awkward it felt to ski the traverse, stand at the bottom of a staircase with your right leg on the floor and your left leg on the fourth step. Then imagine what it would be like to ski over a washboard in that posture. The skiers twitched and jiggled as if they were plugged into something.

At the end of the traverse, the course narrowed and the racers had to shoot through the gate leading to the Zielschuss, a pitch as steep as the in-run for a ski jump. The ground leveled out at the bottom of the hill. The G forces were so intense there that a racer who wasn't completely in control could count on falling backward and placing his butt print in the snow. The locals liked to watch the race from along the sides of the Zielschuss for two reasons: it was close to the finish line, and they were likely to see at least one bone-snapping crash. Todd Brooker, a Canadian racer, rewarded them one year by tipping over at the top of the hill, knocking himself out cold, and tumbling, like a rag doll, to the bottom. Andy Mill nearly packed it in one year, too, in a training run. As he reached the end of the traverse he leaned back in his ski boots. By the time he was halfway down the Zielschuss he was lying so far back that his shoulders dragged on the snow. He went through the compression with his right ski on the snow and he left ski over his head. What could he do? He was a dead man. And then, inexplicably, he bounced up, got a grip on himself, and whooshed through the finish line. It was a religious moment.

"I felt like God had just taken me by the chest with his hand and just pulled me back up on my feet," Mill said years later. The Creator's name often was invoked at the Hahnenkamm; the racers and coaches, many of whom were not otherwise religious, gave Him a lot of credit for what happened on that narrow icy highway.

The Streif was accorded respect in other ways, too. The American racers were so in awe of the Hahnenkamm that, over the years, a tradition had evolved: On the U.S. Ski Team, you were considered a rookie downhiller until you had negotiated the Streif from start to finish. And a training run didn't cut it: You had to make it down on race day. In January 1991, Bill Hudson and Jeff Olson were the only obvious veterans on the team. AJ Kitt's status was the subject of a lively argument. AJ had raced at Kitzbühel once, in 1990. But because snow was so scarce that winter, the race had been contested in two runs, each beginning about halfway up the hill. His teammates, who made up the rules as they went along, contended that AJ wouldn't be a veteran until he had skied the Mausefalle and the Steilhang. Bill Hudson was adamant on this point.

"I'm sorry. I think we still have to consider you a rookie," he told AJ. Being a rookie involved taking a certain amount of crap from your teammates.

AJ snapped, "The rule is that if you finish the race at Kitzbühel, you're a vet. And last year was the race at Kitzbühel."

Being a rookie also meant you had to carry the rookie rock. The rookie rock was a big, flat rock that was kept at a hotel in Mols, Switzerland, where the guys often stayed between races. Each year, at a party called rookie night, the rock was given to the rookies on the team. The only way to get rid of it was to ski Kitzbühel. So being a rookie was a burden, literally. More than any other course on the World Cup circuit, the Hahnenkamm had to be conquered.

But as the team arrived in town, Bill Egan wasn't thinking about conquering anything. Of the five guys he was bringing to the race, three (Tommy Moe, Kyle Rasmussen, and Reggie Crist) had never skied the Hahnenkamm, and one (AJ) had never skied it from the top. The fifth athlete, Bill Hudson, was coming off a knee injury. So Egan wasn't concerned about results. All he wanted his guys to do, he said, was "finish upright."

On Monday night, in a cold drizzle, Egan took a walk through the slick streets of Kitzbühel, alone. Bill was compact and rugged, with hard, muscular legs and a chest that bulged under his ski sweaters. His brown hair was so wispy-thin, especially on top, that it almost wasn't worth the effort to comb it; it fell wherever it wanted to. He had icy blue eyes and a soft and somewhat nasal voice, the voice of someone who wants to get his point across without hurting your feelings. His face was well weathered. The many days he had spent squinting against the white glare of the snow had left deep lines around his eyes, and the many nights he'd spent laughing with his friends at the bar had carved creases around his mouth. Despite the rain, it was a nice night to be out. The air was chill but not bitter, and the village, decked out in pine boughs and bright lights, was alive with people going to dinner or to the bars. Signs of the race were everywhere: Cars bearing ski company logos lined the streets, and banners hanging from shop windows advertised deals on boots, bindings, and other equipment. But Egan, hatless and huddled in a trench-coat, was oblivious to it all. He had a hard decision to make, one involving his kids.

Bill, who turned forty-two years old that January, had created an entire life for himself in sports. He grew up mostly in California, where he surfed and played basketball, a little baseball, and a whole lot of football. When he got out of high school, Utah State offered him a football scholarship, but not a particularly good one. So he stayed in California and played safety for MiraCosta Community College in Oceanside. Bill was wild about the game of football, and ferocious when he played it. He wasn't the sort of safety who arm-tackled people. He whacked them, leveled them, creamed them. ("Creamed" was one of his favorite words.) Bill threw himself at people, even though, in those days, there wasn't that much to throw. He stood five feet seven inches tall and weighed one hundred fifty pounds in cleats. (Jim Tracy, his assistant coach on the ski team, was about the same height; the downhillers called the two men "The Twin Towers.") But he never thought of himself as being small, and neither did anyone else. In his last year at MiraCosta, he was an honorable mention All-America. After junior college, Bill went to United States International University's Cal Western campus on a scholarship. He majored in history and psychology and minored in physical education (he later got a teaching certificate), but what he cared about most was football. Bill wept at the last practice session of his college career. The next day he went into the game and creamed some people. An appropriate epitaph for his football career might be: He Played Way Over His Head.

Bill was too small to play pro football. But he was too hooked on competition to give up athletics, so he decided to learn an individual sport. He chose skiing. When he was still in his senior year in college, he took the winter quarter off and headed to Mammoth, California, to be a night janitor and a ski bum. He learned to ski so quickly that he was soon offered a job as a ski instructor. "That was my demise," he said years later. For the next twenty years, he spent January to June skiing and coaching ski racers in Mammoth. The rest of the year he coached football at Saddleback Community College, near Mission Viejo. Bill had a nice life, more than a grown-up jock could reasonably hope for. Even so, by the middle of the 1980s, he was beginning to feel uncomfortable with it. He was almost forty years old; he felt it was time to devote the entire year either to football or skiing and see how things went.

Over the years, Bill had become acquainted with Theo Nadig, the coach of the men's downhill team. By the mid-1980s, the longtime stars of the downhill team—Doug Lewis, Mike Brown, and Olympic gold medalist Bill Johnson—were near the end of their careers. A new group of racers—Bill Hudson, Jeff Olson, AJ Kitt, and others—would soon take their place. Nadig and Ueli Luthi asked Bill to help whip these new guys into shape and build their strength. In 1989, when Nadig left the U.S. Ski Team (he ended up coaching the Italians), Bill got the head coaching job.

Soon after he took the job, Bill began dating a ski team publicist named Maggie Dyer. Traveling from race to race could be fun, but inevitably it got tedious and exhausting, and Bill often missed Maggie. Being a U.S. Ski Team coach was murder on relationships: Few coaches were married, and none of the three World Cup downhill coaches was. Bill and Maggie kept their relationship fresh by talking frequently on the phone and writing letters. One season, Maggie bought Bill a tape recorder, which he used to make notes for himself on the hill and record his voice for Maggie. She sent him tapes too. Bill, who was not known for his meticulous attention to detail, had trouble remembering which tapes contained ski racing notes and which ones came from Maggie.

Often, when he flicked on the recorder expecting to hear his own voice, he heard Maggie whispering, "Hey, Babe."

To the guys on the team, Bill was more like an older brother than a coach. They didn't always agree with him, but the racers trusted him, and more than that they liked him. They had long since compacted his name from Bill Egan to "Billegan," as in "Billegan's Island." It was a sign of their affection. They were devoted to him because he was devoted to them. When one of them crashed and broke something and couldn't race anymore, Bill tried to tell himself it was part of the sport, to keep a firm jaw, but he was lousy at it. For someone who had spent so much time around football players, he tended to be pretty emotional. When one of his kids got hurt, Bill got hurt too.

The possibility of injury was exactly what he was concerned about that drizzly night in Kitzbühel. The Europa Cup super G race scheduled for the coming weekend in Château D'Oex, Switzerland, was sure to be canceled for lack of snow. If the three American racers there—Jeff Olson, Steve Porino, and Eric Keck—stayed, they would have no race to compete in, and no way even to train. It would be a complete waste. The question, for the coach, was whether to leave them in dreary brown Switzerland, where they would be safe and bored, or invite them to Kitzbühel (they could easily make it in time for the first training run on Wednesday), where they would have an exciting time. The problem was it might be so exciting that it could involve helicopters and leg splints.

Bill had every reason not to bring them to Kitzbühel. Jeff Olson had finished first and second in a couple of Nor-Am super G races in late December, but Bill knew he still had no confidence in downhill. And the Hahnenkamm was no place for him to get it. This course was like a vicious dog: If it sensed fear, it would maul you. Besides, Jeff had a bad history here. Just last year, he had skied into a hole as he was crossing the traverse and fallen, *whump*, on his collarbone, snapping it like a stick. Who knew what he might do to himself this year? As for Porino and Keck, well, neither had skied in a World Cup race in a couple of years. Was it fair to put them up against the best in the world here? Probably not. The difference between Château D'Oex and Kitzbühel was like Little League and the majors; that was how Bill thought of it. What was more, he wanted all of his racers to be extremely careful on the Hahnenkamm course, and he didn't think Keck, a big guy with a reputation for doing crazy things, would be careful. Bill hated the thought of calling Keck's parents—or anybody else's—and saying something like, "I'm very sorry to tell you that . . ." No way. It made no sense to put these kids, these rookies, in danger.

But then, it didn't make sense not to. Bill knew what Jeff, Steve, and Eric would say about skiing Kitzbühel: "Right on! Let's go for it!" He couldn't blame them for being excited. They were ski racers, after all. They were supposed to race, not lounge around in Swiss hotels, waiting for cold weather. What was the point of hauling these kids across the Atlantic if you weren't going to let them race? As Bill strolled in the drizzle, that side of the argument grew stronger and stronger in his mind. Jeff, Steve, and Eric deserved a chance, along with the rest of the team, to compete against the very best. In the last couple of years, most of the Europa Cup downhill races had been canceled because of bad weather; Steve and Eric hadn't raced much at all. Bill didn't feel he could make them wait any longer.

Later, back at the Schwarzer Adler hotel, Bill found Kyle Rasmussen sitting in the lobby, resting his sore leg.

"We're going to have Porino, Keck, and Olson come over here," Egan said. "I can't say no."

By 8:30 Wednesday morning the American downhillers—Jeff Olson, Steve Porino, and Eric Keck among them—were at the top of the Streif, ready to inspect the course.

Steve Porino had felt strange, out of sorts, when he woke up that morning. The feeling had persisted through breakfast and intensified as he inspected the top part of the run, the part leading to the Mausefalle. He tried to pay attention, tried to envision himself negotiating each bump and turn, but he couldn't. All he could think was: I haven't had a single positive thought all day.

Steve was twenty-four years old that winter. He grew up mostly in Winnetka, Illinois, on Chicago's North Shore. He and his three older sisters spent childhood weekends skiing at Wilmot Mountain, a treeless knoll with a vertical drop of 256 feet. It was a hill for city people—"the kind of place," Steve said, "where people crash into the lodge." But it also produced some accomplished slalom racers, Steve among them. As a kid he called himself Steven "Jet Power" Porino. Every day after school he got into the car with his mom or one of his sisters and rode an hour to Wilmot, where he skied under the lights until 9 P.M. He raced well enough at Wilmot to be admitted, during his sophomore year in high school, to Burke Mountain Academy, a school for racers in far northern Vermont. In his early days at Burke he had no interest in downhill, so he competed mostly in the technical events.

He ran his first major downhill when he was seventeen years old. To qualify for the World Junior Championships you had to compete in a downhill, and that year the qualifying race happened to be in Avon, Colorado, at the Beaver Creek resort. Steve, accustomed to Wilmot and the small hills of Vermont, was in no way ready for this downhill, in which racers sometimes got going as fast as ninety miles an hour. "I was," he recalled, "definitely shitting my pants." There were three training runs. In the first, he crashed after he smacked his arm on the base of a gate. He made it to the bottom the second time, but was so exhausted from holding his tuck that his teeth and arms went numb. "I was like a heart attack victim," he said. In the third run, his ski blew off and he fell again. But on the day of the race something was different and he finished about thirtieth, pushing his national ranking above his standing in either of the technical events. In the downhill at the 1984 World Junior Championships at Sugarloaf, Maine, he finished twenty-first.

Suddenly, and forever, he was a downhill maniac.

By 1991 Steve had been on the U.S. Ski Team for four years, but his career hadn't gone far. Because of a lack of snow in Europe, he hadn't raced much, and therefore hadn't improved much. Sometimes he thought about working as a television ski racing analyst, which he might have done well: He was rugged and handsome and was possibly the wittiest guy on the ski team. But he decided that could wait. For now he would seek speed, and victory, and the feeling you get going under the finish banner and looking up to see the numeral one flash next to your name.

But today, looking over the lip of the Mausefalle, Steven "Jet Power" Porino just felt queasy. He looked at the compression below the Mausefalle and measured the roundhouse turn leading to the Steilhang, but the more time he spent on the course the less he thought about ski racing. As he made his way down he began to think about—of all things—vacationing in the islands of the Caribbean. He thought of palm trees, beaches, exotic women. So warm, so relaxing. He knew just how he would work the vacation into his schedule, too—in about an hour, he would start down this race course. Then he would crash, get hurt, and go to the Caribbean to recuperate. He actually thought this. It was a sure thing, as he saw it, that he would fall. He had been in Europe for four days, and still hadn't had a chance to go fast on skis. The last time he had built up any real speed was a year ago, in his last World Cup downhill. Clearly he wasn't ready to ski the Streif. He could not predict with any certainty how serious his injuries would be—he tried not to dwell on that part—but he felt certain they would be severe enough to lay him up for, oh, three or four weeks, anyway.

Yeah, that's it, Steve told himself. The Caribbean.

It was then, about halfway through the inspection, that Steve, as his teammates later put it, "saw God." That is, he realized he would just as soon not visit the islands if it meant going in a body cast. This was not an easy decision for him. As a downhiller, Steve had a certain reputation to uphold—a reputation for always doing the scary, reckless thing, regardless of whether it was a good idea. To back out of the race now would be to violate the unspoken yet sacred oath of the downhiller: I vow to risk everything for kicks. He understood that. But he also knew he could get away with it at Kitzbühel, where almost everyone owned up to feeling afraid. Yes, he was supposed to be a stud. But it didn't mean he had to be a suicide.

After the inspection he got on the radio and called up to Bill Egan, who was standing below the Mausefalle.

"I'm not going to ski today," Steve said. "I'm just light-years away."

Egan, relieved, replied immediately. "OK. That's your decision," he said. "No problem."

The forerunners began making their nervous runs about 10:30 A.M. The second guy tipped over as he left the starting house, bounced back up, narrowly made the next gate, sailed off the Mausefalle, landed, and crashed at the bottom of the hill.

About that time, Eric Keck was near the entrance to the starting house, clicking into his bindings. When he had arrived in Kitzbühel on Tuesday, Bill Egan had told him there weren't enough spots for everyone, so Eric could participate in the training runs, but not in the race. That was OK. Eric just wanted to have his way with that big hairy beast called Hahnenkamm. He didn't care if the results didn't count. As it turned out, he was selected at random as a snow seed. He would start sixth.

The first thing people noticed about Eric was his size. His vastness was the defining thing about him, the central fact of his life. The ski team media guide said he "may be the biggest man (or anything) to represent the U.S. in international ski racing." He stood six feet two inches tall and weighed two hundred fifty-five pounds, practically none of it fat. The circumference of his thighs was such that the skinny-legged Bill Hudson could have fit both of his legs into one leg of Eric's jeans. Eric had hands like a bear's paws, beefy upper arms, a broad nose, and eyes that narrowed into piggy-bank slots when he smiled. Eric was not a great downhiller, and never would be: His size made him struggle through the turny, technical sections of a course. "If all downhill courses were straight, he'd never lose," Bill Egan once said. Being huge had other disadvantages. The ski team never managed to supply Eric with ski clothing that fit him. And when Eric was growing up in Montpelier, Vermont, other kids frequently picked fights with him. (When people see a mountain, they want to climb it.) Eric, for his part, was never one to turn the other cheek. If you wanted a fight, he'd give you a fight.

Eric was the sort of person who was always torn between competing urges. One was the urge to be a good person. Tom and Bev Keck raised Eric and his sister, Heidi, in a Baptist congregation in Montpelier. Eric enjoyed the experience, but like many young people, he quit thinking about religion when he entered his teens. He just figured the Word of God didn't apply to him. And he got along fine that way. After a few years on the ski team, he picked up the Bible again, just for something to read. It can't be that bad, he told himself. Everybody reads it. Well, it wasn't bad at all. Fact was, it was good. He loved it. Suddenly its teachings made a lot of sense. God became real for him again. That was how he put it: God was real. "You can talk about God forever," he said. "It's something that's in man's nature, to wonder if there's something more to life." Now, everywhere he went, the huge Christian carried two Bibles with him—the American Standard and New International versions. They fulfilled his spiritual needs.

But he still had to contend with another urge—the one to have a good time. Some of Eric's teammates couldn't help being amused by his new-found faith. Was this the same Eric Keck who dazzled his friends by farting on lighted matches, shooting flame across the room? No, it was not easy to be a Christian. Once, when Eric and Reggie were living in Sun Valley, Idaho, the police were called to break up a party they had thrown. Quite a few underage girls were found there, drinking. Eric and Reggie were sentenced to perform community service at the dump. They spent most of their time making videotapes of each other bashing in car windshields with a sledgehammer. Another time, after a ski team camp in South America, Eric and Reggie rented a car and used it to chase sheep around a field. Eric would try anything for fun. Once, after a heavy snowfall, he stepped into his skis and executed a double backflip in the layout position. Tim "Swampy" LaMarche, a coach who witnessed the jump, said Keck "looked like a 747 doing a slow roll." Reggie Crist felt Eric was the only person he knew who truly wasn't afraid of anything. That would come in handy in Kitzbühel. Faith in God would, too.

It was almost 11 A.M. and the sky was a cool gray when Eric thrust his gigantic torso out of the starting gate. He sank into his tuck, eased around the first two gates, and aimed himself at the Mausefalle. Dozens of people had stationed themselves in the woods to see the racers go off the jump. As Eric speeded by them, his shiny black skis made a fluttering sound, like birds flocking skyward. And then he took flight, a stocky, twenty-two-year-old man defying nature and reason, gliding on air, his ski poles extended like wings.

But he was too far to the right. Way too far.

He was flying toward the rickety wooden fence on the side of the course. Just when it seemed he would hit, he lifted his knees and pulled himself into a tuck. He cleared the fence by two feet and disappeared among the evergreens.

For a moment there was quiet, as everyone in Kitzbühel drew a breath. And then the people on the hill began to speak at funeral volume, in murmurs and whispers. They spoke in many languages—German, English, French. Did you see that? Where is he? Is he all right? My God. *Ach, mein Gott.* A half-dozen army men in heavy boots clomped after the racer. A Canadian doctor in ski boots followed. Across the course, Bill Egan spoke into his radio.

"Keck's down."

The athlete left a trail of equipment in the woods. One ski was planted in the deep snow like a signpost. Farther down the hill, the other lay flat, the Head logo facing up. A ski pole sprang from the white powder near a tree. And Eric lay on his back next to the fence, as if he were hiding.

He felt all right, considering. He could see his arms and legs spread out below him; they didn't look smashed or twisted. What worried him most was a strange feeling in his mouth. Slowly he touched his gloved hand to his face. He felt something strange, something hard, and on the fingers of the glove he saw blood. Damn. What was that in his mouth? Maybe it's my tongue, he thought. Maybe I ripped my tongue out and it's lying under my nose. Or maybe a piece of flesh peeled off my chin. Keck touched the thing again. Ohhhhh. Not tongue. Not flesh. The strap on his crash helmet. It had slipped off his chin and into his mouth.

He moved the strap. Blood leaked from the cuts in his lips. He had pink wounds on his forehead and a bruise around his eyes in the shape of his goggles. His white racing bib was spotted red like a tie-dyed shirt. His right thigh muscle burned and his thumb felt stiff. Ron England, a Canadian team doctor who had watched the crash from the bottom of the Mausefalle, kneeled by the racer.

"Can you move your arms and legs? Your head?"

"Yeah," Keck said. "I'm all right. Let me up."

Eric struggled to his feet. He looked up the hill, looked at the path he had flown. And then he thrust both arms in the air, drew a deep breath, and let forth a beautiful sound, the sound of a man who was not dead.

"Yeeeaaahhhh!"

The crowd cracked up. Eric felt blessed. The night before, he had read Philippians 4:13: "I can do all things through Him who strengthens me."

"Last night," he said, "I asked the Lord for strength. And the Lord gave the kid strength."

The training run continued. Across the course, Bill Egan was worried. The racers—not just his guys, but all the athletes—were getting way too much air off the Mausefalle. Eric Keck had gone into the woods. Then AJ landed so close to the fence that the buckles on his ski boots rattled, clack-clack-clack, against the slats. Christ, Bill thought, somebody's going to get killed out here. He got on the radio and told Tommy Moe to go easy off the jump. Tommy, already scared out of his mind, obeyed the order so faithfully that he was barely moving when he reached the lip of the jump. He hardly got any air at all.

Bill Hudson would be the next American to start.

"Listen, when you go off the jump, you have to make a very big move, and you have to make sure you don't go right," Egan told him by radio.

"Like Keck?" Hudson said.

"Like Keck."

"Is he OK?"

"He's fine."

At the top, Bill Hudson had to laugh. What a character, he thought. Bill got a kick out of Eric, but he didn't take him seriously as a racer. Eric was too big and too wild to take seriously. It figured that he would go over a fence at sixty miles an hour. It also figured he'd walk away from it.

By the time it was his turn to go, Hudson was no longer thinking about Eric. He was concentrating on the run before him. The timing device beeped and he burst out of the gate. Bill Egan had cautioned him to take it easy, get a feel for the course, but he didn't. It was against his nature to take it easy. Dynastar ski technician Mike Decesaro, who was at the top of the hill that day, would later say that Bill went out of the start as if he were trying to win the training run.

Bill carved through the first two turns, aimed himself at the Mausefalle jump, and pulled up his knees as the ground fell away. Then he went too far right and flew over the fence.

Again the spectators caught their breath. Again the biting cold air seemed to freeze time. Again the hill fell quiet. Again Bill Egan reported to the other coaches that a racer was down. Egan had to get down there. He grabbed his skis, dropped them at his feet, and scrambled to click into the bindings. He was frantic. In his haste he knocked one ski on its side. He had to set it straight and start over.

"Good lord, let him get up. Please, God, let him get up," the coach said. Then he barked into the radio, "You guys have *got* to stop going right."

Bill had gone even farther to the right than Eric had. He had come down on his feet (narrowly missing a big rock), vaulted forward out of his skis, smacked his head on the ground, sheared off the low branches of an evergreen tree, and slid to a stop several feet to the right of the snow fence, not far from a shack where the ski resort stored equipment. He lay there moaning, gasping, rocking slowly from side to side, as if in a nightmare. He was not bleeding. It was hard to tell if he was conscious. People spoke to him but he did not answer, did not open his eyes.

The Canadian doctor, Ron England, examined Hudson, as did a local doctor who was there. They agreed he had to go to the hospital right away. Within moments a yellow helicopter fluttered up the hill, landed at the base of the Mausefalle, and disgorged a couple of paramedics. Slowly, gently, Bill was loaded onto a flat board and carried to the chopper. The paramedics took small steps to keep their footing on the slick race course. Once Bill was safely inside, the helicopter tipped slightly and took off, showering the course in ice. The people at the top of the hill could follow its flight all the way into the village, right to the hospital parking lot, where it alighted less than two minutes later.

Hudson was quickly diagnosed with a collapsed lung. Soon a Kitzbühel doctor, accustomed to seeing serious skiing injuries, inserted a tube in his chest to reinflate the lung and enable the racer to breathe more easily.

That was where it began. Bill Hudson was a broken man, his body a sack of mush. Besides the punctured lung he had a few broken ribs, a shattered left wrist, a compression fracture of two vertebrae, a serious break of the right scapula, and a deep contusion of the kidney, so deep that soon he would begin to urinate blood. Some time later, the doctors discovered that Hudson had also sustained a serious concussion. The whack on the head was affecting Bill's vision: He was seeing double.

David Kiefer, of Laramie, Wyoming, was the American team doctor in Kitzbühel. The athletes liked him because he was a competent doctor, but also because, in his spare time, he raced motorcycles on the street. Kiefer had dumped a few motorcycles in his time, and the guys liked that about him.

When he discussed Hudson's injuries later that day, the doctor likened them to the wounds people get when they go over the handlebars at seventy or eighty miles an hour. That sort of accident, he said, tends to be hard on the hands, arms, shoulders, and especially the head. When he spoke of Hudson's crash, the doctor sounded impressed. "There's a very fine edge between being in control and being out of the course, or being into the fences," he said. "Not much room for error."

Ueli Luthi began the team meeting on time that night, as usual. In Kitzbühel, the athletes met in the hotel dining room.

"Uh, not too great of a day," he said, standing at the front of the room, looking at his feet. Unfortunately we have Hudson in the hospital. I think you guys visited him and you know how he is doing." There was a pause. "I hope we don't have too many of these days."

Then Luthi noted that, for safety reasons, the course workers had made the Mausefalle jump smaller.

The meeting might have been a good time for the racers to discuss how they felt about Bill's crash. Certainly they all had feelings about it. Huddy, as they called him, was their friend, and it pained them to see him so messed up. Besides, most of them had to get up in the morning and ski the course again. They wouldn't have been human if they hadn't feared they, too, would fuck up and wind up riding the helicopter to the *krankenhaus*. At the very least, it might have been helpful to discuss his accident from a technical standpoint—to understand his mistake so they would not repeat it.

But they didn't talk about Bill, not in any serious way. They had all gone to the hospital that afternoon, and though he had looked like hell they had done their best to cheer him up. Eric Keck, sore but not seriously hurt, had used a green marker to write "Hud the Stud" on Bill's left (unbroken) shoulder. Hudson, too, had made a try at a joke: "Keck," he said, "I thought you were the dumbest person in the world, but I am."

After seeing him lying there, Bill's teammates were probably too stunned and exhausted to talk about him anymore. But you also got the sense that the racers felt they weren't supposed to talk about what had happened. Partly it was because they believed they should simply accept whatever happened to them on the race course. "Crashing is part of the sport" was the way they generally put it. Or, as Ueli Luthi said shortly after the Hudson disaster, "That's downhill." In a sense they had to have that attitude: Downhillers had good reason to be fatalistic. Beyond that, they had to maintain the rugged images they had of themselves. Being men, most of the racers seemed to feel—though of course it was never stated—they had to be tough, inscrutable, above emotion. As downhillers, they felt that most other men were somewhat soft. And so when it came to showing their feelings, well, they just didn't. Some might have done so in private, with Bill Egan, or back in the states with the team psychologist, but they weren't about to get touchy-feely here in Kitzbühel, where, you could argue, they needed to do it most. These guys were about as likely to own up publicly to their fears as they were to take up macramé. No, Kyle Rasmussen's leg did not hurt the day he nearly broke it in half in Garmisch. No, Reggie Crist was not afraid of the Hahnenkamm. And no, the downhillers did not want to uncover their feelings about, you know, the Hudson thing.

Steve Porino got up early the next morning, Thursday, to pack his bags. The on-again, off-again Europa Cup race in Château D'Oex was on again, and the coaches had agreed that he and Eric, who was feeling well enough to race, should drive back there and compete. Jeff Olson, who had run the Hahnenkamm before, was going stay in Kitzbühel. The night before, Steve had given an impassioned, almost heroic speech about why he, too, should be entered in the Hahnenkamm race—"Don't worry, I'm ready now, I'm not afraid," etc.—but Bill Egan wouldn't have it, not after Eric and Bill Hudson had ridden those same noble sentiments right into the trees. Like it or not, Steve and Eric were Switzerland-bound.

Shortly before they left, Steve rode the cable car called the Hahnenkammbahn to the top of the race course for one last look around. He was twenty-four years old, and though he was a good skier, he was not a star. This, he knew, might be his last year on the ski team, his last chance to see Kitzbühel. It was a painful thought. Athletes go through their lives assessing themselves by objective standards—what their finishing time was, where they placed, how many batters they struck out or yards they gained. The football player who rushes for fifty yards wants to gain a hundred; the miler strives to break the four-minute mark; the ski racer hopes to finish in the top three in a World Cup race or in the Olympics. But most athletes never become great. Most have a few modest successes and then get hurt or bored or frustrated and begin looking for a dignified way out. Few find one. Not many athletes reach the end of their careers and say, "I didn't achieve as much as I wanted to, but that's OK. It was fun, so I'll just move on." It is hard, when you have built a life around your body, to accept that there are things it cannot do, or will not do, anymore. It's even harder to trade the objectivity of sports for the scary subjectivity of life. Making the transition from athlete to average person is hard, and that day in Kitzbühel Steve Porino was just starting to make it. He trudged up the short, steep slope that led to the starting shack and stood there for a moment, taking it all in. A lot of great racers had pushed out of that shack over the years. Steve had always dreamed of being among them, but somehow it just had never worked out.

When no one was looking, he stepped up close to the old building, raised the sharp end of his ski pole, and, bearing down hard, carved these letters into the wood: s. PORINO.

Not long after Steve and Eric got to Château D'Oex, the race there was canceled once and for all. On their way back to Kitzbühel to join their teammates, the two racers celebrated Eric's twenty-third birthday by driving the van through somebody's cornfield. The downhillers liked to drive their cars in places that weren't necessarily intended for that purpose. A few months earlier, after a training camp in Portillo, Chile, Eric and Reggie Crist had driven to Santiago to go surfing. When the waves died down, they decided to see how far the car would fly if they drove it real fast over the dunes. Pretty far, it turned out.

Later in the drive back to Kitzbühel, Steve and Eric were rolling through a small town when they saw two young women walking on the side of the road, thumbs hanging out. Steve pulled over and the hitchhikers opened the side door.

"What are you doing out here?" Steve asked them as they began to climb in.

"We're on our way to Lucerne," one of the women said, "We just finished a modeling job."

It was then that the two racers looked into the back seat and, in Steve's words, "realized our victory." The racers had not planned to visit

Lucerne, but they agreed they could probably make time to do so. It was important, they knew, to be flexible.

The women really were models. They had their portfolios with them to prove it. They posed for pictures all over Europe, as it turned out. When Steve explained that he and Eric were American ski racers, one of the women mentioned that she had always wanted to visit the United States, but said she wouldn't care to be a model there. America is too prudish, she said. "I like," she said, "to show my tits." With that, she pulled a card from her valise and handed it to Steve. On it was a photograph of the woman, nude from the waist up. Steve's mind was still trying to compute this information when the woman spoke.

"How do you like my tits?" she said.

Steve mumbled that it was certainly a high-quality photograph, but then the women changed the subject and that was the end of that. The racers let the women out near Lucerne, had dinner at a McDonald's, then began to look for the highway to Kitzbühel. Soon they saw a sign saying it was in the other direction. Eric, who was driving, slowed down, then cranked the wheel to make a U-turn. Steve, sitting in the passenger seat, heard a thunk on Eric's door. Then he saw Eric lean out of the window and say, "Ooh, are you all right?"

A woman on a moped had smacked into the side of the van. She was lying in the street, stunned but still conscious. Eric realized that the van was blocking traffic, so he pulled forward to move it out of the way. In doing so he flattened the moped, which had slipped under the wheels after the collision. For a moment he considered just taking off, then thought better of it. The woman, apparently uninjured, then began to pound on Eric's door and scream at him in a foreign language, apparently German. Her chief complaint seemed not to be that he had crushed her moped, but that in doing so he had mangled the Mickey Mouse bell that was fixed to the handlebars. She made it clear she wanted money.

A police officer was summoned. Fortunately for Eric, the officer spoke English. Even more fortunately, he was a ski racing enthusiast, and he knew someone the downhillers knew. The racers knew things were going well when the officer mentioned that he admired Eric's shoes. The cop evaluated the accident scene and then fixed most of the blame on the raving moped driver, who, he reasoned, never would have dented the van if she hadn't been hovering on its flank. The officer then fined her one hundred fifty Swiss francs—then about one hundred ten dollars—and revoked her license. He also fined Eric for making an improper U-turn. Sotto voce, he explained to Steve and Eric that the woman had been on her way to her psychologist when the accident happened. So not only was she a lousy driver, she was crazy. The woman was still wailing over the ruins of her scooter when Eric and Steve roared off to Kitzbühel.

On Friday night the racers in the first seed drew lots for the start of the Hahnenkamm race. The ceremony was held on a makeshift stage beneath a church clock tower. Hundreds of people jammed the narrow streets, drinking and shouting.

Among the noisiest, as usual, were the fans of Franz Heinzer, who rang cowbells and wore white caps and purple sweatshirts imprinted with the slogan, "Ich Bin Franz Heinzer Fan." (AJ Kitt referred to this raucous group as "The Idiots.") Heinzer, twenty-eight, was a fan favorite by process of elimination. Pirmin Zurbriggen, the pious superstar who had won four overall World Cup titles, had retired at the end of the previous season, and 1987 downhill World Champion Peter Müller was thirty-four years old and on wobbly legs. Heinzer, on the World Cup tour since 1981, had won four downhills in his career, but the fans and the press were more interested in what he hadn't won. He had competed in an Olympic downhill only once, finishing seventeenth. And he had finished fourth in the downhill at the Alpine World Championships on three different occasions. After the last time, the unkind press started calling him Franz the Fourth. But now, in Kitzbühel, the fans were on his side; only a month earlier he had won the first of two downhills in Val Gardena, Italy. Maybe, the Swiss fans thought, he was finally becoming great.

A multilingual master of ceremonies introduced the athletes. The crowd clapped loudly for AJ, though not as loudly as they had for the Europeans. Kitt reached into the bucket and drew the number five.

Then the emcee held a microphone in front of him and asked the usual question.

"Does AJ stand for anything?"

"No, not really."
"Well, your parents had a Christian name for you."
"Yes."
"It's a secret?"
"Yes."

Morning came in a drizzle, and by 9 A.M. a gray mist covered the course like a shroud. At the bottom of the hill the snow was sticky and the air cold and damp, the way it is around rushing water in the woods. You couldn't walk without getting wet, and yet you couldn't tell where the wetness came from. From the finish area you couldn't see one hundred yards up the hill. You knew the bright orange gates were up there but they were invisible, wrapped in the flannel fog.

Still, the people in the finish were having fun. They shouted and hooted and drank beer and carried hand-painted signs reading, "Hopp Franz," and "Hopp William Besse." ("Hopp" meant, roughly, "go.") They also drank beer and schnapps and especially *Glühwein*, which they bought at concession stands for forty Austrian shillings. The loudspeakers played "I Wanna Dance with Somebody," by Whitney Houston, and that old song "Poetry in Motion." A couple of Canadian fans painted their faces in the colors of that country's flag. It was a big, crazy party, much like the tailgate parties that take place outside American football games. Soon the fog began to lift, as if pushed up over the top of the mountain by the resolve of the people who lined the course.

The race began on time. Swiss star Daniel Mahrer, number one, finished in 1:59.82, and was immediately beaten by his teammate Franz Heinzer, whose time was 1:58.71. Franz the Fourth was now first. Heinzer's time was still the best when AJ Kitt, number five, got set to go.

This would be AJ's first encounter, in the blur of competition, with the Mausefalle and the Steilhang. Another racer might have been scared (Tommy Moe was) but AJ was just nervous, the way actors are the moment before curtain. In a sense AJ was like a stage performer: He had rehearsed this course, had gone over it slowly each day that week, and had thought carefully about it while watching video at night. And each day his performance had improved: His finishing times in the three training runs were 2:05.41, 2:02.11, and 2:00.54. An actor knows his lines, and now AJ knew his line, the line he would take from start to finish. All he had to do now was give his performance.

It would be wrong to say that AJ did not sense the danger of the course. He knew about Todd Brooker's rag-doll crash in the Zielschuss and Brian Stemmle's near-fatal accident in the Steilhang. But so what? He wasn't about to ski down the Steilhang thinking, Don't hit the net or you'll get killed. What good would that do? AJ thought of the Streif in terms of its technical difficulty, not its ferocity. And he knew he would learn from this experience even if he didn't win. Skiing Kitzbühel, he felt, was so difficult that you couldn't help but improve. If you made it to the bottom, everything you did later was easy. "A cakewalk," he said.

The tones sounded and AJ lunged out of the gate, his shins pushing aside the thin wand that started the clock. He landed softly off the Mausefalle, negotiated the roundhouse right, then fell into the Steilhang, inadvertently skiing through a little hole along the way. No problem. He made the turn well, then crouched low for the long ride through the woods. He handled the Hausberg bump well, but in the traverse he took a lower line than he would have liked. He dropped into the Zielschuss and, several seconds later, ducked under the finish banner. He had made it. AJ was, officially, no longer a rookie.

His time was 2:00.90, fourth place after five racers. AJ took a breather and then got on the radio to give a course report to Tommy Moe.

"Hey, it's not that hard," he said. "It's pretty soft. And, uh, it's actually a little slower today, I think. But the turns are easy. It's pretty soft at the top of the Steilhang. Right where you drop in there's a little hole there. But if you're really committed, you're OK. And the actual Steilhang is not that hard today, either. It's soft, you can hold an edge."

Briefly, AJ talked about the flat parts of the course. And then, his voice rising just slightly, he said, "Everything else is just a piece of cake, so just punch it. A lot of guys are, you know, not skiing so hot, so just believe in yourself and do it, man."

Before each race, Bill Egan skied to the finish area and left a bag of clothing for the downhillers to wear when they got to the bottom. AJ went to the bag now and dropped his helmet inside. Then he picked through the red and blue team jackets until he found the one with his name on it. It felt good to put it on; within minutes after he finished, the cool air had begun to pierce his thin downhill suit. He was satisfied with his run, and felt he had a chance to end up in the top ten, a terrific finish at Kitzbühel. As AJ stood in the finish area, a couple of young fans held out pens and paper for his autograph. AJ signed.

Tommy Moe pushed himself out of the gate: This was it. He had never said, that week, that he was afraid, but you could see that he was. When he talked about the course he called it "interesting," which was about as close as any of the downhillers came to saying it scared them. But most of all he had skied tentatively, as if all he wanted was to make it to the bottom, toss the skis in the van, and get the hell out of Kitzbühel. That was Moe's real goal—to get out of town.

He finished in 2:03.20, almost five seconds behind Franz Heinzer. He wound up in thirty-seventh place, and in one piece. As *Ski Racing* magazine would later put it, he "survived the ordeal without injury."

Just after the twenty-sixth racer, Pietro Vitalini of Italy, left the starting gate, the fog returned, and the organizers suspended the race. After a few minutes the fog rose again. Suddenly the air was noticeably colder and drier than it had been only minutes before. From the top of the hill to the bottom, people watching the race closed the collars on their jackets and clamped their hands under their arms to stay warm.

Peter Runggaldier of Italy, starting twenty-seventh, took advantage of the change in conditions. He whizzed down the hardened track in 1:58.78, good for second place, seven hundredths behind Heinzer, who would hang on to win. Xavier Gigandet, number twenty-nine, finished in 2:00.63, faster than AJ. Erwin Resch of Austria, number thirty-two, was even faster than that.

In the finish, AJ was incredulous. How could this happen? Under normal conditions, few guys outside the first seed could have topped him. After twenty-six racers he had been in ninth place, which, if it had held up, would have been his third-best World Cup finish ever. At Kitzbühel, no less! But now the weather had improved—in downhill, a sudden and precipitous drop in the temperature was almost always good news—and the Xavier Gigandets and Erwin Resches of the world were beating him. And they weren't the only ones. Number thirty-six, Italy's Michael Mair, slipped in ahead of him too. So did Austrian Armin Assinger, number thirty-seven. AJ, seeing Assinger's time, blew up. "Fuck! This sucks!" he shouted. When number thirty-eight, Lukas Perathoner of Italy, finished in 2:00:61, it was more than AJ could take. He left the finish area, disgusted—and in fifteenth place.

As usual, the Mausefalle was having its way with some people. A small hole had formed just below where the racers landed, and everybody who skied through it was having trouble. Atle Skaardal of Norway, one of the favorites, had gone down, *fwap*, as if he had been shot. A Frenchman and a German had also fallen there.

Kyle Rasmussen, his shin still smarting, was the next to crash. He flew off the Mausefalle jump, landed in the hole, and flopped forward. He slid about one hundred feet before getting caught in a net. Immediately he stood up and grabbed his collarbone. But there was no bone there anymore. Just mush. Once more a helicopter fluttered up the hill, and once more an American racer was loaded inside for the flight to the hospital. There, the doctors put Kyle's arm in a sling. That ended his chances of competing at the Alpine World Championships in February. He wasn't going to ski anywhere, not for a long time. He wasn't going to make any money, either.

Only seven more racers got to ski the Streif that day. Racer number forty-seven, Canadian Ed Podivinsky, was in the starting gate when the mist slipped back down over the top of the hill, thickly this time, and for good. After a long delay, the organizers called off the race. After all the anticipation, all the work and fear and struggle, Reggie Crist and Jeff Olson never got to start.

At the team meeting that night, Ueli Luthi congratulated AJ Kitt on his fifteenth-place finish. He also nodded his head to Tommy Moe, who, he said, "made it out of rookieland."

Then Ueli turned to Kyle Rasmussen, who, for the second consecutive Saturday, was attending a team meeting hurt.

"Are you feeling bad, or . . . ?"

"No. Feel all right," Kyle said. Then he said something under his breath.

"Eh? Pardon me?"

"I don't feel like a rookie, though."

"No," Ueli said, "but according to the rule you are still a rookie." Kyle had not skied the Streif in a race, so he was still a rookie. Kitzbühel didn't give anything away, and neither did Ueli Luthi.

Ueli announced the schedule—he always called it "the program"— for Monday. All the downhillers except Kyle and Tommy would drive to Mols, Switzerland, and spend the night there before continuing on to Wengen for the Lauberhorn downhill. Kyle was going home. Tommy, a skilled technical skier, was going to Adelboden, Switzerland, for a giant slalom race. Finally, Ueli asked the racers to settle their bills with the hotel.

"Take care of extras at the desk, eh. If you have made phone calls or signed for drinks, these things must be taken care of." Then he turned to Egan. "Billegan?"

What a week it had been for the head downhill coach. He had begun it by bringing Eric, Jeff, and Steve to the Hahnenkamm. And what had happened? One had skied over a fence, the second never got a chance to race, and the third had had visions of the Caribbean. Then there were the other disasters: Hudson was in the hospital peeing blood and seeing double and Rasmussen was sitting in front of him now, his arm draped in a sling.

"This was," Bill began, "a very trying week. One of the most trying weeks I've ever had. I've been around sports a long time, and I've had a lot of hurt athletes. Too many. Way too many. Unfortunately that's something that goes with elite sports. And you know, it's just part of the game that you have to accept. There are so many brilliant highs in sport. I mean, it's so idiotic, but there are so many fantastic things that happen when you compete well and you have success. But there's always a price to pay. And that price, sometimes, is you get hurt."

Egan paused. The room was, as always when he spoke, quiet.

"You have to accept that fact. And you still have to compete because you guys love it so much. And you have to go hard and try to do your absolute best, because if you don't, it's not going to decrease the chance of injury. And that's a rather dour subject at this moment because of what happened to Bill and Kyle and Eric. And I just hope to God we had it all in one week. I just hope we had our quota."

*   *   *

It was no wonder, after the week they'd had, that most of the downhillers went out that night and got smashed.

AJ, Jeff, Tommy, Reggie, Eric, and Steve went out about 10 P.M. They headed straight for the Londoner, the English pub favored by British tourists, fans of English and American rock music, ski racing groupies, and, especially, tense, overwrought racers. A few dozen people were lined up outside the place when the American downhillers arrived, but with the blessing of the bouncer the Yanks squeezed past all of them. (Savvy bar owners do not keep celebrities waiting in the snow, and in the ski world these young men, who had made a point of wearing their team colors, were indeed celebrities.) The joint was jammed. It was dark inside, and moving from the door to the bar meant doing the lambada with several dozen strangers, which was not something a lot of people there, including the Americans, necessarily minded doing. The Londoner that night must have been the worst fire hazard in Austria. On the other hand, the place was so thoroughly soaked in beer—everything and everyone exuded the sour stink of spilled brew—that the building probably would not have burned well. Most people were drinking the first couple of beers and throwing the third one.

It was a crazy night. AJ Kitt got behind the bar and began serving drinks, accepting in payment whatever people gave him. Tommy Moe, having drunk a lot of beer, stumbled around looking relieved. Eric Keck grabbed some big guy by the throat, and the big guy grabbed him right back. They stood there for a while, clutching each other's Adam's apples and grinning like crazy. Jeff Olson kissed a waitress (he didn't remember it the next day, but his teammates reminded him). Steve Porino met an Italian ski groupie who said yes, *magnifico,* she would love to see his hotel room. He and the woman were engaged in the night's activities when she said something so surprising to him that he repeated it to his teammates at breakfast the next day.

"Please," the woman breathed, perhaps confused about Steve's team affiliation, "speak French to me."

Back at the Londoner, there was an urgency to the partying. This wasn't just a few guys out for a good time. This was an exhilarated, jumpy, somewhat hostile pack of guys on a mission to rid themselves of a week-old, knee-rattling case of the jitters. The Londoner had not become an après-race fixture because of its decor, which was Spartan. Racers drank at the Londoner because of the race, not because of the Londoner. For the better part of a week they jangled their nerves on the slick white serpent called the Streif, and on Saturday night they aired out their feelings in the cramped quarters of the bar. It was something they had to do, and furthermore had a right to do. That was how the downhillers viewed it, anyway. When the racers sucked down the beer they were served without charge by the gracious bar owner, they were treating themselves to a valuable form of therapy. They deserved this; they had been through hell.

And in a way they had profited from it. Downhill is mostly about confidence. Sure, you have to make good turns, but all these guys (except maybe Eric) could turn, and yeah, you have to have stainless steel testicles, but most of them had those too. What few racers had—and what, among the Americans, only AJ had—was confidence in their ability, the serene feeling that they were going to slice down the hill on their feet, not float down in an air ambulance. The only way to get that kind of confidence was to have a redeeming experience on a tough course, and many of the Americans had had one. AJ had. Tommy Moe had, for sure. And so what if Kyle had skied through a hole and broken something? He had trained well, had learned that he could make it to the bottom. The same went for Reggie Crist and, to a lesser degree, Jeff, who was still locked in a cramped box called fear. The Americans had not won anything. Hadn't come close. But they were going to leave Kitzbühel, the ones who weren't injured, better racers than when they had arrived. Most of them had gotten through the finish upright, and that meant a lot.

Still, they needed that party therapy. With the exception of Bill Hudson and possibly Bill Egan, Eric Keck had had the most stressful week of them all, so the course of therapy he prescribed for himself was, to say the least, intensive.

The mess began when Eric and some other men were walking, in the flurrying snow, back to the Schwarzer Adler. The group was near the hotel when a little car passed on the narrow cobblestone street. Someone in the group used his hand or maybe his hip to thump the car as it passed. Some witnesses later said Eric had done it, but the huge Christian denied it. (The exact truth of what happened that night quickly became obscured by confusion, exaggeration, and by Eric's tendency to put a certain spin on the facts of a story.) Some drivers might have kept going, but the Austrian fellow driving this little car chose to stop, burst out, and make something of it. Immediately, and unwisely, he went for Eric, who must have looked guilty. Reggie Crist, who was still in the Londoner when the altercation began, said, "The guy really didn't know who he was fucking with." The fight with the Austrian was, in the beginning, a better wrestling match than a boxing match: The two were grappling, not swinging. Then—in self-defense, mind you—Eric tossed the Austrian through the side window of a parked car. About the same time, the Austrian also received a punch in the mouth. As Eric would put it, "I broke his face in a lot of places."

Having lost the fight, and having extricated himself from the car, the fellow took the only recourse that was left to him: He identified himself as a police officer and, the blood beginning to harden under his nostrils, placed Eric under arrest. The racer was taken to the Kitzbühel police station, where he argued that he was not a bully, but a victim. It was a hard case to make considering that Eric had only a superficial cut to the ear, and that nobody there spoke English. Ueli Luthi was summoned to the police station. Eric told the coach his version of the story, and then Ueli used his German and his considerable charm to talk the athlete out of trouble. Eric and his hung-over teammates left town the next afternoon.

Two Americans stayed behind. Assistant coach Jim Tracy stayed in Kitzbühel with Bill Hudson, who was still lying uncomfortably on his back, seeing double.

5

A Death
in Wengen

On January 17, 1991, Coach Horst Weber hurried to Steve Porino's room at Park Hotel in Wengen, Switzerland, and woke him up. It was 3:30 A.M. Steve, who had been in a deep sleep, didn't know at first what was happening. Weber, a New York ski coach on temporary assignment to the ski team, was standing over his bed, saying something he couldn't make out. The German-born coach, who spoke with an accent to begin with, was talking so fast and so excitedly that the groggy Porino was having trouble understanding him. It was weird. But the really strange thing was that Weber was wearing strips of what looked like electrical tape on his nose and below one of his ears. Only later would Steve learn that the coach had used the tape to cover some sun blisters.

Finally, Steve was able to register what Weber was saying.

"Get up! Get up! Dress like you are going on an airplane! We have war!"

Holy shit, Steve thought. War. He swung his legs off the bed and stood up.

Howard Peterson, the executive in charge of the U.S. Ski Team, had called head coach Ueli Luthi in the middle of the night to tell him the news: A United Nations coalition led by the United States was bombing Iraq in retaliation for Saddam Hussein's invasion of Kuwait the previous August. What would soon become known as the Persian Gulf War had begun. Ueli had awakened Bill Egan and technical coach Georg Capaul and called them to a meeting in the lobby. We have a decision to make, Ueli said. We can go home now or we can stay here for a few days and see what happens. Bill spoke right up. He knew the athletes would want to stay and compete in the Lauberhorn downhill, but with war raging in the Middle East, Americans everywhere would be vulnerable to terrorism. He insisted that the team leave Wengen right away. Bill felt they had to get the kids out of there. Ueli and Georg thought the team probably would be safe in Wengen, but in the end they yielded to Bill.

After the meeting, Bill walked into AJ's room, turned on a light, and said, "Let's go, get up. We're having a meeting."

"What about?" AJ said, squinting against the light.

"We attacked Iraq. We started a war. We have to go home."

AJ was devastated. He would miss the Lauberhorn, which was almost as old and storied as the Hahnenkamm. It seemed likely he would miss the Alpine World Championships, too. And if the war lingered on, he might also miss the World Cup race scheduled for the new Olympic course in Val d'Isère. But as obsessed as he was with his development as a ski racer, AJ understood that some things were more important than ski racing. He got up and began tossing his things into his bags.

For the Americans on the World Cup circuit, it was easy to lose track of what was happening in the world. When they traveled in Europe they almost never saw English-language television. They bought English-language newspapers only infrequently, and when they did read one it was the splashy USA Today, not the dry, news-oriented International Herald-Tribune. Armed Forces Radio was available in some places, but the downhillers listened only to football games. The athletes who represented America in international ski racing competition generally had little idea what America stood for politically, or what its government was doing.

Still, the downhillers knew that President George Bush had set a deadline of January 15, 1991, for Iraq's withdrawal from Kuwait. And yet the trouble had seemed worlds away. That was especially true when the racers were in Wengen. Of all the glitzy, storied stops on the World Cup circuit, Wengen probably was the most idyllic, the furthest removed from the woes of the world. The village lay in the shadow of three pointed mountain peaks—the Jungfrau, or young woman; the Mönch, or monk; and the famous Eiger, or ogre. (In local legend, the Monk guarded the young woman from the terrible ogre.) Some of the downhillers felt it was the most beautiful place they visited. It was definitely the quietest. In winter, the town was closed to automobile traffic; to get there you left your car in a village below and rode up the hill in a quaint, rickety train. Of course, all this peace and quiet came at a price: Wengen was self-consciously highbrow, even stuffy, a resort for people who don't look at the prices on the menu. If you had the money and you could tolerate the stuffy attitudes, it was a great place to get away from the world. After a few days in Wengen you could almost forget there was a world out there at all.

Which was what happened to the downhillers. There they were, spending their days gliding down a snowy mountainside in Fantasyland, while somewhere in the Mideast, the soldiers of the United Nations coalition were sitting on hot sand, sipping water to stay cool, and waiting to kill, or die. So when the war began—when the war, in effect, came to Wengen—the racers naturally were shocked.

Tommy Moe certainly was. After Bill awakened AJ he turned to Moe, AJ's roommate in Wengen, and said, "Tommy, get up. We have to pack and get out of here. The war has broken out, and we're history."

Moe, normally a heavy sleeper, jumped out of bed yelling, "Bullshit! Bullshit! We can't leave now! This is bullshit!" But he had no choice. Within minutes his bags were packed and he was ready to leave.

The team had to get to Zürich to catch the plane home. The first train normally didn't leave Wengen until daybreak, but the village agreed to run a special 6 A.M. train for the Americans. Egan had never seen his athletes work so hard to leave a place. They didn't say anything; they just worked. Reggie Crist and Steve Porino shuttled the gear from the hotel to the train station and the others loaded everything into a boxcar. The athletes were assisted by a few drunken Italians and Yugoslavs who were arriving back at the hotel after a night in the bars. The team was ready to go in plenty of time.

The athletes and coaches had one of the few laughs of the day when Horst Weber arrived at the train station. Weber, who had lived in the United States for many years, was wearing a Bavarian sweater and a German farmer shirt. He didn't want to leave any doubts about his true nationality, just in case the group happened to meet a terrorist. Seeing him, Bill said, "You don't want to be associated with us now, huh?" Later, at the Zürich airport, Eric Keck decided he, too, should travel in disguise. He pulled his pants up around his belly button and tried to look as unhip as possible on the theory that any terrorists hanging around the place would mistake him for a European.

And yet none of the guys really felt like laughing. The war had completely disrupted their lives. They had no way of knowing when it would be safe to race in Europe again. Next week? Next year? And what were they supposed to do while they waited? Yes, the war really screwed things up. Of course, some of the younger guys—Reggie, Eric, Tommy—had more on their minds than ski racing. They were thinking about getting shot at. Nobody could believe the United States would need to institute the draft for this war. The fighter pilots would drop a few bombs on Baghdad and Saddam Hussein would wave the white hanky, right? Probably. But who knew? In December and early January, Reggie Crist had thought a lot about the possibility of a war against Iraq. He was no hawk, that was for sure. But if the U.S. got into a war, wasn't he supposed to fight? He couldn't decide. Tommy hadn't thought much about war at all. Now that it had begun, he couldn't stop thinking about it. He hated the idea of getting ripped away from his cool, comfortable world and being stuck in a desert somewhere. Where the hell was Iraq, anyway? Tommy's teammates didn't make things any easier for him. They tried to make him believe the armed forces always drafted Alaskan ski racers first.

The downhillers left Zürich about five hours after Ueli had gotten word that the war had started. Their travel plans were supposed to be a secret, lest the crazies discover what plane they were on and blow it up. But as it happened their plans weren't secret at all. When the plane arrived in New York, the cable news channel CNN was waiting for them. Egan was interviewed first. Then the TV people said they would like to interview two athletes. Everybody wanted to do it, so while CNN waited, the guys drew straws. Eric Keck won. The TV reporter asked him how he felt about coming home.

"We're sorry we had to come back, but ski racing doesn't seem very significant compared to what's happening in the Persian Gulf. We definitely wish all those guys the best," he said.

It was ironic that Eric had been chosen as team spokesman. In two weeks in Europe, he had taken only one complete downhill run.

* * *

In Wengen, training for the Lauberhorn downhill went on. The conditions were tricky on Friday, the day after the Americans left town. The snow was thin, and the course workers had watered the track in many places to make it hard. The racers got a stiff, choppy ride, especially at the end of the course, which was already among the most technically difficult on the circuit. At the bottom of the course, the racers had to cross a narrow bridge at high speed, then carve through three sharp turns, slowing down all the way, before dropping off a ledge into the finish. (People watching at the bottom could see only the last three or four seconds of the race—the time it took for the racer to set up for the last jump and ski under the banner.) Because the racers rode such a hard edge, the turns quickly got chewed up. For the racers in the back of the field, the turns in that section would be challenging. The length of the course was also a test. At two minutes and thirty seconds in length, the Lauberhorn downhill was a half-minute longer than any other course on the World Cup circuit. Racers arrived at the finish exhausted.

The sport was trying an experiment that day. Normally, anyone who was in the field for the training runs was permitted to compete on race day. But here, only the top thirty finishers on Friday would be allowed to ski on Saturday. The idea was to create a sort of super-race, a made-for-TV event in which viewers would see thirty stars or near-stars, and no also-rans. A lot of the racers didn't like this. Nobody wanted to be excluded from the race just because he had an off-day on Friday. Besides, the athletes were accustomed to holding back something until race day. Under these rules, they would have to go all-out on Friday, too. In a meeting held that week with representatives from the Fédération Internationale de Ski, the sport's governing body, some of the veteran racers expressed their reservations. Some of the younger guys, they said, might push too hard in hopes of qualifying for the race. Someone could get hurt. And yet, they went along with the plan in the end.

Austrian Gernot Reinstadler wore bib number forty-four that day. Reinstadler, twenty years old, was among the young Austrian racers who were expected to take the place of stars like Helmut Höflehner and Leonhard Stock. He had made his way through the junior ranks—he was the Austrian junior champion in giant slalom and the combined in

1988—and was now getting experience on the World Cup tour. Nobody expected Reinstadler to win at Wengen, or even come close. But everyone felt he was a promising kid.

Reinstadler, who wanted very much to qualify, skied fairly well that Friday. He came into the last section carrying good speed, and made the first turn cleanly. But then he got into trouble. He started the second turn late, making it hard for him to get ready for the finish jump. To handle that jump well, a racer had to finish the last turn and then aim his skis straight off the ledge. Reinstadler never finished the last turn. He was still sliding sideways, to his right, when he caught air. His momentum carried him toward the tall red safety net on the side of the course. He landed halfway up the net. He was going perhaps forty or fifty miles an hour when he hit. His right ski caught in the net, trapping his right leg while the rest of his body kept going. He twisted violently around, then slammed to the snow. He slid limply down the hill and stopped. A thick smear of blood, a narrow red carpet, stretched from the fence to the racer.

After a moment Reinstadler stirred. With effort he sat up and looked at himself, looked at the blood trailing up the hill. And then he lay down again, unconscious.

Gernot Reinstadler died early the next morning of massive internal injuries. The force of the crash had snapped his pelvis and nearly severed his right leg. The doctors tried to save him with surgery, but it was no use. He lost his body's entire blood capacity several times over. Reinstadler was the first person to die in World Cup downhill skiing competition since Frenchman Michel Bozon crashed in Megève, France, in 1970. The sport's organizing body canceled the Lauberhorn and everybody packed their things on the train and went home. Competition would resume Monday at the Alpine World Championships in Reinstadler's home country.

The accident was not forgotten, of course. The Wengen race organizers and the people at the Fédération Internationale de Ski would spend a lot of time and energy trying to account for the death. But there was no explaining it, and no excusing it. Downhill is a perilous sport; people get hurt all the time. But Reinstadler should not have died in that crash. He was not going fast when he fell. He did not make a serious mistake. The amazing fact is that he did not even miss a gate. But the worst tragedy, the thing that shamed the race organizers the most, was that Reinstadler got hurt not by sideswiping a tree or a spectator or a course worker. He was killed when he hit a safety fence, a device that was meant to save his life. Instead of deflecting the racer back onto the course the netting trapped him like a fly.

The Americans learned of the tragedy the next day, either from TV sports reports or from someone else who had heard. It was stunning news, of course. Almost all of them remembered Reinstadler. At Garmisch earlier that year, the Austrian had raced right after Bill Hudson (Reinstadler had placed fortieth). Tommy Moe had competed against Reinstadler on the junior circuit; he didn't know him well, but the little he knew of him he liked.

But even those who didn't know Reinstadler personally could still say they knew him, because he was just like them. The Americans were young men gaining experience in a sport that required nerve and skill and, above all, experience. So was Reinstadler. Week after week the Americans went out there and tried to improve their turns, tried to find ways to shave a few tenths off their times. So did Reinstadler. In a sport that humbled people, the Americans wanted to be great. So did he. Reinstadler had wanted to be great. He had died trying. Each of the American downhillers coped with it in his own way. Tommy Moe tried not to think too much about it. Steve Porino mostly felt surprised. He viewed what he and his teammates did as routine, unremarkable. He knew it could be dangerous, but he felt that the danger generally was overstated. Until Reinstadler's accident, it had never occurred to him that a person could die in downhill training. Reggie got a videotape of the crash from a neighbor and watched it several times. The tape startled him at first. How could Reinstadler have died in such a mild accident? In the end, the pictures of the crash made Reggie respect the sport more than ever. AJ dealt with the crash in his usual methodical way. He was careful to avoid seeing it on videotape, and he didn't discuss it with anyone. He reasoned that if he talked about it he might get spooked, and if he got spooked he wouldn't ski well. Fortunately for him, it was easy to avoid the subject. He was back in the United States, far from the racing world.

That was the key, really, to the way all the American downhillers handled Reinstadler's death. They were lucky—they hadn't been there when it happened. They hadn't seen the trail of blood, and they hadn't spoken to Reinstadler's shocked Austrian teammates. They would not be attending the funeral. For them, it was easy to keep from feeling too much. This was different from their usual reaction to accidents. Usually they simply laughed at crashes, which didn't seem callous because nobody they knew had ever been killed until now. They had always laughed because the crashes looked funny, and because, thank heaven, they weren't the ones crashing. The giggling was a defense mechanism, a way of saying, "It didn't happen to me." But when Reinstadler died, they distanced themselves even further than that. Instead of saying "It didn't happen to me," the downhillers told themselves, in effect, "It didn't happen."

The death seemed to haunt Bill Egan much more than it did his athletes. Maybe it was because he, unlike the downhillers, was old enough to fear and respect death. Or maybe it was because of what he saw in the newspaper. A short time after the accident, Bill happened to see a copy of a European daily that had covered the Lauberhorn. The paper had a picture taken immediately after the crash. Better than anything Bill could think of, it symbolized the futility and senselessness of Reinstadler's death, and illustrated the shocked and confused way witnesses had reacted to it. In the foreground, the athlete was shown lying unconscious. And in the background, a man in heavy boots could be seen running up the hill, past the racer. The man was carrying a shovel.

He was going to cover up the blood.

About the time Reinstadler died, Bill Hudson was moved to a hospital in Innsbruck. He expected to be there just long enough for the doctors to give him the once-over. Then, he figured, he would be on his way home.

But his bruised kidney was still a concern. In Innsbruck, he was told he would have to stay in bed for a few days so the doctors could keep an eye on him. That was the first blow. Bill was bored and lonely and wanted desperately to go home. Then came a second blow. Bill had had double vision ever since the accident. In Kitzbühel, he would look at the ceiling over his bed and see two sprinkler heads instead of one. The doctor there told him it would clear up. But now, in Innsbruck, he got a second opinion.

"You did some damage to a nerve," the doctor said. To Hudson it looked like two doctors, one on top of the other.

"When's it going to get better?"

"Well," the doctor said, "we're not sure that it is going to get better. It might stay like this."

It might *what?* Hudson was stunned. In all the days he had spent lying in hospitals, he never imagined he might have hurt himself so badly that he wouldn't be able to race anymore. He considered injuries temporary: They slowed you down for a while, and then they healed and you started skiing again. He had always been an athlete, and he had just assumed he would continue to be one. But maybe things wouldn't work that way this time. Maybe his vision would not improve. And if it didn't . . . Well, he wouldn't let himself think about that. As a downhiller, Bill had a lot of experience in denying that he felt fear.

After a week, Bill was told he could go home, but only if a doctor accompanied him as he traveled. Fine, he said. Just get me out of here. With the doctor at his side he flew to Zürich, then changed planes and continued on to Los Angeles. He reclined on a stretcher the whole way. A friend of the family flew him in a private plane from Los Angeles to Sacramento, where his mother lived. He checked into the hospital at the University of California–Davis.

Bill's girlfriend, Kathrin Burkhart, arrived from Park City a few days later. When he saw her, he began to cry. He couldn't even say why, exactly. He had imagined he would happy to see her, and he was, but he hadn't been ready for anything like this. When he finally quit gasping he thought: That was weird. There would be many more times in his recovery when the depth and strength of his feelings would surprise him.

Oh, but it was wonderful to have Kathrin there. Shortly after she arrived, Bill took his first shower since the accident. In Austria the nurses had bathed him with sponges, which felt all right but didn't really make him feel refreshed. They hadn't even tried to wash his hair, which by now looked and felt as if he had dunked his head in oil. So the moment he felt up to it, he shuffled to the bathroom, turned on the water and stepped under the spray, only to realize that he could not possibly wash himself. His broken left wrist was wrapped in plastic to keep the cast dry, and because of the broken shoulder he couldn't raise his right arm at all. Bill stood under the water for a couple of minutes, thinking it over, seeing double through the steam.

He called out, "Kathrin . . ."

Bill Egan had been back in the United States only a few days when Howard Peterson, the ski team's chief executive, asked him if he wanted to take his athletes to Saalbach, Austria, for the Alpine World Championships. The threat of terrorism no longer seemed as real as it had a week earlier, and the Austrian authorities had agreed to guard the athletes in Saalbach, which put everyone at ease.

Well, Bill said, I'd like to take them back to Europe, but not to Saalbach. Instead, he wanted the guys to skip the championships and spend a week training for the World Cup race to be held on the new Olympic course in Val d'Isère. In his opinion, it was too late to go to the World Championships. The competition was already beginning in Austria. If the downhillers tried to go now, they would arrive brain-dead from jet lag. They wouldn't do well, and they might even get hurt. Bill couldn't cope with the thought of another racer getting banged up. He told Peterson that he didn't think they should go. AJ Kitt, who was in Rochester, resting and watching the war on TV, felt the same way. He had even told friends that he would decline any offer to go to Saalbach. No way, he said. I'm not going.

In the end, they went. Howard Peterson respected Bill's opinion. But these were the World Championships, and he felt the U.S. Ski Team should at least make a showing. On January 23, six days after the down-hillers left Wengen, the ski team announced that a small team of athletes would return to Europe for the competition. AJ Kitt and Reggie Crist would race in the downhill. (After the Hahnenkamm, Tommy Moe had gone to a giant slalom race in Adelboden, Switzerland, and stretched the ligaments in his ankle. Though he could have raced, he and Bill Egan agreed that it would be best if he didn't.) So would Nate Bryan, a technical racer with a little downhill experience and a lot of nerve. Bill and AJ weren't happy about the decision to go back, but they never seriously thought of boycotting the event. Instead, they decided to go to Austria and see what they could accomplish. As AJ would say later, "I thought maybe I could pull a good result out of my ass."

Bill was told that the route the athletes took to Saalbach would be kept a secret for security reasons. He and his guys were instructed to wear clothing that would not clearly identify them as Americans or American ski team members. At the Innsbruck airport, they were told, they would be met by an Austrian fellow who would quietly escort them to Saalbach. It would be very clandestine, very hush-hush. No one would know they were on their way to the World Championships.

When the downhillers got to Innsbruck, they were met by a guy wearing a ski parka covered with Saalbach and World Championship patches. So much for discretion.

The team arrived in Innsbruck the morning of the super G race, so the athletes couldn't possibly compete. Downhill training began the next day. Everywhere they went that day, Egan, Jim Tracy, and Ueli Luthi were greeted warmly by the other coaches. Yes, the European and the American teams were rivals. But they were also part of the same community, the same little world. The athletes didn't often strike up friendships—it's hard to be chummy with someone when all you can think of is beating him down the hill—but the coaches did. They attended coaches' meetings together, cooperated in videotaping training runs, and even shared an occasional drink or meal. The European coaches would have felt sorry if their American friends couldn't have come to Saalbach. Besides, the event wouldn't have been the same if world politics had kept the Americans, or anyone else, from attending. After all, you couldn't have the World Championships unless everyone in the world came. In a season of loss and disappointment, the Europeans' hearty greetings made the American coaches feel good.

Security in Saalbach was tight. Guards escorted the Americans everywhere they went. *Everywhere.* One day, Reggie Crist skied into the finish area and was met, as usual, by a security person.

"I'm just going to bring these over to the ski room," Reggie said, picking up his downhill boards. "I'll be right back."

"I'll go with you," the guard said.

"That's OK. It's right over there," Reggie said, pointing to a building a few yards away.

The guard followed him anyway.

The downhillers soon began to joke about the security. They referred to their visit to Saalbach as "Operation Snowball." Everyone chose a code name. Nate Bryan was Cheetah. Reggie was Scud. Ueli was Black Eagle. And so on. On the hill, you could hear the Americans talking to each other by radio.

"Black Eagle, Black Eagle, this is Scud. What time is inspection?"

"Don't be a focking asshole."

The other coaches got a big kick out of it. One night, Ueli and Bill considered going to the coaches' meeting incognito—in noses and glasses.

But that was all that was fun at the World Championships—for the Americans or anyone else. The mountains were breathtaking and the snow was adequate, but the mood was dark. The Austrians, still heartsick over the death of Gernot Reinstadler, understandably found it hard to be cheerful hosts. They put on parades and presented music, but the festivities somehow fell flat. Things were no more joyful on the hill. Downhill training brought a string of serious injuries. Lars-Boerje Eriksson of Sweden, popular among the American downhillers, skied into a small hole and hurt his knee so badly it was thought he might never race again. A brilliant nineteen-year-old Norwegian named Kjetil Andre Aamodt got injured the same way. Norway's Lasse Kjus broke his jaw. These were great racers and popular guys, and their loss saddened everyone. Egan, who felt he had seen far too many helicopters already that season, thought the thwock-thwock-thwock of the rotors was going to drive him mad.

Bill, still a basket case over the Hudson debacle, was determined that none of his guys get hurt. He urged them not to take any chances in training, not even chances that would significantly improve their times as the week went on. Just make it to the bottom; that was the idea. That was all right with them. The downhillers were so addled from air travel that they felt as if they were skiing underwater. Bill believed you could do a lot of things with half your faculties, but making seventy-mile-an-hour turns wasn't among them.

After each terrible day of training, the coaches would return to their rooms for a terrible night of television. The hotel in Saalbach had the cable channel CNN, and the Americans looked to it for news of the war.

Had the ground war begun? Was Israel under attack? A few Israeli athletes were competing in Saalbach, mostly to warm up for the 1992 Olympics. The Americans had to feel for them as Iraqi scud missiles streaked toward Israeli cities. Yes, the war was a considerable distraction for the downhillers. Bill Egan would say later that he could understand why many sporting events were canceled during World War II. Sports just didn't matter in the midst of that tragedy. It was the same now. What happened on the ski slope didn't seem all that important.

On race day, AJ started first. When he got to the finish line he looked at his time and jokingly raised his arms in victory. Hooray, he was in first place. He didn't stay there. AJ, who would later say he had "jelly legs" during his run, ended up twentieth, and he felt lucky to have done that well. He hated the course, which was set by former Swiss star Bernhard Russi, the same person who had designed the new Olympic course in Val d'Isère. If the Olympic course had as many slow, sharp turns as this one did, AJ didn't think he would like it much. But he and Bill did not blame AJ's mediocre result in Saalbach on the course alone. Bill would later describe his star athlete's performance with a single word: "Shitty." The other Americans did little more than show up. Franz Heinzer, no longer Franz the Fourth, won the gold medal.

The World Championship downhill may have been a disappointment for the Americans, but it was a disaster for the Austrians. Early in the week, a lot of people felt that veteran Austrian downhiller Helmut Höflehner had a realistic chance to beat Heinzer. Höflehner was skiing well, and besides, he would have the advantage of competing in front of the home crowd. Then his father suddenly died. Though he was devastated, Höflehner resolved to compete in the downhill in the belief that his father would have wanted him to. He skied well in training—he won the first training run—and everyone anticipated a touching and dramatic finish in the race. Höflehner had tears in his eyes as he stood in the starting gate on race day.

Höflehner pushed crazily out of the gate, trying to get the extra bit of speed that might help him win. But as he did the tails of his skis crossed and he was thrown off balance. He dumped a half second, maybe more, before he got going again. In an effort to make up the time he skied out of control and missed a gate.

It had been that kind of season for Austria.

*　*　*

After the World Championships, the downhillers made the long drive into France for two World Cup races in Val d'Isère, a downhill and a super G. Now, this was going to be a very big deal indeed. The French had spent five years and several million dollars building a new downhill course for the 1992 Olympics. The course had already attained the status of national monument, like the Eiffel Tower.

For the Americans, this was a chance to practice for the Big Moment, their chance at glory. If they skied well now, they would have confidence going into the games.

AJ Kitt was particularly eager to ski the course. When he was about ten years old, he had tried to calculate the year that he would win an Olympic gold medal. Let's see, he thought, in 1988 I'll be nineteen years old. That's probably too young. But in 1992 I'll be twenty-three. That sounds about right. I'll win the gold medal then. Now that he was older, AJ could see things didn't work that way. Because experience was so important in downhill, as in everything else, most racers didn't reach their peak until their mid-twenties. Still, he thought he was capable of finishing in the top three in 1992. As always, he'd do his best and see what happened.

Tommy Moe, who had missed the World Championships so he could rest his injured ankle, was back with the team now. He was under a lot of pressure in Val d'Isère. For a couple of years, people had been telling him 1992 was his big chance for an Olympic medal. The new course was said to favor downhillers with excellent technical ability, and Tommy was just such a skier. Dynastar, his ski sponsor, was even designing a special downhill ski to suit the course. OK, Tommy thought. That's exciting. But in a way, he wished people would quit talking about medals. He had never finished better than thirteenth in a World Cup race. He felt he could do well at the Olympics, but a top-three finish might be too much to expect. Still, Tommy didn't let the talk get him down. He was optimistic and easygoing by nature. He just wanted to get onto the hill and have some fun. Jeff Olson and Steve Porino also rejoined the team for the Val d'Isère races. Reggie Crist was there, too. The French were comparing the new course to Kitzbühel's Hahnenkamm layout. The Americans couldn't wait to see if the comparison was apt.

The new Olympic course was on the same mountain as the old World Cup course, the one Bill Hudson had crashed on in December. But it was on a different part of the mountain. The World Cup downhill, known as the OK, meandered down the west side, sloping slowly and gently toward the finish. The Olympic course was carved out of the north side. The Face de Bellevarde was not so much a slope as a cliff: Standing at the top, you had the sensation that you could throw a rock all the way to the bottom. The risk of avalanche after a storm was so great that the Face was usually closed to recreational skiers. Carving a race course into this big gray rock had been quite a feat, requiring bulldozer drivers with the nerve and balance of downhillers.

The start, which was near the start of the OK course, was like other downhill setups. The racer left the gate and screamed straight down a long, steep pitch, reaching almost seventy miles an hour in the first few seconds. After that, the course looked unlike any track the American athletes had ever seen. At the bottom of the first steep pitch was a long left turn that required the racer to set the edge of his right ski and, basically, hold on for dear life. Then the ground disappeared, and the skier rocketed off a steep jump. After a couple of sharp turns the racer confronted an odd twist called the net turn, a steep, slick right turn that emptied out onto a road. The road was bordered by a tall red snow fence—a good thing, because without it anybody who fell off that road wasn't going to stop tumbling until he reached the Office de Tourisme in the center of town.

After another roundhouse left turn (by now the racer's overworked right leg would be as limp as a cooked noodle) the skier had to prepare for the strangest and most controversial set of turns in downhill racing. Course designer Bernhard Russi, the former Olympic downhill champion, was known for adding gimmicks to his courses. For the 1989 Alpine World Championships in Vail, Colorado, he had built a series of banked turns that required the racer to bounce off the walls like a bobsledder. He called this section Rattlesnake Alley. Some people thought it added color and intrigue to the sport. Others thought it was like putting a windmill on the putting greens at Augusta National. Russi's downhill course in Saalbach had such a sharp turn near the top that several racers actually skied a few feet up the snow fence and kept going, like skateboarders making a slick turn in a pool. The gimmick on the Olympic course was much grander, and much more troublesome for the racers. About twenty seconds from the finish, the zooming racer suddenly had to make a sharp right turn, followed by an even sharper left turn between two enormous rock outcroppings. It was like skiing into a maze. The rocks, part of the natural landscape, were covered with heavy padding, so anyone who lost control in that section probably would bounce off them and come out whole. Still, the racers could see from inspection that a lot of people would not come out standing up.

The finish was as conventional as the start. The racer made a couple of short turns and then skipped off the finish jump, whose landing was long and steep, the way the downhillers liked it. If you crashed off this jump, you'd land softly and slide forever. This safe design was carefully planned. The downhill would be the first big event of the games; the French wanted the athletes to sail into the finish like graceful birds, not twist in like smoking warplanes. Carnage would be bad for the image of the games.

In the first training run, AJ finished forty-eighth. He didn't feel he was skiing brilliantly—he still had not recovered from the back-to-back transatlantic flights—and yet he blamed the course layout more than he blamed himself. He hated the Face de Bellevarde. Downhill, he said after his training run, "should not be a struggle to ski around obstacles." And this, he felt, was an obstacle course. Instead of riding a flat ski and making challenging high-speed turns, as he did in every other downhill, AJ found himself repeatedly gaining speed and then slamming on the brakes, like an aggressive driver in heavy freeway traffic. He really had to slam on the brakes to ski through the rocks. In this section, the course was no faster than the average giant slalom, which to a downhill purist like AJ was insulting. The finish jump was no special thrill either, in his opinion. He felt Russi should speed up the approach to the jump so the racers would fly farther—say forty yards instead of twenty or thirty. Why not? The landing was smooth. Anybody who couldn't handle a little air shouldn't be in the race to begin with.

The French liked to say that the Face de Bellevarde course would set the standard for downhill racing in the future. That was exactly what AJ was afraid of. In his opinion the sport was getting too conservative. The great old courses—Kitzbühel, Wengen, and so on—would always be around, but he doubted anyone would build a new one as challenging.

The threat of lawsuits, such as the one Brian Stemmle was pressing at Kitzbühel, was too great. Gernot Reinstadler's death in Wengen, AJ believed, would further inhibit course designers. In the future, he thought, downhills would be full of Rattlesnake Alleys and rock mazes. And he didn't think the sport would be better for it.

Some members of the press figured AJ disliked the layout simply because it didn't suit his style: He had a reputation as a glider, someone who floated on the snow, and this was a highly technical course. AJ thought they were wrong. His complaint went much deeper than that. He wouldn't have minded a course that was merely technical, but this one was something else. He was a downhiller, and this was a go-cart track. Comparing this to Kitzbühel was a serious insult to Kitzbühel. It disappointed AJ to think the Olympic downhill, the greatest event in his sport, would be contested on such a gimmicky track.

Tommy Moe also had a hard time with the Face de Bellevarde. He hacked his way through the first training run, slowing down so much in the rock tunnel that he couldn't have been hurt even if he had fallen. He finished sixty-third, but it didn't bother him. He told *Powder* magazine, "I'm not gonna run home with my tail between my legs. I like this sport too much to let the negative stuff get to me." Steve Porino, starting from the back of the field, had even more trouble than Tommy did. By the time he left the gate, the light was so flat that every little bump and dip came as a shock. The rock tunnel was pitch-dark and the snow inside it was rutted and covered in death cookies. All Steve could do was throw his skis sideways and hope to remain upright until he hit daylight again. He managed it. The course wore him out. His legs went numb about fifteen seconds from the finish; his feet could do little to influence which way he went. "My skis suddenly became luggage," he said.

After a second training run, a storm moved in and dumped several feet of snow on the Face de Bellevarde. The racers spent two days in the Hotel La Becca, playing cards, reading paperbacks, doing stretching exercises in the hallways, and wishing the snow would stop. It didn't. The organizers canceled both races. The American downhillers left Val d'Isère knowing little about the Olympic course, other than they couldn't do anything about it now. No more races were scheduled on the Face de Bellevarde before the games. When it came time for the big event, the Americans flyboys would have to wing it.

6

Losing

The downhillers entered the last part of the World Cup season looking ahead, which was a good thing. If they had stopped to add up their losses, they might not have been so enthusiastic. Bill Hudson had gone into the air and come down in pieces; Kyle Rasmussen and Tommy Moe had skied through shallow holes and were hurting; Jeff Olson had skied into a deep one and was hurting worse; Eric Keck and Steve Porino had not skied much at all. Perhaps most disappointing, the racers had not fulfilled the promise of December, when several of them had finished in the top fifteen in World Cup races. Bill Egan, who had counted up his losses plenty of times in his life, never said so to the racers, but he was upset about it, and worried.

His kids weren't, though. The month of March brought new opportunities, shiny white. The first was a downhill in Aspen, Colorado, on a course most of the Americans knew and liked. The race was known as "America's Downhill." After that the team would jet off to Lake Louise, Alberta, Canada, for the last two downhills of the World Cup season. They could leave January and February in Europe behind them; it was sunny and warm in North America. They were home now. The phone calls were cheap, the waitresses spoke English, the postal system made sense (relatively speaking), and the American downhillers were going to kick some ass. That was the plan anyway: Look ahead.

At least one American had reason to feel genuinely optimistic. AJ Kitt arrived in Aspen still high from the U.S. Alpine Ski Championships—

the racers just called them the nationals—which had just been held in Crested Butte, Colorado. Only the Americans and a few Canadians had competed. AJ had won everything, or at least everything that mattered to him. He had won the downhill, barely beating Tommy Moe (Eric Keck, Steve Porino, and Reggie Crist were third, fourth, and fifth). The super G victory had been even more satisfying. The course had one particularly challenging turn, a bump called Panorama that threw several racers way off line. In his usual thorough inspection, AJ determined that he would need to set up for the turn long before he got to it. It paid off. The headline in the next day's *Denver Post* said, "Kitt outthinks field for second victory." The *Post*'s account of the race began, "May we present, for the second straight day on the victory stand, AJ Kitt, the thinking man's ski racer." AJ's father, Ross, who had urged his young son to develop "fast brains," made a special place for the article in his scrapbook.

AJ and his teammates couldn't wait to start practicing, but they had to. On Wednesday, which was to have been the first day of training, the seams split in the gray ski over Aspen, and the snow fell in clumps. (If you want snow, schedule a downhill.) There was no hope for training that day, and not much hope for Thursday, either. The race was scheduled for Friday.

At the team meeting Wednesday night, Ueli Luthi said the race organizers had scheduled two training runs for the next day. But he wasn't hopeful about the weather.

"There is another system who might move in tonight," he said, in the way only he could. "This is not the most ideal situation. We have to do everything in one day now to get ready for a race. It means a lot of effort from you guys. It means a lot of concentration. I think if we go the right way about it, it's no problem."

The best thing about Aspen, from the racers' point of view, was not the downhill course or the challenging skiing trails or even the carefully groomed young women. It was the food.

At every other stop on the tour the downhillers had to eat whatever the hotel happened to be serving that night. Often the food was not good. Sometimes it was not immediately identifiable. And there was never enough of it. (You've heard the gag: What terrible food! And what small portions!) Aspen was different. In Aspen, the athletes (all of them, not just the Americans) ate dinner in a different restaurant each night, for free. The race committee arranged for the free meals as a way of introducing the racers to the community, and of promoting the race. The racers paid for drinks and left tips; that was it. And in a town where dining well was an essential part of living well, the food was no minor fringe benefit. The American downhillers, who, no kidding, thought more about getting fed than getting laid, couldn't have been happier if the race organizers had provided party girls.

These weren't cheap meals, either. Among the restaurants providing free food were the Caribou Club, Mezzaluna, Syzygy, Steak Pit, Guido's, Skier's Chalet, Maurice's, Lauretta's, Carlos & Pepi's, Pepi's, Poppie's, Primavera, and Ute City Banque (stop at the banque on your way there). It wasn't unusual for the American downhillers to consume more than one thousand dollars worth of food in a single evening. *Urp.*

The bill was more reasonable that Wednesday night in Aspen, but only because the racers dined at a relatively inexpensive place—Cantina, an extremely popular Mexican joint. AJ was there with his father, Ross, and his cousin Alison. Tommy Moe brought his father, Tom Senior, and his stepmother, Tyra. For the first time all season, AJ and Tommy had the pleasure of being with family members before a race. The Europeans had the support and friendship of their families all the time, but for the Americans it was a rare treat. Skip Merrick and Spencer Eccles, young racers who hoped to make the World Cup downhill team, joined the Kitts and the Moes at the restaurant. This was no ordinary night. When the downhillers ate together as a team, away from family members and guests, anything went. Guys shouted at each other, snatched rolls from the basket as soon as it was placed on the table, bickered over servings of rice or potatoes, and talked endlessly about their two favorite subjects, football and women. They didn't actually throw food at each other, but only because they valued eating it so much. But at Cantina, AJ and Tommy and the others were on their best behavior. They graciously shared the chips and salsa with their guests and raised their voices only enough to make themselves heard. They were in public now, not in the fraternity-house atmosphere of the team hotel.

Nobody in the restaurant seemed to recognize AJ and Tommy. These guys were not stars, not by Aspen standards. In this town, it wasn't unusual to bump into Chris Evert or Martina Navratilova, so seeing a couple of ski racers was no big deal. Still, the restaurant was happy to have them. After dinner the racers signed a poster for the owner and strolled out, leaving behind a sizable stack of fives and tens as their tip.

The first thing Eric Keck did when he arrived in Aspen that week was check the schedule of worship services at the local churches. And then he called and left a message about the services for Ole Furuseth, a Norwegian racer and devout Christian. Eric spent a lot of time that week in his room, reading his two Bibles. His curiosity about God was insatiable. But Eric did something that week that might be interpreted as a little devilish. One afternoon he answered the phone in AJ's room when AJ wasn't around.

"Hello?"

"Hello, AJ?" The voice was a woman's.

"Yes," Eric lied.

The woman identified herself. Eric recognized the name as someone AJ had dated that week. He chatted with her for a moment. Then the woman said, "It doesn't sound like you."

"I have a cold," Eric said. "Listen, I really enjoyed our date the other night. I wish we'd done a little more."

The woman was quiet for a moment as she thought that over. Then she said, "Well, we could go up on the mountain."

"I'd like to have you on my mountain," Eric said.

By now, the woman could tell the guy on the phone wasn't AJ. This was a typical downhiller gag, the sort of thing the guys did to each other at every opportunity. AJ wasn't upset when he heard about it. What did it matter? It wasn't as if he was in love with the woman.

From the way AJ Kitt's father told stories about his increasingly famous and frequently reckless son, it was apparent that he admired the craziness as much as he did the fame. His favorite involved racing—not on skis, but in a car. AJ was always wild, and he always wanted to go fast. Ross, who owned a company that published municipal law books, could understand that (he often had that half-nuts look in his eye himself), but he didn't want the kid tearing up the streets of Rochester in the family car. So when AJ was about seventeen his father signed him up for race training school at Watkins Glen, the well-known track in upstate New York. Ross' idea was to let his son get his thrills in a controlled environment.

AJ, strapped into his seat belt and wearing a motorcycle helmet, really took to the sport. His drove a small white sports car, a zippy little thing with four cylinders and a turbocharger. With his skiing experience he considered it easy to find the fastest line around the track. Indeed, he completed the first few laps so quickly that his father, driving another car, soon lost sight of him. AJ was hauling ass, and loving it. After a few minutes Ross squealed around a corner and saw a yellow flag, the signal to drive slowly. A moment later he saw a black flag, the signal to stop. He was pressing the brake when he noticed a small white sports car tipped onto the driver's side, its engine whining and wheels spinning. The car's spoiler and front bumper lay on the asphalt. Wow, Ross thought, somebody has really screwed up his car.

And then Ross noticed his son standing next to the wreck.

AJ told his father he was all right, then explained what had happened. He was making a high-speed left turn, he said, when the wheels on the left side of the car ran over the round plastic bumps, called turtles, that defined the width of the track. At that point, the car, as ski racers liked to say, "got light": Instead of gripping the asphalt, the tires came off the road and the entire car jumped to the left. When the rubber finally grabbed the road, the vehicle rocketed nose first into a wall. AJ estimated he was doing 85 miles an hour at the time.

The impact blew off several parts of the car and stuffed the right front wheel into the engine compartment like the landing gear on a 747. The vehicle ricocheted off the wall, flew 135 feet, and landed on its nose, shattering the windshield. Then it bounced across the track and rested on its side, the wheels churning at the ground. "It was like an A-ride in an amusement park," AJ said later.

When the ride ended, AJ was suspended in his safety belt like a rock in a sling. The moment he got his senses he turned off the ignition, tossed the keys out the window, and climbed out. An ambulance was called to the scene, but there was no need for one. "Never mind me,"

AJ said. Then he pointed at his father, who was a little excited, and said, "Just make sure he's OK." Later, when Ross had calmed down, he and AJ each grabbed a beer and posed in front of the wreck, like a couple of hunters with their trophy buck. Later, Ross hired a flatbed truck to drive to the track and haul the car back to Rochester.

Ross delighted in telling this story. Yes, AJ had demolished a $15,000 car, but so what? He was punching it; that was what counted. Ross's son was an aggressive driver, somebody who took risks. In the end, the story did not embarrass AJ; it glorified him. As father and son were leaving the track, a Watkins Glen employee told AJ to come back sometime and "drive a car that can handle you."

The weather in Aspen was mixed on Thursday morning. The sky radiated blue over the town, but there were clouds over the mountains. Shadows stretched across the peaks, casting a silvery blue light that you don't see anywhere else in nature. As the racers rode up the lift early that morning, they found that it was still dusting snow near the top of the mountain. Off in the distance, a thin gray cloud partially blocked the sun, so that it seemed the whitish sunlight was peeking through cellophane. On the race course, two groaning tractors, connected by a cable, struggled to pack down the new snow. Farther down the hill, course workers used shovels to clear the track. They were careful not to move the red downhill gates, each of which was imprinted with the name of the sponsor, Subaru. At 11:30 A.M., ninety minutes late, the first training run finally began.

AJ wore number three that day. He was fighting the flu—he said his legs felt as wobbly as they had felt during the Alpine World Championships, when he was suffering from jet leg—but it didn't show in his skiing. When he left the start, he felt he was leaping off the top of a long flight of stairs: It was that steep. Then the course flattened out, and AJ glided for thirty seconds over some of the easiest, and most boring, terrain on the World Cup circuit. (Any good weekend skier could handle the speed.) Here, AJ kept a low profile and hoped his skis were running fast. Curtis Bacca, the ski technician for Head, thought of Aspen as his greatest challenge of the year, his Kitzbühel: Smart ski preparation never mattered more than it did here. After leaving the flats, AJ passed a tall sign. "America's Downhill," the sign said. Next to those words was an arrow pointing to the left. The Aspen downhill was the only World Cup course with road signs.

The course soon got more interesting, and considerably more difficult. About fifty seconds into the race, AJ encountered the pitch called Aztec. There were only two turns on the thirty-four-degree pitch, but one of them, a right turn, was among the trickiest on the tour. The turn was sharp, the hill frighteningly steep, the speed high enough to blur the vision. It wasn't the sort of place where people crashed and got helicoptered off, like the Mausefalle in Kitzbühel. Rather, Aztec tripped people up—knocked them off balance and threw them off line. Skiing Aztec poorly was like having some wise-ass kid step on the back of your sneaker and give you a flat. It was hard to get your momentum back. If you screwed up here, you probably wouldn't win. Because this was the first training run, AJ negotiated Aztec slowly and deliberately, just to get a feel for the terrain. He would add speed in the second run.

Two other turns made a difference. In the section called Strawpile, AJ had to ski fast toward a fence. Then, just when it seemed he would cream it, he had to make a sharp right turn back across the hill. Coach Jim Tracy described the turn as "ballsy." It was a fair description. AJ made the turn cleanly, then entered a roundhouse right turn called Norway Island. The turn didn't look tough, but it had a mean history: A few years back, in a women's event, seven members of the Swiss team had crashed there. After that, Norway Island was known as Cheesehead Corner. From Norway Island, it was only a few seconds to the finish. AJ finished eleventh, which was about where he wanted to be. The hottest racer that day was veteran Swiss racer Peter Müller, who ended up in first place by almost half a second. Müller always did well in Aspen: He had won the race four times and finished in the top fifteen five other times.

The rest of the Americans had predictable results, with two exceptions: Jeff Olson skied better than expected, and Tommy Moe skied a lot worse. Jeff, who started sixty-fourth, came in twenty-seventh, and Tommy, number thirty-three, was fifty-third. The coaches had expected the results to be the other way around. Then again, Tommy's ankle still bothered him, and Jeff . . . well, it was never easy to explain anything Jeff did.

Bill Egan watched the first training run from the bottom of Aztec, the meanest section of the course. Other coaches watched with him. None of them liked what he saw. Indeed, anybody standing close to the cluster of coaches got a quick lesson in multilingual cursing. First, an American racer would screw up the turn, and Bill, standing there in his ski boots and sunglasses, would mutter, "Shit!" Then a German or Austrian guy would blow the turn and you'd hear a coach say, "Scheisse!" The Swiss trainer would yell "Schisdreck!" when his guys fouled up. And the French coach murmured, "Merde!" The trainers weren't being unkind: In the first training run, Aztec tripped up just about everyone.

In the second training run (won by Austrian Helmut Höflehner), AJ was doing the muttering. He was fast on the top, but got progressively slower as he went on. He started his turn late in Strawpile and ended up missing a gate, which drove him crazy. To AJ, missing gates was inexcusable. It showed a lack of concentration, and he couldn't abide that. In the finish he felt miserable, physically and emotionally, and it showed. He stood apart from the other racers, gazing up the hill.

As he stood there, a reporter approached him and said, "Mind if I ask you a couple of questions?"

AJ didn't look at him. "Not right now," he said.

Boy, those guys pissed off AJ. Couldn't they see he was unhappy, that he didn't feel like talking? What was wrong with them? AJ never considered that the reporter was merely trying to do his job, and that he had no other time to do it because the racers were available for interviews only after the practice runs. Nor did it occur to AJ that by clamming up he had passed up a chance to promote the race, and the sport, and himself. AJ earned most of his money endorsing products, not competing in races. His sponsors valued him only to the extent that he got his name in the paper and his picture on television. If he disappeared from public view—if he became a nobody—they would have no use for him. So it was unwise for him to shun the press, even when he was having a bad day. But he couldn't see that just now. He was, as usual, focused on the task, on the scary work of wringing tenths of a second out of a race course. He did not stop concentrating just because the run was over. People who knew AJ knew he was a dedicated athlete and a decent, fair-minded, and yes, outspoken, person. But this stranger, this reporter, didn't know anything about AJ. To him, the athlete just seemed rude.

The coaches and athletes met that night in a room at the Aspen

Meadows Hotel, where they were staying. Bill and Ueli stood near the television set, holding their notes in their hands. Most of the the racers sat on the carpeted floor or in chairs. A couple sprawled on the bed.

Bill and Ueli felt a lot of pressure in Aspen. The next day's race was the only World Cup downhill scheduled in the United States that year, and the press and the fans expected the Americans to do well. But doing well meant one thing to the press, and quite another thing to the coaches and athletes. If AJ finished, say, fourth, he would consider it a brilliant race, a real success. A fourth-place finish would duplicate the best result of the career. But the press wouldn't play it that way. The papers would emphasize the failure angle. They'd acknowledge that it was Kitt's best finish of the season, but they would add how disappointed he was that he hadn't quite made it onto the podium. (Those pathetic Americans, they never make it to the podium, they'd say.) And if rookie World Cup downhiller Reggie Crist finished, say, seventeenth, he'd spend half the night making delirious celebratory phone calls to his friends and relatives, and he'd pass the other half partying his brains out in the bars. The papers, however, would report his finish in the last paragraph, way back there on page 14-D: Among other Americans, Reggie Crist was seventeenth, Tommy Moe was thirty-first . . . And so on.

The coaches knew how important it was to get good publicity for the sport. But in a way, they didn't give a damn what the press, or even the fans, expected. In their opinion, the press didn't know anything about the athletes, or, for that matter, the sport. And they were mostly right. In all the United States, only *Denver Post* reporter Charlie Meyers and the staff of *Ski Racing* magazine covered downhill in a meaningful, ongoing way. Which is to say they actually had met most of the racers and knew something about them. But even Meyers and the *Ski Racing* reporters generally stayed home during the European part of the World Cup tour. When the athletes raced in, say, Val Gardena, their coverage was usually put together with press releases and wire stories. As for the rest of the press, well, it drove the coaches nuts. Lots of newspapers ignored World Cup ski racing fifty-one weeks a year, and then, when the Aspen race came along, published articles about the sorry state of the U.S. Ski Team and its thin chances of winning. Oh, the coaches hated that! Not that they argued with the overall accuracy of the stories. The downhillers, who presumably were out there to win, never did. No, what rankled the coaches was that these newspapers acknowledged nothing but victory. They would not hail the progress of an AJ Kitt, or the potential of a Tommy Moe or a Kyle Rasmussen. If you didn't win, you didn't matter, period. Bill and Ueli couldn't help but be bothered by it.

The racers' poor reputation was on the coaches' minds at the meeting.

"I think you guys are ready," Ueli told them. "I'm looking forward to tomorrow's race. Just go after it, eh? I mean, we are here on home turf, and it'll never be better than tomorrow, so let's go and do it."

Bill felt the pressure much more than Ueli did. As head coach, Ueli's job was largely administrative. He communicated with the ski team office in Park City, made sure the downhillers and technical skiers got to each race safely, decided when it was time to promote a racer from the minor leagues to the World Cup tour, and so forth. Yes, he also spent time with the athletes, but he never got emotionally involved with them the way Bill did. When the racers went to the gym to play basketball, Bill played with them. When they watched video, Bill was there, offering encouragement. When they went free-skiing, Bill often went along. He knew all about their personal lives—and they knew about his. So he had a much more personal stake in the team's success than Ueli did. But the team hadn't had much success lately, and now Bill was exhausted. The long season had worn him out. There had been days—most of them in Kitzbühel—when he had wondered if the job was worth the trouble. Coaching was supposed to be fun, but lately it hadn't been. Now, in Aspen, Bill desperately wanted the guys to do well, and not just because the press and the fans wanted them to. Mainly, Bill was hoping they could recoup some of the losses of the past two months. They needed to feel good about themselves when the season ended, and so did he. So even though he really felt like grabbing his girlfriend Maggie and catching the next plane to Mammoth, California, Bill managed to find some inspirational words for the racers.

"I saw some good things today, too," he began. "To be perfectly frank, I think you guys are a little stronger relative to the field than I've seen. I saw some really good things happening. And I think you can put it together now. It looked as if, you know, you were training and you were training intelligently. So now tomorrow let's make it happen. I mean, it is America's Downhill and all that.

"And also, there's a lot of negative shit running around. A lot of negative people. I have a hell of a lot of faith in you guys, and you know that. And you should have a hell of a lot of faith in yourselves. This is our hill. Let's show them tomorrow. Let's stick it in their ear. And let's stick it in their ear with our skiing. OK? And then we'll leave here with a good feeling. Let's give it our best, huh?"

This was the headline in *Ski Racing* magazine after the race: "Heinzer homers in Aspen downhill." And the Americans didn't come to the game.

That winter, the Swiss hero was in the sort of groove most athletes never find. He beat Atle Skaardal by just twenty-six hundredths of a second, but to those who watched him go by, who saw his sleek body crouching low and his gloved hands thrust down the hill, it seemed he would win by a whole minute. Why did anyone else even try? In the finish, Heinzer looked—as he always did—a little surprised he had won. To be precise, he looked as if he had been unconscious all the way down the hill, only to be revived moments after he sliced under the banner. "I was lucky to win this one," he told the press. Yeah, sure. He was magnificent. The Americans admired him and at the same time resented the hell out of him.

AJ, who raced second, felt sick during his run, and it showed. He turned lazily, making himself late for some gates. He managed to finish eighteenth, which, in his opinion, stunk. Not that he blamed himself. He had skied well in the weeks leading to the race. But in the finish, he seemed less angry than he had been when he missed a gate in training. It was as if he was resigned to what had happened. A reporter asked him if perhaps the pressure had gotten to him. Kitt shook his head and said, "Nah." No, he never thought about that stuff. He was sick, that was all. Another reporter asked if he was disappointed. "Sure. It's always disappointing when you don't do as well as you know you could have done," he said.

The rest of the team just collapsed. Reggie caught an edge and nearly tipped over in the flats, which is the skiing equivalent of walking along a new, smooth, dry sidewalk, stubbing your toe, and falling down. Tommy was mediocre, Jeff just bad. Eric finished sixtieth, only to learn he had been disqualified for leaving the starting gate too early. "Oh well," he said after the race. "It's not like I won." Skip Merrick, a young kid, was sixty-second; Steve Porino, who almost tipped over in a flat section on the bottom, was sixty-third; and Todd Kelly, another young guy, was sixty-seventh, five seconds behind Heinzer. However, Kelly did beat the only Hungarian in the field.

After the race, the athletes loaded their skis onto their shoulders and dragged back to the ski room to put them away. They didn't speak, didn't blink. They were wooden, all of them. Dead souls. Of course they were. Losing wears you down. It can turn into a habit and then degenerate into a way of life. In the worst cases, it becomes into an identity: You didn't only lose; you're a loser. For athletes in a slump, losing is a force unto itself, a power they can't control. It becomes a mysterious, uncontrollable phenomenon. Athletes on losing streaks often quit believing in themselves and place all their faith in the sinister energy of the streak. The more they lose, the more they believe they'll lose. And they're right. Losing is a degenerative disease. In Aspen, the American downhillers were in the advanced stages of the disease. They had lost and lost big, and it felt lousy, especially in front of what amounted to a hometown crowd. Tommy's father and stepmother were there. AJ's dad was at the race. So were Steve's parents. Almost everybody else had friends in town.

As Steve waited for a ride back to the hotel, he went through some mail that his mother had brought him. He opened one envelope to find that an airline had sent him a special bronze frequent-flyer pass.

"That's all I've gotten this year," he grumbled. "A bronze from an airline."

Bill Egan was grim-faced when the racers arrived for the team meeting that night at the Aspen Meadows. In a way, Bill didn't blame himself for their poor performance. They were the downhill racers; he was just the coach. But of course he did feel responsible for what had happened. In his speech the night before, he had pronounced his athletes great— "I saw some really good things happening, and I think you can put it together now"—and then they had gone out and exposed him as a fraud. That was how it felt, anyway. Bill had been so despondent after the race that he had wondered aloud if the ski team would let him stay on. His most important job as a coach was to motivate people, to get more from them than they knew they could give, and he obviously hadn't done it very well. So he felt as miserable as his kids did. And yet he didn't feel like giving up. Over the years, Bill had had lots of thrills in coaching. He had helped lousy football players become decent ones and good football players become great ones. He had helped AJ finish fourth at Cortina and had coached Bill Hudson to thirteenth place in Kitzbühel. When he told the racers he felt they could put all it together, he wasn't trying to con them. He really believed it. Bill was an optimist, and optimism was an important qualification for any coaching position, especially a job coaching a team as raw and inexperienced as his was.

Bill delivered his speech that night in a near whisper, frowning and toeing the carpet. Again, his kids were all around him. Nobody looked into his eyes, but everybody paid attention.

"OK, listen up," he began. "OK, um, I'm proud of you guys. And I'm proud of myself. And we have to be proud, because we worked so damn hard. And we have some shitty days occasionally, or we have a day when we're a little bit disappointed, like today. And we should be disappointed, because we're too good to have that kind of day. There were some positive things about today, but there were some negative things, and I like the fact that everybody was a little pissed off. Because you know that you can beat these guys. And we have just got to pick our intensity level up a little bit more. We have to do something, because I put my pants on the same way any coach does. And," Bill said, pointing to AJ, "Franz Heinzer's no better than you are. He's good right now, right? But he's not any better than you are. And it goes the same for all of us. We know that. OK?

"It can be, it can be difficult now if we wimp out. This is a test of our character. There's going to be a lot of people saying we are just the shittiest team they've ever seen. And it's going to be be coming down big-time. And I don't give a shit about it. And I don't think you guys should either. OK? Because it's not your fault. You guys are not shitty athletes. And it's not my fault. I'm not a bad coach. I'm not great, but I'm not bad. So we must—we must—do better. And we will. Because we want to."

Bill paused. "For the next two weeks, I want you to do something, and after that you can point the finger anywhere you want. But for the next couple of races I want you to point your finger at the number one problem. You look in the mirror, and you know the person to blame for your inability to be as good as you can be. I'm going to work harder. That's one thing fortunately that not being successful does for you. It makes you work harder. At least it does as long as you have hope. And I have dreams for you guys."

The room was still. After a moment the coach went on.

"We are young. We're young. You guys haven't had a hell of a lot of experience in the World Cup. You look at the guys who did really well today. Some of them have just had tons of experience. OK? So it's going to take a little bit of time. But on the other hand, we're not *that* young. OK? We may be a little bit inexperienced, but if we really learn from these experiences, we can really make quantum leaps forward. I want you to be really critical of yourselves, because that's what makes winners. As I say, it doesn't bother me that you're a little disappointed.

"You guys have to shoot for the moon now. You have to shoot for the moon. In the next couple of weeks we can make it happen, and we can learn a hell of a lot and be ready to go next year. I don't want to end up walking out of Lake Louise and having people badger us, saying we're the shits. And I don't want us walking out with our heads between our legs, saying, Yeah, we are. Because we aren't. We're going to learn from this experience and we're going to come back next year and be a little bit better. A little better. Not just one or two of us, but a lot of us.

"So what are we going to say to these people when they start talking to us? All I can say is, keep your cool. They *don't* understand what we're going through. They don't understand where we're headed. And one day when we're good, they can ask us how we got good, and it'll be easy to talk to them. So right now, I would say just keep your cool. Try not to say anything that's silly. Say I'm lousy. I'll take the heat. Tell them Egan's a nerd coach, and if they ask me I'll say, Yeah, they're right. OK? OK? And keep working, guys. We're not . . . that . . . far . . . away."

A day or so later, the downhillers met at Denver's Stapleton Airport for the flight to Canada. After they checked in their luggage and their hefty ski bags, a few of the guys went back outside to sit in the cool, fresh air. AJ, Steve, and Reggie were sitting together on a bench when a small blue car pulled up to the curb. The passenger door opened and Jeff stepped out. And then the driver's door opened and a handsome young woman got out. Jeff's teammates looked her over.

As Jeff carried his bags to the curb, AJ asked him under his breath, "Did you close the deal?" In downhiller lingo, fucking was known as closing the deal.

Jeff just smiled.

The woman was helping Jeff carry his things to the curb when she noticed the handsome blond racer sitting on the bench. She did a double take.

"Reggie?"

Reggie did a double take of his own. Jeff's girlfriend turned out to be an old friend, someone Reggie had met while attending summer school at the University of Colorado. He gave her a hug. For a few minutes Reggie and the woman stood and chatted while Jeff watched, pretending he wasn't surprised. Then the woman said goodbye, kissed Jeff, got in her car, and drove off.

A few minutes later, on the plane, Jeff couldn't hide his curiosity. "So," he asked Reggie, who was sitting in the row in front of him, "you knew her?"

What Jeff wanted to know was whether Reggie and the woman ever had been, you know, involved. They had not, but Reggie didn't say so. He thought it might be fun, as he put it, "to push Jeff's buttons."

"Yeah, we were in school together," he said. "She's a really nice girl."

"Yeah, she is," Jeff said, leaning back in his seat.

"And," Reggie said, "she's a great lay."

The flight was awful. The plane rocked and lurched like a rowboat in surly seas. Even the flight attendants got in their seats and buckled up. More than once, the plane plunged so far that people shrieked. The captain made an announcement, but the noise of the engines drowned him out. Virtually every team was on this plane. If it went down, the World Cup downhill circuit would be wiped out, kaboom.

But the crazy-ass downhill maniacs weren't worried, were they? Actually, one was. Of all the Americans, the person most unnerved by the ordeal was not jumpy Tommy Moe or claustrophic Bill Egan, but Eric

Keck, the huge Christian. Eric's teammates were surprised to see him so rattled: He was so large, and so tough, that if the plane had spun in, they would have expected him to emerge from the burning rubble, dust himself off, and walk away. But here he was, in his window seat, saying his prayers and bitching at the pilot.

"What's the matter with this idiot?" he said, presenting his fear as anger. In this crowd, anger got more respect.

Eric kept griping. After a while, AJ, sitting right in front of him, wheeled around and snapped, "Shut up, Keck. We're still flying, aren't we?"

AJ could always be counted on to apply logic to the situation. Yes, they were still flying; AJ was satisfied with that, and would be right up to moment the wings snapped off. Then, probably, he would try to calculate the chances of the plane's coming down on something soft. Really, though, he could see no reason to complain. It was a little windy. So what? Sure, the plane had been jumping like popcorn in a popper, but it hadn't bothered him a bit. The real reason he was angry at Keck was . . . Eric, with his loud whining, had woken him up.

7

"The Mountain
Is Skiing Me"

For sheer beauty, few places on the World Cup circuit rivaled Lake Louise, Alberta, Canada. The ski area was set on majestic, bald-headed Mt. Whitehorn, an eighty-seven-hundred-foot peak deep inside Banff National Park. Except for a few houses, stores, and hotels, the park belonged mostly to the animals: Skipjacks darted through the trees and moose moseyed along the roads. This was no Aspen: Nobody went out on the town because there was no town to go out on. Most of the downhill teams stayed in the Château Lake Louise, a sprawling, 101-year-old hotel overlooking Lake Louise. A glacial peak rose from the water; hotel guests occasionally were fortunate enough to see a section of ice snap off and splash down into the icy blue. Afternoons, people could ice skate on the lake or cross-country ski around it, with only the sound of the wind to distract them.

Lake Louise, site of the last two downhills of the year, was remote in every sense. Because the ski area was so far from where people lived, few spectators were expected at the races. Nor would the races be shown on American television (though some people in northern states would be able to pick them up on Canadian TV). For the Americans, the competition in Lake Louise was another big opportunity, one last chance to make something of a hard and confusing year. But if they intended to achieve something, they would have to do it almost completely alone.

* * *

124

On the first day of downhill training, Tommy Moe, Reggie Crist, and Kyle Rasmussen gathered to watch some of the first-seed racers go off a steep jump near the top of the course. This was the place where guys would really get air, the place where photographers would set up for dramatic pictures. The takeoff was flat and the landing steep, so that going off the thing was like shooting off the end of a table, and coming down was like landing halfway down a flight of stairs. You wouldn't want to lose your balance going off this thing, no, sir. The jump was simple in the way that skydiving was simple: If the parachute opened, you'd be fine. Tommy, Reggie, and Kyle pretended they weren't scared, of course. That morning, they observed a downhill ritual that could be called Making Something Seem Like It's Not a Big Deal. In this case, the ritual involved standing on the lip and insisting that the jump wasn't that big, that you wouldn't fly that far, and that everything would be fine, no matter what.

Tommy—who was skittish about getting air, and who therefore was among the most eager participants in the ritual—watched a guy blast off the jump. Then he said, "It looks sweet, man. I can't wait to run this race."

Reggie, who had been standing a few feet away, skied over and said, "What do you think, Moe?" Reggie used interrogatives to express many of his feelings, especially nervousness.

Tommy replied, in his disjointed, verbless way of speaking, "Nice and smooth. High speed. Snow."

Kyle—his broken collarbone mostly healed—skied over and joined his teammates. The three young men seemed to be doing a lot more wiggling and shaking and stretching than they actually needed to do to prepare for the race. Fear clings to you like a sand spur; you have to try to shake it off.

A racer went off the jump. He made a series of noises as he passed. His skis went *ssshhh* on the snow. He went fwoosh when he passed. And his skis went *clap* when he landed. His flight lasted until three Mississippi. The Americans watched him until he was out of sight.

Kyle said, "That's not bad at all, eh, Moe?" Kyle and Tommy were good friends. They usually roomed together, and they once enjoyed a long, drunken fishing trip together in Alaska.

"No, it's no sweat," Tommy said.

Another guy hit the jump: *Ssshhh. Fwoosh. Clap.*

Kyle shook his head. "It's pretty fast."

Later that day, the Americans lost a guy during his first training run, but not on the jump at the top of the hill. They lost him at the bottom.

Skip Merrick was a twenty-one-year-old kid from Sun Valley, Idaho (Reggie Crist's hometown), a skinny, smallish, dark-haired guy with a slightly pointy nose and a gentle manner. On the ski team, he was best known for swiping the American national downhill championship from AJ Kitt at Crested Butte, Colorado, in 1990. While AJ was standing in the finish, hugging his skis and accepting congratulations on his first national title, Skip came from the back of the field and took the first-place trophy. On the national TV broadcast of the race, AJ looked like a guy who had returned from an invigorating week's vacation in the Bahamas to discover that someone had stolen his house. It was easily the highlight of Skip's career.

Skip had started only one World Cup race in his career—the one in Aspen the week before. He had finished sixty-second, a hundredth of a second ahead of Steve Porino. Bill Egan and Ueli Luthi had decided that, in Lake Louise, the final training run would serve as a qualifying race, with the youngest and least accomplished athletes vying for spots in the real races. Skip, who felt he could do much better than he had done in Aspen, was eager to qualify.

Near the finish, however, he had to absorb a small bump, really just a ripple in the snow. Most guys skied over it with ease, but Skip got a little light on his feet, and when he touched the snow again he caught an edge and went down hard. He smacked face-first into the hardpack and slid across the finish line. His time was 2:10.41, which is worth mentioning because he actually beat one guy: Graham Bell of Great Britain.

Skip got off the course under his own power, but the twinge he felt in his knee made him worry that something might be wrong. And something was: The medial collateral ligament was torn. 'Bye, Skip. 'Bye, season.

That afternoon, as dozens of World Cup skiers ate lunch, a stocky, narrow-eyed, curly-haired man ventured into the spacious dining room at Château Lake Louise. The fellow, who had just received a rubdown, wore only a white terry-cloth bathrobe and flip-flops. When the racers saw him, some stared, some chuckled, and some laughed so hard they couldn't chew their prime rib. The underdressed gentleman then affected a supremely bored look, turned, and strolled out.

Italian skiing superstar Alberto Tomba was, as the racers would put it, a piece of work. In a sport full of daredevils and smart-asses, Tomba was by far the most outrageous character. Off the snow, he was a notorious egomaniac and lecher. He wore expensive boots, a black cowboy hat, and a stubble of beard that was meant to be sexy. He traveled mostly by helicopter, waving down at his teammates, who trudged from race to race in cars and vans. He loved women, or at least always had a use for them. On the plane to Calgary, he squatted in the aisles to check out the legs of the flight attendants. When he got to Lake Louise, he introduced himself to some of the local women by saying, "You will come home with me tonight." He did that in lots of places. Sometimes it worked. Once, the White Circus went to Canada for a race at Whistler Mountain, British Columbia. All the athletes motored to the race in rickety, crowded buses. All, that is, except Tomba. As the buses trundled down the highway he zoomed by in a rented convertible, a woman on each arm. God, they resented the bastard. The racers felt better a few minutes later, when they spotted Alberto on the side of the road, explaining everything to a Mountie. In many ways, Tomba was trouble.

Even so, he was a genius on the hill, arguably the most powerful technical racer who ever lived. Tomba specialized in slalom and giant slalom, but he had come to Lake Louise to race in the super G. Tomba, who won two gold medals at the 1988 Olympics in Calgary, was one of the few athletes in the world who actually lived up to his billing. He did not merely ski a race course. He murdered it. He blasted through slalom gates like a SWAT team going through a locked door. In the giant slalom, he used his edges the way speed skaters use their blades, gaining speed with every step.

Tomba tended to be overweight, which meant he got out of breath easily. When he won a race, which he did regularly, he liked to ski to the middle of the corral, drop to his knees, catch his breath for a moment, and then clasp his gloves together in thankful prayer. The religious image was appropriate: Tomba was probably the second most popular figure in Italy, behind Pope John Paul II. Italian families showed up at Tomba's races hours early in hope of glimpsing their hero as he warmed up; little children stood at the base of the hill and, when they saw him, yelled "Berto! Berto!," using the same plaintive, admiring tone of voice their grandparents might have used to shout "Papa! Papa!" Sometimes even Tomba didn't seem to know the difference between himself and the pontiff. At one slalom race, he opened the windows to the starting shack, leaned out, and blessed his fans, pope style. Pope Alberto I.

The American downhillers marveled at Tomba's success, and at his physique: They referred to his upper legs, accurately, as "stumps." But he never competed in the downhill, which, as far as they were concerned, meant he was at least part wimp. Nor did he normally enter the other speed event, the super G; the one in Lake Louise would be his first of the season. The reason was, simply, that the events were too dangerous and he didn't want to get hurt. What he told the press, in his usual flippant way, was that his mother would not let him compete.

That week in Lake Louise, Tomba had his first and only encounter with another unforgettable ski racing character: Eric Keck. It was a great moment, one that the Americans believed proved which man was a true giant and which was a poser. It happened in the hotel weight room. The huge Christian was already there working out when Tomba, trailed by a half-dozen photographers, made his entrance. The Italian limbered up in a big, theatrical way, just in case anyone hadn't seen him come in. He wore a very skimpy pair of shorts ("bun-huggers," Eric called them), suitable for the French Riviera, and a tank top. Grandly, he moved to the bench press machine and set the weight at the highest level. Then he limbered up some more. Finally, Tomba took his place on the bench and attempted to lift the bar. It wouldn't budge. He smiled and laughed as if he hadn't really been trying. He tried again. This time, grunting, groaning, and arching his back, he managed to lift the weight, hold it for a moment, and set it down. He sprang off the bench, grinning and flexing his muscles for the cameras.

Eric, who had been watching the whole show from the stair machine, couldn't stand it another minute. He stomped over to the bench press machine, lay down, and banged out ten quick repetitions, hoisting the load like a bag lunch. He then got up, dusted off his hands, smiled at Tomba, and walked out of the gym.

* * *

The racers had a comfortable stay at the Château. Afternoons, they rented skates and played hockey on the lake. (One day, the Americans played the French, but nobody kept score.) Evenings, they stayed in their rooms, playing hearts and watching movies on the tube. A young racer named Brett Grabowski took a shine to a waitress who worked the lunch shift, but he didn't do anything about it, unless you count looking at her and talking about her a lot.

The training was not as pleasant for most of the Americans. Eric Keck, warming up on a public trail, swerved to avoid someone and crashed at fifty miles an hour. It took a while to clear the cobwebs, but he eventually decided he was OK to race. Reggie Crist—who had won a Nor-Am race on a shorter version of this course in December, and therefore hoped to do well in the World Cup race—had an encouraging first run, finishing a little over three seconds out. But he was inconsistent: He didn't improve his relative standing in either of the next two runs. And Jeff Olson was just miserable. He finished sixtieth, seventy-second, and sixty-fifth in the training runs, and he didn't expect to do much better in the races. One evening, he watched himself on video and said, "It's making me sick."

Only AJ skied really well in training. He evaluated the course in his usual careful way, and, in the three training runs, produced the following results: third place, second place, first place. In that order. In the wax room, a lot of the ski technicians who joined the betting pool were putting their money on AJ to win the whole thing.

The night before the first race, Bill Egan made his comments brief. "We've had pretty good training the last couple of days, and you guys have to give it your best shot tomorrow. That's all I can ever ask of you, that you give it your best shot. Let's make it happen."

March 15, 1991 was a gorgeous day in Banff National Park. The sky was pale blue and the hot yellow sun poked through clouds as thin as gauze. The finish corral was covered, as usual, with sponsors' names—Xerox, Molson Canadian (the major sponsor), CBC Sports, Fuji Film, Diet

Coke, TAG sports watches, Olivetti, Reimer Express Lines Limited. But except for the TV cameras and a few coaches and reporters, there were no spectators. The first racer would be greeted in the finish by little more than polite applause.

AJ, who wore number three, finished in 1:58.36, and for the first time in as long as he could remember, looked at the scoreboard to find himself in first place. He was ahead by well over a second. Still skiing along, he crouched low and pumped his fist several times. Then he jumped out of his skis so he could hold them up for the camera. He moved into the coaches' area to watch the rest of the race. Hannes Zehentner, whom he had just beaten, pounded him on the back and said, "Good run."

After most races that season, AJ had picked up his skis and disappeared into the crowd of coaches and racers in the finish, just another guy wearing a bib. Here, he would learn how differently people treated racers who did well. As soon as AJ left the finish corral, teammate Skip Merrick, who had hobbled up the hill on his injured knee to watch the race, pounded him on the back and said, "All right, AJ!" A few people who had skied over to watch the finish of the race craned their necks to see him, and a coach from the Swiss team gave him a congratulatory nod. AJ smiled and nodded back. For AJ, this was indeed a beautiful day; the sun seemed to be shining on him alone. He unzipped the front of his downhill suit and was taking off his gloves when an announcer from the Canadian Broadcasting Company approached him, microphone in hand. A cameraman followed. AJ made the cameraman wait while he put on his Ray-Ban sunglasses. Ray-Ban was one of AJ's sponsors.

"With AJ Kitt of the United States, and a very happy man," the announcer said, in announcer-speak. "But you can't be too happy until everybody's down, right?"

"Right, yeah, you gotta wait for Heinzer, and Niklas Henning had a couple good training runs, too."

"AJ, you nailed this course all during training. Did you feel you could have a super run today?"

"Yeah, for sure, I mean, my worst training run was third. I think whenever, you know, that's the case, you always have to have confidence going into the race."

"Well, hang in there." The announcer faced the camera. "A very anxious AJ Kitt as he waits at the finish line, hoping for a World Cup victory." When the cameraman gave the signal that he had stopped shooting, the guy said, "Thanks, AJ," and walked away.

Ueli came on the radio a couple minutes later and congratulated AJ. French racer Adrien Duvillard patted him on the back, as did some other early finishers. Eric Keck, who was in the back of the field and therefore wouldn't race for another hour, skied over to AJ and whooped his approval. Eric was wearing a neck warmer bearing a picture of the Teenage Mutant Ninja Turtles.

AJ said, "It has been incredible standing here."

From where he stood, AJ could see several sections of the course. One by one he watched his competitors ski down. If he was nervous, it did not show. Kristian Ghedina, number four, didn't come close to beating him. William Besse, the fifth racer, didn't either. Daniel Mahrer, number six, finished thirty-three hundredths out, and AJ looked relieved. Racer number seven, Rob Boyd, the Canadian, had a bad run, considering it was his home slope, and finished twelfth. Peter Wirnsberger and Berni Huber finished out of the top twenty. AJ was in first place after nine racers. Someone in the finish area told him, "It looks like you're going to get on the podium," meaning it appeared he would finish in the top three. "I don't know," he said. "You have to look out for Höflehner."

But he had to look out for Franz Heinzer first. He skied tenth. The way he had been going, AJ didn't expect to beat him. He didn't think it was impossible or anything; he just didn't expect it. Which was wise. Heinzer finished fourteen hundredths of a second ahead of him. A few minutes later Atle Skaardal, of Norway, surprised Heinzer by finishing in 1:58.08, pushing him into second place, and AJ into third.

The race was not over. AJ believed that success in downhill racing came from skill and careful preparation and quick thinking and, of course, nerve. But ahead of all those things he listed experience. The fact was that the people who skied the best had also skied the most. Well, Helmut Höflehner had experience. The Austrian was thirty-one years old that winter. He had won his first World Cup race in 1983, in Lake Louise. Racing seventeenth, he had skied like a madman, lost control halfway down the hill, landed on his backside, bounced up, and won the race, edging out Franz Klammer. AJ was fourteen years old at the time.

Höflehner had since won nine more races. He had seen the courses on the World Cup circuit again and again and again. AJ still occasionally got lost trying to find them.

Höflehner's experience prevailed that day: He sneaked into third place by a tenth of a second, knocking AJ off the podium. The American was right: You had to look out for Höflehner.

After the race, a crowd of reporters surrounded AJ, who had equaled the best finish of his career. One TV journalist asked, "What goes through your mind when you're standing there, watching guy after guy come down the hill?"

"You have no control over what the other guy does," he said. "You only have control over what you do. So you just stand there and watch and see what they do."

"Still," the reporter said, "a pretty good day for AJ Kitt?"

"Yeah, sure. I'm pretty happy."

"What does AJ stand for?"

"Nothing."

Jeff Olson finished forty-fourth that day, more than three seconds behind the winner. To say he was disgusted would not adequately describe the depth of his misery. He was sad, disappointed, confused, completely at a loss. He was also, standing in the finish, in a mood to talk about it.

"I know what fast downhill's like, and every time I come down this year, I know I'm not fast. I just get to the finish line and I'm like, not this time. Why I'm slow isn't a big secret. It's just that I can't . . . change it."

He was having trouble with his right turn. He could turn to the left, but when he tried to turn right, his ski lost its grip on the snow and he dumped speed. After that, every little bump and ripple threw him off line. He practiced and practiced, but nothing helped. Of course, Jeff's problems went way beyond his inability to make a right turn, and he knew it. He wasn't just doubting himself as a ski racer. He was questioning his worth as a person. Sure, it hurt him when he skied poorly. What hurt him more was that Jeff the human being couldn't seem to do anything to help Jeff the ski racer. When he said, "I haven't made a good right turn since . . . I don't know when," he wasn't really talking about the mechanics of skiing. He was talking about self-confidence. Jeff didn't believe in himself anymore. This was the ultimate crisis, the sort of problem that ends athletes' careers. Certainly he knew how to make a right turn; he had been making them all his life. What he needed was strength of will, but he apparently didn't have enough. He wasn't just losing ski races. He was losing self-esteem, shrinking in the mirror. In downhill, he said, "you have to take the bull by the horns, and just do it." But he couldn't get a grip on that bull. Jeff often wondered if his near-crash in Val d'Isère was to blame for his troubles. Who knew? "Sometimes you don't realize that you're holding back," he said. "It's almost subconscious, you know? You think you're pumped up and you're ready to go, and then you do these little things, ticktock ticktock, all the way down, that are not assertive. When I look at the video, I see indecision." But even seeing himself make a good turn didn't give him the confidence that he could do it again. Nothing did. "I'm trying real hard not to let myself go crazy, because I could, very easily."

Jeff paused to watch a racer ski into the finish.

And then he said, "The mountain is skiing me. I'm not skiing the mountain. I know that, and I'm just trying to work through it."

Kyle Rasmussen wore number forty-one that day. Downhill racing seemed like a brand-new sport to him. He felt uneasy on his skis, out of balance, as if he were wearing two left boots. Instead of skiing, as he usually did, he found that he was thinking about skiing, which of course ruined everything.

He figured it was natural to feel strange after being off skis for two months. Kyle had missed the competition of the World Cup tour, but he had not missed being on the road, not a bit. His wife, Linda, was going to school, so he stayed home with Anthony. The kid was seven months old when Kyle got back from Kitzbühel, and therefore was about as delightful as he was ever going to be. While he kept an eye on the baby, Kyle did some cooking, mostly because it was one of the few things he could do with one hand. He made what he would later refer to as "awesome gourmet meals," including deer stew, unusual sausage dishes, and exotic spaghetti sauces. He gained a few pounds during his convalescence.

After a few weeks of cooking and playing with the baby, he decided to test the healing collarbone by going fishing. To Kyle, fishing was one of the most important things in life, right up there with downhill racing, deer hunting, and family life, though he wouldn't have wanted to rank them, especially not on the first day of bass season. Kyle dreamed of being a professional bass fisherman after he was finished being a professional ski racer. Actually, he said, fishing for a living would be a lot like skiing for a living: You got sponsors, you drove to the competition site and practiced for a few days, and then you got out there and punched it. Or cast it.

But when Kyle went fishing late that January, he was after steelhead, not bass. It had always frustrated him to be in Europe, competing in some race, when the steelhead season opened in California. But this year he would get his chance to fish, if only with one hand. Some of his friends who attended Chico State invited him to Chico to drink beer, watch the Super Bowl, and fish for steelhead, so off he went. He was doing that last thing, fishing for steelhead, when, as he would put it later, "I sort of re-broke the collarbone."

He was having a good day until then. Nobody around him seemed to be having any luck, but he had caught five steelhead. Then Kyle's luck ran out, too. He was sitting on the edge of the river, just watching the water go by, when BAM! A big steelhead took off with his lure. Few things could excite Kyle like the whine of a fishing reel, so naturally he jumped to his feet to fight the fish. But because he was holding the pole with his good arm, he had to push himself up with his bad one. He had just put his weight on it when he heard a pop and felt a terrible searing pain, much worse than anything he had endured in Kitzbühel. He lay back on the bank, gripping his shoulder and groaning. Meanwhile, he lost the steelhead. After a few days the bone quit hurting, and by March Kyle was ready to race again.

Sort of. He didn't have any trouble with the scary jump near the top of the hill. But halfway down the course in Lake Louise he was in forty-third place, which, since he was wearing number forty-one, meant he was even slower than some of the snow-seed racers. He finished sixty-second, almost five and a half seconds behind the winner. He beat only two guys, an Englishman and a Japanese.

"It was like coming back from the summer break and training down-hill," he said after the race. "It just wasn't there, you know?"

Back at the hotel that night, Ueli Luthi called the meeting to order.

"OK, guys," he said, and the racers settled down. "First of all, congrat-ulations to AJ." The downhillers applauded heartily, and AJ smiled and nodded. Then Ueli urged the rest of the racers to "take the finger out a little bit tomorrow." Out of their asses, he meant.

Bill Egan's only advice was that the guys push harder out of the start. From where he stood in the starting shack, it didn't seem that they were getting much momentum off the top. "Let's get it on," he said.

Bill also reported that he had been talking to Bill Hudson, who was recuperating in Park City, Utah. Hudson had a message for them. "He said, 'If you guys don't get results tomorrow, you're a bunch of pussies.' "

Hudson had arrived in Park City in February. His mother, Sally, drove him to Utah about a week after he got out of the hospital at University of California–Davis. He complained a lot about how slowly she drove. There was nothing between them and Park City but the desert and the gleaming highway narrowing into the distance. If the car went off the road, it wouldn't hit anything, for God's sake. Couldn't she punch it?

When at last they arrived, Bill moved into an apartment with his girlfriend Kathrin Burkhart and her two roommates. The doctors had told him not to do anything for a few weeks, and it was an easy order to follow. He couldn't move his shoulder or back very well, and he still saw two of everything, one on top of the other. So for the first two weeks he stayed in bed while Kathrin cooked his meals, dressed him, tied his sneakers, and so on. If he got hungry when she was at school—she studied nursing at the University of Utah—one of her roommates fixed something for him. Kathrin thought Bill was a good patient. He didn't ask for much.

Bill and Kathrin talked all the time about how Bill felt physically, but they didn't talk much about the accident itself. That didn't surprise Kathrin; Bill never said much about ski racing. He spent so much time thinking about it and worrying about it and actually doing it that when he was away from it, he preferred to discuss something else. The most he said about the crash was that he didn't remember it. He recalled Bill

Egan radioing up to the start after Keck's fall and telling him not to aim to the right when he went off the jump. He remembered approaching the Mausefalle. After that there was a gap in his memory, a place where the tape was erased. The next thing he could remember was waking up in the hospital, seeing a group of doctors, and conking out again.

And yet it was clear that the accident had frightened him. He watched a lot of movies on video, and was shocked at how many of them made him cry. He never used to cry at movies, but now he couldn't plug in a tape without a box of Kleenex next to the bed. Once, Kathrin asked him to listen to an Eric Clapton song she liked. Bill listened to it and wept. God! he thought. What is going on with me?

For a while he was angry at himself for crashing, but that had passed. He had made a mistake, simple as that. In downhill, mistakes could be painful. Once in a while he tried to reconstruct the accident in his mind, to see if he could figure out what had gone wrong. He would ask himself, What if I had taken off ten degrees to the left? Would I still have gone over the fence? How about fifteen degrees? But that kind of thinking didn't get him anywhere. It didn't heal his broken bones. There was nothing to do now but get well.

After two weeks in Park City, Bill began to insist on doing things for himself. He was tired of being bathed and fed and dressed as if he were a child. It was humiliating. Sometimes, when Kathrin tried to help, he told her, "That's OK. I don't need you anymore."

What he wanted to do most was drive. Early on, his doctor had given him an eye patch so he could see normally. In a month in bed, Bill had done nothing but read books and watch movies and cry. He'd had enough. He wanted to go places. For someone in his condition, it was a lot to expect. The eye patch took care of the double vision but caused a problem with depth perception. Kathrin was so worried that he would have an accident that she tried to get him to go to a parking lot and practice for a while, like a teenager getting ready for his driving test. He refused.

When he first began to drive, Bill was not what anybody would call agile. He had to strain just to bend over far enough to get into the car. Once he managed to work his way into the seat, he still had to find a way to steer. He couldn't lift his right arm because his shoulder was smashed, so he used his broken left wrist to lift his right arm onto the wheel. And off he went, a very dangerous one-armed, one-eyed young man. The irony was that one of the places he often drove himself was to physical therapy.

Eventually the bones got better, but the eyesight didn't. It scared the hell out of him. When he first got hurt, Bill had feared that he would never ski race again. Now it occurred to him that his fate might be even worse than that. Double vision would affect everything he did, forever. Somehow he managed to joke about it: He told Kathrin he liked having double vision because he always saw two of her. And yet she knew Bill was scared. He always went by himself to see the orthopedist and the physical therapist. But he always asked Kathrin to go with him to the eye doctor. He figured he might need a friend there.

He was right. During one visit, the doctor told him there was only a fifty-fifty chance that his vision would repair itself. If it didn't get better, he might need surgery on a muscle behind one of his eyes. And there was no way to know how much the surgery would help.

Bill Egan, who spoke to his friend from time to time, was worried, too. He knew the racer was determined to come back, but he wasn't sure it was a good idea even if his vision corrected itself. Hudson had had a series of bad head injuries—one in Val Gardena a few years back, the concussion in Val d'Isère, and now the one in Kitzbühel. Egan hated to think what the next one could do to him. The coach didn't know why ski racing was so damned important anyway. It was just a sport. It wasn't worth dying for.

"I think," Egan said in Lake Louise, "that it's time he found something else to do with his life."

The weather for the second race in Lake Louise was perfect for free-skiing and sunbathing, but too warm for downhill. The sun shone brightly in a cloudless blue sky, softening the race track in some places. The guys skiing from the back would have to look out for deep ruts, especially in the turns. It was a fine day to watch a race, but again, few people did.

Jeff Olson, the first American to compete, had another lousy race, though not as lousy as the first one.

He wore number fifty-nine, but was chosen as a snow seed and therefore started among the early racers. Generally, Jeff succeeded in concealing his frustration when he skied badly: He wasn't the type to abuse his helmet or shout foul words. But when he failed to break the two-minute mark (he finished thirty-fifth), he couldn't help himself. He skied over to the far end of the coaches' area, stepped out of his skis, and kicked them hard. The kick didn't even scratch them. A struggling downhiller could always take comfort in knowing that he would have to get pretty angry to wreck his equipment.

When he composed himself, Jeff got on the radio and gave a brief course report. He concluded it by saying, "Just stay on top of it. Just do what you do."

Helmut Höflehner took the early lead, but didn't keep it. Franz Heinzer, racer number five that day, skied another fantastic race and beat the Austrian by sixty-two hundredths. Heinzer glided through the finish and stopped close to the coaches' area, spraying snow all over the coaches and athletes—including Jeff, who seemed to enjoy the baptism. "Sprinkle me with your stardust," he said, wiping his face.

Skip Merrick, hobbling around the finish on his injured knee, saw Heinzer's time and said, "If AJ beats that, I will kiss his feet. I will kiss his feet if he beats that time."

At that moment, AJ was not thinking about getting his feet kissed. Instead, he was wondering if he was going to make it to the race at all. To get to the start at Lake Louise, the racers had to take a chair lift halfway up the mountain, then ski down to a second chair lift that would carry them nearly to the top. They had to grab a T-bar to ascend the last few hundred yards. When AJ arrived at the second chair lift, it was stopped. Something was wrong with it, and the lift attendant didn't know when it would be fixed. "You'd better ski down and take the other chair," the guy said. AJ knew which chair he meant—the two-seater that groaned up the side of the mountain. It took some time to ski down and board the lift. And it took even longer for the old, slow chair to mosey up the hill.

Shit, AJ thought. He would be lucky to make it to the top in time for his start. If he was late, he'd be disqualified. At the very least, he wouldn't have enough time to warm up. It was a beautiful day, sunny and quiet, the sky a luscious blue, but AJ was oblivious to that. This lift was crawling up the hill like a dying man through the desert, and AJ was pissed, pissed, pissed.

He got to the start ten minutes before his name was called. He liked to be there at least thirty minutes ahead of time. He did some quick stretches and, with help from Edi Waldburger, the Rossignol ski technician, clicked into his skis. AJ moved toward the starting shack. Everything was happening fast, too fast. Bill Egan told AJ to forget about being late, just think about the race. AJ tried, but he was rattled. Shit! When he got into the gate he thought he was concentrating, but he wasn't. AJ liked to do things his way—deliberately, moderately. Even when he played golf, he went to the first tee fifteen minutes early so he could warm up and start thinking about his game. Now he had to rush, and that wasn't part of the plan. He couldn't adjust. He tipped over in the second turn, and that was that. The last World Cup downhill of the year, AJ's last, best chance to win a race, was history. Heinzer had won again.

For an instant, AJ was furious. The next instant, he accepted what happened. All right, he told himself. It's just one race. These things happen in downhill, and you have to accept them. He got up, skied through the next gate, then did a daffy—a sort of airborne split—off the jump. At least he could say he went out with style.

In the finish, AJ was approached by Chip and Pepper, smooth-talking, long-haired twin brothers who hosted a TV show for hipsters. They wanted to do an interview; would he mind? Not at all, AJ said, donning his Ray-Bans. The twins, bearing microphones, got on either side of AJ, and the camera rolled. Here is a transcript of the interview:

CHIP: "So what happened?"

AJ: "Well . . ."

PEPPER: "Underwear too tight?"

Tommy Moe was tired, and he skied that way. He got wide in some of the turns. Also, he caught an edge about where Skip Merrick did earlier that week and nearly crashed as he entered the finish. He ended up twenty-fourth—not bad, but not nearly what he was capable of.

"This sucks," he said in the finish. "I hate getting beat."

The World Cup ski season was long—five months and many thousands of miles long—but Tommy's season had dragged on longer than most people's. He had spent the previous summer and fall skiing in New

Zealand and Argentina, and then had joined the team in Colorado in early November. He had landed on his rear in Garmisch, held his breath for a week in Kitzbühel, and tweaked his ankle in Adelboden. Now he was exhausted, and glad it was all over.

"I don't know," he said, peeling off his downhill bib for the last time that season. "I just don't have the hunger that I had in December, man. I'm tired. Toward the end of the season you're just like, 'Oh, man, two more weeks.' You know? I'm taking this summer off, man."

Bill Egan came to the team meeting that night in a lousy mood. The downhillers had been gathering each evening in a second-floor sitting room with a high ceiling, dark wooden furniture, and long, weighty velvet curtains. It was a vast space, but that night Egan's anger filled it. When a couple of the athletes showed up a minute or two late he chewed them out. If twenty-fourth place was the best they could do—and that day, it was—to hell with them. They deserved to be chewed out.

It wasn't just this race that was eating Egan, of course. It was the whole disastrous season. What was wrong with these guys? Did they think he enjoyed living out of a suitcase half the year, eating hotel food and talking to Maggie by phone every few days? He didn't. He didn't do this job for the money, for God's sake. The World Cup season was over now. Opportunities had been lost. Time had been wasted. In his football-playing days, Bill had succeeded by giving more of himself than other people were willing to give. Squandering chances ate him up.

"Being mediocre," he told his athletes, almost spitting, "sucks. I don't like it, and I won't stand for it. I won't do this if you're mediocre. You guys are too good. I can't accept it, and I won't accept it."

8

Summertime, and the Living Is Extremely Easy

Summer was always a leisurely season for the downhillers. The warm weather gave them time to see their families and friends, recover from lingering aches, take a few college courses, forget what little French and German they had learned, and play games in which they weren't expected to be the best in the world. The team got together to work out only three times in the 1991 offseason. The first workout, held in San Diego, California, was known as a "dry-land" camp because it didn't involve snow. The male downhillers and technical racers attended, and so did a few members of the women's team. The athletes spent several days playing volleyball, surfing, learning tai chi for balance and concentration, and running sprints. Later, the downhillers flew to Norway to ski on a glacier. (In past seasons, the team had held its midsummer training camp in Chile or Argentina, but prices in South America had gone way up so the team had to find an alternative.) Thor (pronounced "Tore") Kallerud, a native of Norway who coached the American men's technical team, made the arrangements. The athletes did a lot of free-skiing in Norway, just to get a feel for the snow. They also practiced giant slalom to work on their turns.

Bill Egan really liked the way Reggie Crist skied at that camp. For the first time, Reggie was turning in a long, clean arc, instead of rushing into the turn and jamming on the brakes so he could make the next gate. Finally, the downhillers skied for a week in Switzerland. The on-snow camps kept the racers from getting rusty. But for most of them the summer was just for fun, a chance to prepare for the new season by not thinking much about it.

For Eric Keck, the huge Christian, no preparation would be necessary. He would not be returning to the U.S. Ski Team. When the coaches met to choose the athletes for the upcoming year, they did not save a place for him. Eric had competed in only three World Cup downhill races the previous season. He had been disqualified in Aspen and had finished fifty-eighth and fifty-seventh in the Lake Louise. Probably his most significant achievement had been vaulting over a fence in Kitzbühel and surviving. The coaches could no longer justify spending money trying to turn him into a world-class downhiller. Eric was told he could go to the Beaver Creek resort in Colorado in November 1991 to try to qualify for the World Cup team, but he wasn't interested in last-ditch opportunities. The racing life had become a bore. He had spent two or three years traveling to Europa Cup races that always seemed to be canceled for lack of snow, and Nor-Ams were no longer a challenge. Eric had always felt the life of a ski racer was frivolous, and of course he had often proved it. Well, he had had enough. What good was he doing the world by gallivanting around Europe, running over mopeds and farting on matches? None. It was time to go to college, time to get serious about life. That summer, Eric arranged to attend Saddleback Community College in Mission Viejo, California, where Bill Egan had coached football. The huge Christian planned to try out for the football team in the fall.

Eric didn't think he would miss downhill much. He insisted the sport had never scared him, not even when he lay stunned in the woods in Kitzbühel, unsure if he had bitten off his tongue. Besides, he knew he would find thrills in other sports. "Kayaking down the North Fork River in Idaho is like going over two hundred Mausefalles," he said. But Keck's teammates couldn't help being affected by his loss. In Eric, Reggie Crist was losing his best friend on the team, the one person who could always make him laugh, no matter what. Eric and Reggie had often roomed together on the road, and for a while the huge Christian had even lived with Reggie in Sun Valley and dated his younger sister. Life on the road would be a little more lonely for Reggie now. The other guys would also feel the loss; even though they hadn't all taken Eric seriously, they had all liked him and gotten a kick out of him. But now the legend was gone. A young Californian named Todd Kelly would be taking Eric's place.

Todd had a bright future, especially in super G. The downhillers all knew and liked him and felt he would fit in just fine. Still, things wouldn't be the same without Eric Keck. The crazy-ass downhill maniac team would be a less crazy, considerably less devout, and a whole lot smaller without him.

Bill Egan married Maggie Dyer on June 1, 1991, in Park City, Utah. A justice of the peace performed the ceremony in Maggie's backyard. Tommy Moe was there. So were Jeff Olson and AJ Kitt. Bill Hudson desperately wanted to come, but he had already accepted an invitation to another wedding, in California. Instead of hiring a wedding photographer, the couple put cameras on the tables and asked the guests to snap pictures, which they were happy to do. It was a cold, rainy day, a bad day for an outdoor wedding. Still, everyone thought the weather was appropriate. If you want snow, hold a downhill. If you want rain, get married outdoors.

Tommy Moe was accompanied to Bill Egan's wedding by his girlfriend, Megan Gerety, a nineteen-year-old downhiller on the women's team. The couple spent most of the summer together, living in a way that could have been made into a TV show called Lifestyles of the Blond and Jobless. For a while they vacationed in Hawaii, where they got tans and ordered tropical drinks and cavorted in the surf. Then they headed up to Alaska (Megan was a native) to delight in the springlike weather. It was an easy life. Tommy was taking the summer off, man.

Tommy's father, always torn between running his son's life and letting him drive it himself, was fond of Megan, but he didn't approve of the relationship: He wanted Tommy to love skiing alone. Tom Moe, Sr., married three times, thought women could wait. Tommy, young, handsome, and hot to trot, didn't think so. He got along famously with Megan, who resembled a young Mariel Hemingway and possessed a reckless streak as wide as any male downhiller's. (Bill Egan was afraid to watch her ski because she was so wild.) So the guy known to his teammates as the Golden Child kept enjoying that careless summer, the summer of his twenty-first year, never considering how blessed he was to be athletically gifted, good-looking, wealthy for someone his age, and completely free. Didn't everybody live this way?

Right on the Edge of Crazy

When he wasn't vacationing in Hawaii or Utah, Tommy was kay-aking, playing tennis, or riding his mountain bike. His pleasure in sports put him in great shape. It also got him hurt. One day in Alaska, he was speeding along on his mountain bike when he lost control and went over the handlebars. Snap! Broken collarbone. That put an end to the one-man, summer-long Alaska Sports Festival. He also had to miss the September training camp in Norway, but attended the camp in Switzerland in October. Unable to do anything athletic for a while, he hung around the house and learned to cook. Why not? Go with the flow, man.

Early that summer, Kyle and Linda Rasmussen and their son Anthony moved into a house near Kyle's grandfather's ranch in Angels Camp, California. The house was more than one hundred years old and was set on a paved road, far from anything else. At night you could hear the wind whistle and the coyotes howl and the frogs croak. The place was creaky and drafty. There was no air conditioner to cool the hundred-degree days, and the tap water was bad.

Still, Kyle was happy there. Many days he stuffed his little boy into a backpack and went bass fishing in his grandpa's irrigation ponds. The fish were feeding, so it wasn't unusual for Kyle to catch twenty in an hour. Anthony, propped up on his dad's back, watched quietly. Sometimes Kyle turned around to find him asleep. The boy had had his first birthday that May. One day he picked up a pole and dipped the end into the water, as if to fish. His father couldn't have been happier if he'd sat at the piano and played Mozart.

Kyle and his family were living in the house rent-free, so Kyle felt he ought to lend a hand on the ranch. After that it was hard to find time to fish: Kyle worked for his grandfather, Bill Airola, seven days a week, sunup to sundown. In the spring the ranchers brought the cattle in and put bells on them. Then they drove them into the hills for summer grazing. Kyle often rode a horse named Seagram. (Tommy Moe visited Kyle for a few days and found horseback riding to be something like skiing Kitzbühel—what happened wasn't entirely up to him.) Kyle didn't mind the work, except that it left him no time to train for ski racing. Finally, in July, he summoned the nerve to tell his grandfather he couldn't work for him anymore; he had to get in shape. Bill Airola took it pretty well.

With all of those things happening, Kyle and Linda didn't have much time to themselves. One night, the Rasmussens decided to do something they hadn't done in a long time: go into Stockton and have a night on the town. They left Anthony with Kyle's grandmother Bette, put on their going-out clothes, and were just about to drive away when Kyle's friend Keith Rakoncza, who was going out with them, spotted a deer walking by the road. Kyle and Linda hadn't been out together in a long time, but Kyle hadn't killed a deer in a long time either. Several months, as a matter of fact. Also, it was bowhunting season, and Kyle had not yet felled a deer with a bow and arrow, though he had spent a lot of time trying. What he figured out, as he looked down the road at that big brown buck, was that bowhunting season would be over soon but Stockton would still be there. So he left his wife sitting in the car, grabbed his bow, and jumped into Keith's pickup to go after the deer. Keith drove, and Kyle stood in the truck bed.

They followed the buck for a while, which wasn't easy because it was dusk and the deer blended in with the grass and the trees. Then the animal made a mistake: It ran forty yards up a hill and stood there, its profile to the hunter. With the skyline as background, Kyle could see his prey clearly. Normally when Kyle hunted, he wore camouflage clothing, but at the moment he was wearing a nice pair of jeans, a dress shirt, and his best cowboy boots. It felt strange to hunt in that outfit, but not strange enough for him to stop.

He drew his bow, aimed, and shot the buck right in the neck, killing it instantly.

If Kyle had missed his shot, he and his wife and friend probably could have gone ahead with their plans for the night. But now that the Rasmussens had a dead deer lying on the property, Kyle thought it would be best to just go ahead and skin it. He put on some old clothes and went to work. Linda, who admired Kyle's aim but not necessarily his timing, went down to his grandparents' house to wait. Kyle planned to take her out when he got finished, he really did, but by the time he had the buck skinned it was 11:30 and Linda was asleep.

There would have been enough meat from the deer to feed Linda for weeks. Except that she didn't care for deer meat.

*   *   *

Jeff Olson spent most of that summer in his condominium in Park City, Utah, pining. Oh, he did other things, too. He took classes at the University of Utah and kept himself in shape by playing basketball and lifting weights. But mostly he pined. He had planned to marry a former U.S. Ski Team member that June, but in the months before the wedding things started to go wrong—not in any specific, fixable way, but in a sort of chronic, degenerative, inoperable way. At first Jeff's fiancée wanted to be married, and then she didn't, and then she did, and so on. Anyway, the wedding date came and went and Jeff was still single. Pretty soon the relationship ended for good.

Jeff was blue for a long time. On what would have been his wedding day, he and Steve Porino were driving home from a camping trip in southern Utah. On the hour he was supposed to be married, Jeff rolled down the window and began to scream, just to let the tension out. He kept screaming for a long time; Steve joined in to keep him company. About that same time, Jeff's parents, Jack and Val, visited him in Park City. He looked so sad when they said goodbye that, on their way out of town, they impulsively bought a cocker spaniel puppy, then headed back to Jeff's house and handed it to him. The dog raised his spirits a lot. Steve, who was renting a room from Jeff, came up with a name for the puppy: Betty. Betty Cocker.

The last year had made Jeff feel sort of old. At twenty-five he had already been through what felt like a divorce. And after his miserable year on the slopes he wondered if his athletic career was ending, too. He was a ski team veteran, and yet he had never won a race in Europe, which made him feel guilty. Sure, he'd been hurt, but in downhill, who hadn't been? He couldn't, and didn't, blame injuries. He blamed himself. Well, he told himself that summer, everything is going to change now. This would be Jeff's year. He knew it had to be. If he didn't ski fast this year, he wouldn't be invited back.

Love comes, love goes. Somewhere a relationship ends, and somewhere else a new one begins. Steve Porino met a woman that spring.

A Park City photographer named Lori Adamski-Peek asked Jeff and Steve to come to the mountain to pose for the ski resort's promotional brochure. (You can never get enough square-jawed racer-hunks in promotional brochures.) All the racers had to do was glide down the hill while Lori fired away. Sounded good to them. Lori had also asked two women to pose. One was Holly Flanders, a former U.S. Ski Team member. The other was Kristina Kjeldsberg, a student at the University of Utah. Lori, who knew Steve was unattached, had told him a lot of nice things about Kristina. When he met her, Steve understood why. Kristina was not talkative, but when she did get around to saying something, she inevitably came across as a charming, thoughtful, levelheaded, highly intelligent woman. Kristina was working toward a degree in material science engineering, with an emphasis in biomaterials. She had never recorded a grade lower than A in her college career. As it happened, she also was tall and fair and very striking. As Steve put it, "I thought she was hot." They rode the chair lift together a few times. Steve wanted to get to know her better, but that would have meant asking her on a date, which wasn't the sort of thing he was known for rushing into. Steve also was bright and good-looking—he had a movie-star's cleft chin and brown hair that always looked freshly tousled—but he was not overburdened with self-confidence. He met plenty of women who interested him, but instead of asking them out, he simply considered whether to ask them out. While he sat around considering, the women met other men and got married and had families, and Steve stayed single. As impressed as Steve was with Kristina, he wasn't taking any chances that first day, on the ski slope. And the next time he saw her, he didn't ask her out either. Or the time after that. Steve bumped into Kristina at parties several times in the next few weeks, but he never did anything more than charm her.

That summer, Steve and Bill Hudson took classes together at the University of Utah. (Bill was still having vision troubles, but they didn't prevent him from going to school.) They had sociology class at 3:30 P.M. and economics at 7. To kill time after sociology, they liked to go to the mall, catch a movie, and dine at the Chick Fil-A. One day Steve decided he had waited long enough; it was time to call Kristina. Trouble was, he didn't have her phone number. He also had no idea how to spell Kjeldsberg. But he knew it began with a K, and he figured the number would be listed in the Salt Lake City phone book. He and Bill found a public phone and opened the book to the Ks. Bill started at the end and Steve started at the beginning. They went through every K-name in Salt Lake

City, looking for one that sounded like Kjeldsberg. After fifteen minutes, Steve found it. He dropped a quarter into the slot and dialed the number. Kristina answered.

"Hello?"

"H-h-h-hi, this is S-S-S-Steve P-P-Porino," he stammered. (Steve later said, "I felt like I was doing my Woody Woodpecker imitation.") Then he said something like, "I'm just kind of down at the mall, I was just kind of wondering what you were doing."

"Not much. What's going on?" she said.

Soon, he relaxed enough to ask if she would like to have dinner with him that night. It was an audacious question, considering it was already 5:00 P.M. Kristina was not offended, but declined the offer anyway: She had to study. You do not get a degree in material science engineering with an emphasis in biomaterials without putting in some long nights at your desk. She said, however, that she was available for dinner the next night. Great, Steve said. The next day they bought groceries and she made him an excellent meal. The evening went well. Steve and Kristina ended up spending most of the summer together.

Only much later did Steve learn that Kristina had been wondering if he was ever going to call. She didn't plan to wait forever. Just before he called her from the mall, she had called Lori the photographer to ask for his number.

Bill Hudson didn't tell anyone when his vision began to clear up. He was afraid it wasn't really happening. The two images he saw, one on top of the other, seemed to be moving closer together each day. And it seemed he didn't have to tilt his head so far anymore to see clearly. But what if he was wrong? What if he wasn't getting better at all? No, he wasn't going to talk about it until he was sure.

One day he went to a doctor and took a series of sophisticated vision tests. As Bill remembered it, the doctor looked at the results and said, "It doesn't seem to be getting better at all."

Bill felt the world imploding. "What?" he said. "It feels like it's getting better."

The doctor looked at the charts again. Wait a minute, he said. I made a mistake. You're right. It is getting better. And, he said, it probably will continue to get better.

What a mistake! But Bill didn't care. It was true: He was getting better. By midsummer, his vision was as good as it ever was. Soon he began to work out with weights. The broken shoulder had left his upper body slightly deformed, but who cared? Now he felt he would race again.

Not everyone felt it was a good thing. Bill's accident had damaged a lot more than his bones and organs: It had rattled some of the people who loved him. More than once, Sally Hudson called Kathrin and said, "Do you think he's going to race again?" Sally prayed he wouldn't, at least not in the downhill. Sally felt her son could have been a great slalom or giant slalom skier. It seemed to her that this was an opportune time to change disciplines. There was not much chance of that: Her son had the heart of a downhiller.

Kathrin didn't care for downhill, either, now that it had almost killed her boyfriend. But she didn't want to discourage Bill from going back to it. She didn't want him to quit now and spend the rest of his life wondering if he had done the right thing—which she knew he would do. Besides, as fearless as Bill was, as little as he cared about his own safety, Kathrin felt even he had limits.

"If he's so freaked out that he gets in the starting gate and thinks, 'Wow, I can't do this,' I don't think he'll do it," she said.

Bill definitely wanted to come back, but the decision was not his alone. Bill Egan, for one, was still skeptical. How many times could a guy whack his noggin before it killed him? At first, Egan felt Hudson should go back to school and keep his head out of trouble. But as the racer's condition improved, Egan's feelings changed. If the guy was well enough to compete, Egan would support him. But the coach wanted to be sure Hudson would be all right. The ski team made a deal with the athlete: If you want to race, get clearance from a neurologist.

So Hudson did just that. During the summer, the doctors told him he could race without putting himself at serious risk. As far as Hudson was concerned, that was that. Discussion over.

But it wasn't the end of it, not really. At the downhillers' first on-snow training camp that summer, in Norway, the coaches treated Bill as if he were made of porcelain. At least it seemed that way to him. Finally,

Hudson couldn't take it anymore. He sat down with Egan and Ueli Luthi and said, "I'm tired of hearing about the accident. It's not an issue. So from now on, when I'm on the hill, I don't want to hear about anything but skiing." The coaches said they understood, and from then on they did as he wished.

But Bill hadn't really put the accident behind him, not yet. If he wanted to bury the memory once and for all, there was still one more thing he had to do. He took care of that last detail in Norway. He was skiing fast, really fast, for the first time, making the kind of long, sweeping turn that only the best skiers know how to make, the kind of turn that leaves tracks in the snow so deep you can see them on the way back up the chair lift. He was on the ground, but he was soaring.

And then, as the racers liked to put it, he ate shit. He came over a bump, landed, and caught his edge. His ski shot out to the side. He pulled it back in, then caught the edge again and got high-sided—tossed forward off his horse. Bam! He went down. The skis scattered. When Bill stopped sliding he shook the snow out of his ears and got up. That was important: He got up. No need to call that helicopter. He put his skis back on and made his way down the hill, a little surprised, but not hurt. No, not hurt.

Bill Hudson had crashed and laughed. He was a downhiller again.

From March to August, AJ Kitt lived in a house in upstate New York with some buddies and his dog, Speed. It was the first time he had lived away from his parents, and he liked it. He passed most of his days water-skiing and playing golf. He also played softball in a couple of leagues. During this time he also had what he described as a "stupid" relationship with a young woman. A few days after they met she accompanied him to Utah for Bill Egan's wedding. After he traveled with her for a few days, AJ figured out he didn't much like her, and that was that.

Later in the summer AJ bought a three bedroom, two-and-a-half bath condominium in Boulder, Colorado. He chose Boulder because his aunt sold real estate there, because the market seemed strong, and because he wanted to have Colorado residency so he could eventually attend college at the University of Colorado, his parents' alma mater, without paying the high out-of-state tuition rate.

Besides, he wanted to make his life in the west. Even though he had always lived in the east—in New York, no less—AJ liked to think of himself as a westerner. He liked the open spaces, the skiing, the independent way of life. Now that he actually owned property there, he felt justified in wearing jeans and cowboy boots if he wanted to. His teammates, especially Kyle Rasmussen, a born Californian, refused to treat him as a westerner. So what if he owned property in the Rockies? To them AJ was just a scruffy-headed New Yorker doing a poor imitation of a cowboy. That's what they said to get on his nerves, anyway.

AJ—who felt he actually did a pretty good cowboy imitation—had plans that went way beyond condo ownership, way beyond wearing jeans and cowboy boots. He wanted to own a ranch, preferably in Wyoming. His idea was to buy property from an experienced rancher, and then hire someone to tend to the ranch while he was away. Ideally the place would be an hour or two outside Jackson Hole, one of his favorite ski resorts. In the winter AJ's hired men would run the ranch. In the summer AJ would work part-time on his property, and spend the rest of his time as he always did—waterskiing, driving fast cars and motorcyles, drinking beer.

And what did he plan to raise on the ranch? Not horses. Not cattle, like Kyle Rasmussen's grandpa. No, AJ wanted to raise buffalo. He planned to buy a few head, let them graze the land, and invite people in to see them. Someday, perhaps, people cruising U.S. 26 would see billboards saying, "AJ Kitt's Buffalo Ranch, Next Exit. We Hope You Like Them, But It Really Doesn't Matter If You Don't, Because We Do." If the venture didn't make money, he'd just write the whole thing off. AJ had thought it through, and he was sure he wanted buffalo. "They're cool animals," he said. "They've been abused and I want to help them out." It was wonderful to be twenty-two, single, sort of famous, and rich enough to buy expensive two-thousand-pound beasts just because you liked their style.

And yes, he was rich enough, or nearly so. After one season in downhill's first seed, AJ qualified as a minor skiing celebrity. As such, he got lots of attention from people who were trying to sell things. Rossignol and Salomon and Raichle paid him large retainers to use their equipment; he could count on that money every year. And they paid big bonuses when he skied well. But there was more. That summer he was paid

$3,500 to make an appearance for Head sportswear. For Ray-Ban, his headgear sponsor, he appeared at a trade show in Las Vegas and posed for a picture that was later used in a magazine advertisement. Once in a while he took a small fee to appear at ski shops in New York. These things added up. Among the downhillers, only Tommy Moe, the Golden Child, came close to earning as much money as AJ earned. Kyle Rasmussen had earned only $6,000 as a skier the previous year, but then he got a lucky break: Visa, the credit card company, paid him several thousand dollars to appear as a downhiller in a commercial that would be shown during the Olympics. Even though AJ had far more money than most of his teammates, they didn't resent him because they felt he had earned it. Besides, AJ was too discreet and private to boast about what he had. He did not walk around bragging about his plans to buy buffalo.

That summer AJ was just beginning a relationship with Rolex, the glitzy watch company. Rolex was among the more subtle supporters of ski racing. It gave money to junior racing programs, but did not insist, as other firms did, that everything on the hill, and most things off the hill, be emblazoned with the company name. That summer AJ was given a chance to meet with top company executives at the Rolex offices in New York City. He felt self-conscious—"like a cheeseball," as he put it—because all he had with him to wear was a blazer. It wasn't his fault; the meeting had been arranged on the spur of the moment, and he hadn't brought a suit with him. He enjoyed the experience despite the awkward feeling. AJ, who spent most of his time tramping around Europe with a bunch of crazy kids, found that he liked sitting in the offices of a big, world-famous company and hobnobbing with some obvious grownups. Later, the Rolex people even gave him a watch.

As much as AJ liked the condo and the appearance money and the Rolex watch—and he liked them a lot—he understood that downhill racing was not about material things. It was about winning. And even though he was slightly famous, he still had not won anything. Well, OK, he was the reigning national champion in downhill and super G, but really, so what? Everybody already knew he was the best speed-event skier in America. To be a success in ski racing he needed to win against international competition, to win on the World Cup circuit. To put it succinctly, he had to beat Franz Heinzer.

He believed he could. AJ viewed the previous season, his first in the first seed, mostly as a learning experience. He raced on six World Cup downhill courses, three and a half of them (Garmisch, the top half of Kitzbühel, Aspen, and Lake Louise) for the first time. Heinzer had done well because he was a great skier, no question, but also because he had competed on those courses many, many times. He had experience. Well, now AJ had some too, and he intended to put it to use.

He figured a change in his equipment would help him, too. AJ started using a shorter ski over the summer. He had spent the previous year on 230-centimeter skis; now he was on 220s. The new skis were easier to turn. On the longer skis he had felt as if he was piloting the Queen Mary. Now he felt he was driving a zippy sports car.

This was, of course, an Olympic year, the year America would pay attention to downhill again, but success at the Albertville Olympics wasn't AJ's first priority. That was partly because he disliked the course. It was also because he knew he couldn't count on winning any single downhill race, Olympic or otherwise. The competition was too fierce, the conditions too unpredictable for any racer to do that. The Olympic games were held only once in a great while (after the Albertville games, the next Olympics would be held in Norway in 1994, and after that in 1998), so in a sense any victory was a freak victory. Not that he didn't want to win a gold medal—he did. If he had a great race and became an instant national celebrity and an almost instant multimillionaire, he would take it like a man. But he wasn't going to take out any big bank loans with Olympic riches as collateral, that was for sure.

No, AJ Kitt's most important goal for the season was to win a World Cup race. He believed that was more realistic. There were nine downhills on the World Cup schedule that season, which meant nine chances to win. Val d'Isère, the first race of the year, seemed a particularly good prospect for a victory. The race would not be held on the Olympic course, but rather on the old World Cup course, which AJ liked. He had finished in the top three in all three training runs there the year before, but on race day he had skied badly, and had been slowed down even further by the wind. He was angry about that now; he wanted to get even with the race course. So as the team prepared to board a plane for Europe in late November 1991, AJ was thinking about revenge.

Yeah, Val d'Isère, he thought. Winning Val d'Isère would be fine.

9

Winning

When the downhillers drove into France that December, three months before the Albertville games, it already looked Olympic. A handsome wire sculpture in the Olympic colors had been erected near Albertville, and the Olympic rings had been painted on the highway. Merchants were also beginning to cash in on the excitement. Kyle Rasmussen, who was behind the wheel, stopped to get gas at a convenience store near Val d'Isère. When he, Jeff Olson, and some of the other racers went inside, they found Olympic pins, games, sweatshirts, T-shirts, and postcards. The downhillers were both wowed by the incredible display of merchandise and turned off by how tacky everything looked. Reggie Crist picked up a doll named Magique, the Olympic mascot. The doll, no doubt the pride of the Olympic organizing committee, was a star-shaped fellow with black eyes, a thin red smile, no nose, a blue jumpsuit, and a cone-shaped hat with a tassel. Reggie and his teammates quickly pronounced the doll goofy. On the price tag there was a note: "Made in Indonesia."

The American van soon twisted up the narrow mountain road into Val d'Isère, rolled through the center of town, and pulled up to Hotel La Becca. The athletes unloaded their equipment in the shadow of the mountain. As they worked, they could see the slick, creamy Olympic downhill course snaking from the summit of the Face de Bellevarde to the base. This, not the Olympic rings or Indonesian-made dolls, was the only symbol that mattered. For a moment, Jeff and Reggie paused to admire the red-bordered slope, which was beginning to disappear in the dusk. Here, three months from now, someone would ski his way to unimaginable riches and fame and glory, and the American downhillers couldn't help dreaming it would be one of them. After they finished carrying their skis into the garage beneath the hotel, they gathered by the fireplace in the cozy dining room for a meeting with the coaches.

"Now the season starts," Ueli Luthi said. "I think it's very important to get focused into the season and approach things in the right way. We have to start notching up now. The Olympics are not that far away anymore."

But the racers would not have to contend with the Face de Bellevarde yet. This week, they would be skiing another hill—the old downhill course, the site of World Cup downhills since 1969, and of other races since the mid-1950s. The downhillers got their first look at the so-called OK course on Wednesday morning. It had a few tricky spots. The first was the Collombin jump, which wasn't really a jump, but rather a gradual falling away of the earth. Instead of being tossed skyward, the racers simply ran out of ground. Most of them glided one or two feet over the snow for more than one hundred feet, touching down softly, like herons on water. The jump was named for Roland Collombin, the great Swiss racer of the 1970s. One year he lost his balance going off the jump, crashed, broke his back, spent a year recovering, came back to Val d'Isère, and broke his back there again. On the World Cup downhill circuit you had to do a lot to get something named after you.

The rest of the course held some bad memories for the Americans. Just below the Collombin was the jump Jeff Olson had gone off backward the year before, messing up his mind for a whole season. Below that was a high-speed right turn where Kyle Rasmussen had biffed it two years earlier. His skis got out from under him and he slid feet-first into a fence. He broke his left thumb and sprained his left ankle and knee and missed three weeks of racing. A few seconds after that fast right turn, the athletes would finally come to the compression, where, in 1990, Bill Hudson had whacked his head and wound up in the hospital, weeping and puking. During inspection, Bill took a long look at the compression. He wanted to ski it just well enough so they wouldn't name it after him.

*   *   *

Where, Bill Hudson asked himself, are the butterflies? He didn't feel anything fluttering around in his stomach as he inspected the downhill course Wednesday morning, the first day of training, and he couldn't understand why. For the first time since his accident in Kitzbühel he was sliding down a World Cup course, wearing his bib and his downhill suit, but he wasn't a bit nervous. For eleven months he had anticipated this moment, had dreaded it, really, and now . . . nothing. As he glided from gate to gate he felt serene, as if he were taking the relaxing first run of the day in Squaw Valley, his hometown. Today, Bill was one mellow Californian. It was frustrating, in a way. He wanted to be nervous. If he was scared now, he reasoned, maybe he would be confident when he got into the starting gate.

He wore bib number sixty-seven that day, which ranked him among the also-rans. That didn't help his confidence much, because he felt he was better than they were. But it wasn't just that he thought he was better. He expected to be the best. Bill expected to win every race he entered. He couldn't stand it when he didn't win, which of course was most of the time. His teammates were familiar with his bad temper. They all had different ways to describe it. When he was really seething, Todd Kelly would say, "Look out. Huddy has the crazy eye." Bill Egan would say he was "red-lining," as if Bill were an engine about to blow. And then, *kaboom*, he would. One time, after a run in Kitzbühel that didn't meet his standards, he skied through the finish and began furiously kicking a fence, as if it were an animal he was trying to kill. Jeff Olson had to tell him, "Hudson, mellow out, man." The only thing that did was make him turn his wrath from the fence to his teammate.

But these days Bill was in better control of himself. In early December the downhillers had stopped in the French village of Valloire for a Europa Cup super G race, a minor race that the team used as a warmup for the season. Hudson had a mediorce run, finishing back in the pack. This was understandable; after all, he hadn't raced in almost a year. When the race was over, he got the crazy eye, but that was as far as it went. He never blew up. Instead, he thought it through. You have to be patient, he told himself. You were hurt. Just do the best you can and try to have fun. For Bill it was progress, a small but important step.

When he finished his inspection that morning in Val d'Isère, Bill took off his skis and took the tram back to the start for his first training run. He had long since decided to disregard his instincts and take this easy. Every electrical impulse in his brain told him to punch it, go crazy, but he was not going to listen this time. He told himself, If I had taken it easy at Kitzbühel I might never have been hurt.

He waited, but the butterflies never came. Bill went out of the start calmly. He made the first several turns with ease, then, as he approached the Collombin jump, curled up his body so he wouldn't fly far. Actually, he was so careful that he didn't fly at all. As he skied away from the Collombin he rolled his eyes and said to himself, "Geez, what was that?" He stood up in the compression, slowing himself way down. The next two turns, the ones that had tripped him up the year before, were easy at such a low speed. Bill glided through the finish several seconds behind the fastest racer. That was embarrassing, he thought.

But God, that was fun, he told himself. That's why I do this. Because it's so much fun.

AJ Kitt finished among the top racers all week. After dinner Friday night, the night before the race, Bill Egan was excited. "I think this may be it," he said, meaning Saturday might be the day AJ would win. The thought made him so anxious that he went out with some other coaches that night and got drunk, just to put it out of his mind.

AJ went to bed about 8:30 that night. He read a book for a while before switching off the light. In his first days on the World Cup circuit, he couldn't sleep the night before a race, but over the years he had learned ways to calm himself. On this night, he shut his eyes and skied the course once in his mind. AJ often took imaginary downhill runs. After inspecting a course, he liked to find a quiet place where he could stand and envision the ideal line down the hill, the way that would lead him to victory. Doing this helped him get to know the course and took his mind off his nervousness. A lot of downhillers took these mental runs. Fans arriving early for races often saw athletes standing in the finish area, leaning on their ski poles as if they were asleep. But they weren't asleep; they were just thinking. Now, as AJ lay in bed, he concentrated especially hard on the middle third of the OK course—the tower turn, the meadows, and the compression. His imaginary run was soothing, flawless, the only perfect one he made that week. There was no need to take the mental chair lift back to the top and ski the course again. Bill Hudson, relaxing in the next bed, was still reading by lamplight when AJ fell asleep.

AJ awoke at 5:00 A.M., took a leak, and lay in bed for a while, thinking about the race. Again, he thought about the middle third of the course. He had made a mistake in the compression last year, and he was determined not to do it again. Once or twice he thought about winning, but he chased the thoughts away. AJ believed you weren't supposed to think about certain things before a race, and coming in first was one of them. If you thought too much about the result, you might not pay enough attention to the process, which would practically guarantee a poor result. AJ always concerned himself with the process—making clean turns, finding the right line, gliding softly on the snow. He would have plenty of time to think about the result when he crossed the finish line.

He got up and ate breakfast at 7. Hotel La Becca was a small, two-story pension owned by Dominique and Beatrice Tempesta. The couple served the same breakfast every morning: dark, rich coffee, yogurt, cheese, orange juice, and toast and croissants with jam. AJ polished off the meal in fifteen minutes. He noticed that his teammates were quieter than usual; nobody was laughing or joking or fighting over the croissants. The downhillers were always serious on race day. After breakfast, AJ rode the tram to the top of the hill and inspected the course one last time. Then he rode back up again to begin his warmup. AJ's warmup program was always the same. Twenty minutes before the race he heated up his muscles with a series of exercises—leg dips, jumps, stretches, some running.

That morning AJ walked to a steep slope next to the starting area and ran up and down it until he began to sweat inside his downhill suit. Ten minutes before the race, Edi Waldburger, the Rossignol representative, helped him into his skis. Five minutes before the race AJ fastened the buckles on his boots. Like most downhillers, he tightened his boots almost to the point where they cut off the flow of blood to his feet. When he moved his legs, he expected his skis to move too; that would happen only if the boots fit tightly. Finally, AJ pulled his goggles down over his eyes. He always did that last because he found that the lenses fogged up if he put them on too soon.

AJ wore number thirteen, which he considered his lucky number because he was born on the thirteenth, in September. He was about to enter the starting gate when he heard someone say that one of the snow seed racers had finished in 1:57. That struck him as a surprisingly fast time. Otherwise, he made no effort to find out how the racers ahead of him were doing, for the same reason that he hadn't allowed himself to think about winning the race. At 10:48—beep, beep, beep—AJ was gone.

Immediately he made a mistake. The course began with a fall-away right turn. To ski it well, a racer had to set the edge of his left ski in the snow and ride that edge all the way around the bend, like a figure skater carving a long arc. AJ got too far into the turn before he set the edge, so when he finally did, he had to set it hard, which slowed him down. It's all right, he told himself. It wasn't a big mistake.

He flew a long way off the Collombin jump and he felt fast in the flats. In the meadows, he skied exactly the line he wanted to ski. For those fifteen or twenty seconds gravity was his plaything, instead of the other way around. Bill Egan, standing in the meadows with some other coaches, danced around in his ski boots when AJ flashed by. About that time, Austria's Leonhard Stock, the racer ahead of AJ, skied under the finish banner. His time, 1:56.18, was the best of the day. Stock, a veteran racer who had won the Val d'Isère downhill the year before, pumped his fists and hoisted his skis and posed for the cameras. It looked like he had won again.

Stock was still smiling when AJ soared off the tunnel jump. For the first time that week AJ stayed in his tuck as he entered the compression. The speed surprised him and he slipped, but quickly caught himself. He made the compression turn cleanly, popped off the last jump, and tucked under the finish banner. A flagpole blocked his view of the clock, but even with the pole in the way AJ Kitt could see what he needed to see: the order of finish.

"1," the clock said. He had beaten Stock, the 1980 Olympic downhill champion, a respected veteran, by forty-nine hundredths of a second. Youth is beautiful but tactless.

Right on the Edge of Crazy

AJ pumped his fists in the air, nearly falling over as he did. In the finish, the crowd shouted with surprise. At the top of the hill, the Austrian coaches went dead silent, as if they had just been informed of an air raid on Innsbruck. AJ clicked out of his skis and held them over his head, making sure to face the photographers as he did. Then he leaned the skis against his shoulders and smiled as the shutters winked. There were many racers to come, but it was unlikely that any of them could beat AJ's time.

The reporters scrambled toward him. A low fence separated the racers and coaches from everyone else. The reporters had to press their hips against the fence and lean forward to speak to him. They held microphones and tape recorders near his mouth, so many that he couldn't see where some of them were coming from, couldn't tell which hand belonged to which person. Most of the reporters spoke stiff, formal English, the kind of English you speak when you've learned it in a classroom. They asked questions all at once. How did you train for the race? Where are you from? Did you know that you had the fastest time at the halfway point? He tried to answer them all: I did a lot of giant slalom training to work on my turns. Rochester, New York. Of course not.

One of the reporters said, "What does AJ stand for?"

"Nothin'," AJ said.

In the midst of all of this, Canadian racer Brian Stemmle strode up to AJ and shouted, "Fuck, AJ! Yes, sir!" Then he shook AJ's hand and was gone.

AJ was still preening for the press when Tommy Moe, number twenty-nine, began his run. He skied better than he had all week. He made a mistake on the tunnel jump, flying so high that he thought, "This might be a fucking death wish." Then he landed, *ka-POW*, and was grateful that his knee ligaments didn't snap. When Tommy sliced through the finish and found himself in eleventh place, he, too, raised his arms over his head. Then he threw back his head and let out a whoop, which made his teammates crack up when they saw it later, on videotape. Tommy was a little disappointed when two racers skied well and bumped him down to thirteenth place, but not disappointed enough to take back the whoop. In the finish he yelled, "AJ won that bitch!" It certainly looked like he had.

All the other Americans made it to the finish, with varying degrees of success. Reggie Crist missed a gate halfway through and wound up skiing lazily down the course, standing up, chin in his chest, as if leading an alpine funeral procession. Kyle Rasmussen finished way back, almost four seconds behind AJ. Then he stepped out of his bindings and kicked his skis. Steve Porino finished way back. So did Todd Kelly, the new guy on the team. Jeff Olson finished in twenty-seventh place, third best among the Americans. He generally did something like that the moment everyone was sure he was washed up. Bill Hudson, wearing number sixty-three, finished fortieth, which pleased everyone except Bill Hudson.

Many other racers came down after Bill, but none could beat AJ's time. By finishing first, AJ became the first American man to win a World Cup downhill since Bill Johnson did it at Canada's Whistler Mountain in 1984. AJ's time, 1:55.69, was a course record. Leonhard Stock was second, and the unbeatable Franz Heinzer was third. In Aspen, nine months earlier, Bill Egan had told the team, "Keep working, guys. We're not that far away." He had been right.

That night AJ and his teammates gathered in the center of Val d'Isère for the awards ceremony. It was sort of a rehearsal for the Olympic awards ceremonies in February. The top three finishers, AJ, Stock, and Franz Heinzer, were called, in the order they finished, to a stage, where they stood on a podium. For a moment AJ stood alone, smiling and waving. His teammates and coaches, who occupied the middle of a crowd of perhaps two hundred people, cheered and shouted, "Yeah!" and "All right, Al!" A dozen camera flashes popped when AJ held his arms over his head. Then Stock and Heinzer joined AJ in the limelight. The audience cheered the three of them for several minutes. Behind the racers, the Olympic course was bathed in white light. Jean-Claude Killy, France's 1968 Olympic hero and the organizer of the Albertville games, shook hands with each man. AJ was given a heavy crystal trophy and an envelope containing his prize money—34,650 francs in cash, about $6,475. The race organizers later doubled the prize money. AJ also earned about $50,000 in bonus money from his sponsors.

At last, the athletes turned to their right and watched as the flags of their countries were raised. A tape-recorded version of "The Star-Spangled Banner" was played on the public-address system. After a few notes the music abruptly stopped, as if even the tape recorder couldn't believe what it was playing.

"C'est O.K. pour AJ Kitt," the headline in Val d'Isère paper said the next day. The paper called AJ "l'héritier," or descendant, of Bill Johnson. AJ snorted at that. As far as he was concerned, Johnson was Johnson and AJ was AJ, and the two had nothing to do with each other. Yes, they were both considered excellent gliders, and they had both won their first World Cup race at age twenty-three. But that was about it. Johnson was a talented guy, but he lacked the self-discipline athletes need to stay successful. AJ, of course, was Mr. Self-Discipline, the consummate professional ski racer in a country where most people didn't know there was such a thing as a professional ski racer. Johnson had been one of the best downhillers in the world for three months in 1984. AJ had the potential to stay on top for several years. But AJ never compared himself to Bill Johnson, and he hoped young racers would not model themselves after AJ Kitt. AJ never wanted to be anybody but AJ.

The front-page headline in the Swiss newspaper *Blick* said, "Kitt stahl Heinzer die Show"—"Kitt steals Heinzer's show." That about summed up the European attitude: It was Heinzer's race, he owned it, and had AJ stolen it, the little snot. Actually, what the paper called AJ—and this was supposed to be flattering—was "stiernachen," or "bull neck." A photograph inside *Blick* showed Ueli Luthi crumpling a pack of Marlboros. He had promised the racers he would quit smoking if one of them won a World Cup race. Now, after smoking for most of his adult life, he was keeping the promise.

Both Blick and another Swiss paper, *Zeitung*, gave AJ's full name as "Alvar Junior Kitt." AJ went crazy. Alvar? Where did they get that? AJ accused his teammates of revealing his real name, but they didn't own up to it. Alvar? Jesus Christ. Now, Alva Ross Kitt IV didn't seem so bad.

Sports Illustrated made him feel better by calling him simply AJ. But in AJ's mind the magazine committed its own sin. In the back of that week's issue it published an item saying, "SWOOPED to an unexpected victory . . . AJ Kitt," etc. Next to the item it ran a picture of AJ catching air at Val d'Isère.

AJ read the item, looked up, and said, "That's bullshit. It wasn't unexpected."

Alvar had a point: It wasn't unexpected. AJ had been tap dancing around the victory podium for a couple of years, as everyone in the ski world knew. But the rest of the world didn't notice. It always happened that way. When Bill Johnson won the gold medal in Sarajevo, a lot of papers said he "came out of nowhere" to win. People always seemed to come out of nowhere to surprise a popular press that wasn't paying attention. The truth was that Johnson had been the favorite to win in Sarajevo: He had won the Europa Cup downhill title in 1983 and a World Cup race in Wengen just before the Olympics; he had a fast pair of skis; and he was skiing better than anyone else. But it had made great copy to say he shocked the world, so the press said it. If AJ Kitt went on to win a medal in the Albertville games, somebody probably would say the same thing about him. But he knew better. He and his teammates had traveled too many miles and broken too many bones to believe that people came out of nowhere to win downhill ski races.

AJ's win changed everything. For one thing, it changed the thinking of his teammates. For the first time, they knew, really knew, that it was possible for an American to win a World Cup race. That was important, because they definitely had to believe it before it would happen. You simply could not pole out of a World Cup starting shack thinking you were going to come in fifty-sixth and end up winning. The morning after AJ's victory, U.S. Ski Team Alpine Program Director Dennis Agee sent a fax to France. After congratulating AJ he wrote, "The rest of you guys, good job, the program is working." Actually, the victory said more about AJ's program than it did about the ski team's. And yet, because he had won, the rest of the guys felt they could win, too, eventually. Most of them had beaten AJ at least once in their careers. What was to stop them from doing it again?

The win also changed AJ. Before, he had been a very good racer, a guy with lots of potential. Now he was a winner. It was an important step. Potential doesn't mean a thing. Every athlete has potential, but few ever get a Wimbledon trophy, or a Masters green jacket, or an envelope stuffed with francs. When athletes win, they distinguish themselves not just for a day, but forever. Bill Johnson would be known as the 1984 Olympic downhill champion as long as he lived. Likewise, Jack Nicklaus would always be U.S. Open golf champion. And of course, just like losing, winning is a mysterious and powerful force, something that gets easier each time you do it. That's what athletes mean when they mention momentum. Once they've won, they can't help thinking they'll do it again. Winning changes the way athletes think about themselves. It tells them, You were right to believe in yourself. You are for real. Certainly AJ felt that way about his victory. His fourth-place finishes in Cortina, Italy, and Lake Louise, Canada, had helped him build confidence in himself. But the victory in Val d'Isère had done something more. It had confirmed, in the most significant way, that AJ's program worked.

He felt the weight of his achievement in other ways too. Overnight, every ski racing fan in Europe learned his name. So what if most of them had learned it wrong? Everywhere the Americans went for the next couple of weeks, people would see their team jackets and ask, "Kitt? Kitt?" The guys would say, "No, not Kitt," and then they'd point to AJ, who would smile his magnetic smile and say, "Kitt." Beyond that, he was now acknowledged as one of the best ski racers in the world, a worthy adversary for the Heinzers and Skaardals and Stocks. Already the press was asking if he thought he could win again the next week, in Val Gardena, Italy. Sure, he would say. Why not? And if he could beat Heinzer in Val d'Isère, what was to keep him from doing it in Val Gardena or St. Anton or Garmisch or Kitzbühel or Wengen . . . or at the 1992 Albertville Olympics?

10

Jumping
the Camels

Air. That was what the crazy-ass downhill maniacs thought about when they thought of Val Gardena, Italy, traditionally the second stop on the World Cup downhill tour.

The course in Val Gardena (also known by its German name, Groden) had a steep start, a tricky, turny bottom section, and a terrifying high-speed finish schuss, in which the skier shot like a bullet toward the bottom, awaited by a crowd of thousands. As Bill Egan inspected the finish slope on the American team's first day in town, in mid-December 1991, he said, "It's the one place on the World Cup tour where you don't want to catch an edge. You're hauling ass here." Bill Hudson, who was making a career of catching edges in places where it was best not to catch them, had caught an edge there a couple of years back. It was his first World Cup concussion.

But never mind the finish schuss: Val Gardena, a flowery valley in the shadow of the craggy Dolomite range, was about air. About halfway into the course, the skier reached the famous camel bumps, which commanded the kind of respect from downhill racers that Heartbreak Hill got from Boston Marathon runners, and that Augusta National's Amen Corner got from golfers. The camels were, simply, three big, rolling bumps spaced about thirty yards apart. Approaching these jumps at sixty or seventy miles an hour was something like driving a runaway car down a steep San Francisco street: You zoomed downhill, hit a bump, flew for a while, and then hit another bump.

Right on the Edge of Crazy

For years, downhill racers made a point of not getting much air in the camels: Instead of jumping from hump to hump, they tried to keep their skis on the camel's back. Skiing this way was like flying an airplane through extreme turbulence. It was frightfully hard work, and you came out of it with your eyes crossed and your fillings loose. Finally, about 1980, an Austrian racer named Ueli Spiess got an idea: He would absorb the first bump, the gentlest of the three. But when he reached the second bump, he would launch himself into the air and fly over the crest of the third—a leap of forty or more yards. People on the tour were sure he would end up hospitalized, and a few thought he should have been institutionalized just for considering such a thing. Even so, Spiess went for it, and made it. He never won the race, but he forever changed the way people skied the course. His daring leap made everybody feel obligated to jump the camels. You looked like a sissy if you didn't. Not everyone handled them as well as Spiess did. Over the years, the snow on the top of the third camel bump was dented by many a rear end. Bill Johnson, 1984 Olympic gold medalist, never successfully cleared the third hump. In fact, in December 1986, he blew out his knee trying, and his career was never the same. Later, an Italian racer crashed in the camels and swallowed his tongue. He was dead on the course, but the doctors got his heart going again and saved his life.

Now, in 1991, two runs were scheduled on the first day of training. AJ Kitt, as usual the first American to ski, made the long leap over the camels with ease, just as he had done the year before. When he landed, he punched the sky as if he had just scored a touchdown. The extra movement slowed him down, but he didn't care. This was just a training run, and he was excited. Leaping the icy canyon was that exhilarating. AJ skied easily through the meadows, and made the right turn into the finish schuss.

And then things went wrong. He was in his tuck, screaming down the long, icy incline toward the finish, when the wind pushed his goggles just a smidgen out of whack. When the wind hit him, his eyes filled with water and he went instantly blind. Suddenly he was skiing with an aquarium on his head. If the terrain had been flat all the way down he might have kept going, but he knew he would soon reach the finish jump, and he wasn't interested in going off of it blindfolded. If he couldn't see it, he couldn't survive it. So, in a brilliant act of self-preservation, AJ lay down on his side. He did not panic. He simply put himself down the way an experienced motorcyclist might lay his bike down to avoid a disastrous wreck. He went off the jump on his back, so he got almost no air. He slid through the finish on his side, then got up and dusted himself off.

"I'm fine," he said on the radio, interrupting the coaches' heart attacks.

As much as anything he had done to take the top prize in Val d'Isère, AJ's controlled crash showed why he was a winner. A downhill course could surprise you; it could throw you off line or trip you up or knock your glasses out of whack. But if you were smart, if you thought things through, you could often—not always, but often—keep skiing. Or at least you could save yourself so you could ski the next day. AJ skied the last seventy-five yards on his back and finished seventh in the training run.

Back up the hill, the Americans kept bounding over the camels. Tommy Moe, Kyle Rasmussen, Jeff Olson, and Bill Hudson, all of whom had made the leap in previous years, also landed safely; Bill, who had legs like springs, cleared the third hump by fifty feet. Steve Porino and Reggie Crist didn't have any trouble either. On the tour, the Americans had a reputation as superb jumpers, and for good reason. Skiing was mostly a recreational sport, not a competitive one, in the United States, so most American kids grew up skiing just for kicks—going fast, leaping off moguls, doing stunts in the air. In Europe, meanwhile, kids began going through slalom gates as soon as they could balance themselves on skis. They worked on their racing technique all their lives. That was why Bill Egan often said, "The Europeans are the better racers, but the Americans are the better skiers."

The last American to confront the camels was Todd Kelly, who had replaced Eric Keck on the team. You had to be a certain kind of nut to jump the camels. Fortunately, Todd was that kind of nut.

Todd, who had turned twenty-two in November, had sparkling blue eyes and fine, straight red hair with natural blond streaks. He was, like all the downhillers, in excellent physical shape, and yet he was not lean: You didn't need to see baby pictures to tell he had been a pudgy child. He wore a gold hoop earring—not through his earlobe, but through the small wedge of flesh that covers the opening to the ear. (Only after he got the earring did he learn that he could have damaged the nerves in his face by punching a hole there.) Even with the earring and the cherubic build, Todd gave the impression of someone much older than he was. Ski technician Curtis Bacca, who was thirty years old, once razzed Todd by saying, "I hope I don't look like you when I'm forty."

With the departure of Eric, the huge Christian, the role of team character was unassigned. Todd, of Squaw Valley, California, naturally assumed it. His qualifications as a character went way beyond his looks. Todd had a unique way of saying things. Basically, when he said something, he meant the opposite. For example, if he planned to purchase, say, a new shotgun (he recently had caught the hunting bug), he would point his finger at you and declare, "I'm not buying a new shotgun when I get home. I'm not." Todd was the sort of fellow who liked to have lots of neat things; among the other items he definitely was not going to buy were a new water ski, hunting clothes, and a parasail. When something awful happened, Todd liked to say, "I'm so pissed." But he was never really pissed. Todd seemed too good-natured, or maybe just too eccentric, to get really angry about anything.

Todd, the son of a former U.S. Ski Team coach, had made exaggeration his life's work. He loved music, but he even overdid that. It was not enough for him to travel with a boom box and a few compact discs or tapes, like the rest of the guys. No, he wouldn't leave home without his huge Bose Acoustical Wave Music System, a tape player and radio powered by ten batteries. He also brought along a Sony portable CD player (with remote control), two sets of headphones (one for use when he was free-skiing, the other, a studio-quality set, for special listening moments), and sixty-seven CDs. Todd's taste was eclectic—he liked everything from Frank Sinatra to the heavy-metal group Metallica. If Sinatra had an exact opposite, Metallica was probably it.

About once a week Todd revealed his quirky side to the public. One thing he couldn't stand—one thing that really did piss him off—was sweating into his downhill suit. He hated the sensation of his cold salty sweat against that tight green suit. None of the downhillers liked that feeling, but Todd was the only one who disliked it enough to do something about it. Each time he finished a race he lowered the zipper on the front of the suit and pulled it off his shoulders. Then he stripped off the top half and stood there half naked, steam rising from his furry red chest. The sight of him always raised a few eyebrows in low temperatures.

On the morning of the training run in Val Gardena, though, Todd was concerned only with the camel bumps. He had been thinking about them—worrying about them, really—since he'd gotten to town. During inspection that day, he scarcely looked at the other parts of the course. Coming, as he did, from a ski-racing family, Todd had learned early to fear and respect downhill's most famous obstacles—the Collombin jump in Val d'Isère, the Mausefalle in Kitzbühel, and of course the camel bumps in Val Gardena. His heroes were Franz Klammer, the Austrian icon, and Steve Podborski, one of the Canadian madmen known as the Crazy Canucks. Another was Leonhard Stock, who would be competing here this week. These were the racers who dominated downhill racing when Todd was a kid. He had seen all these men jump the camels, and now he would jump them too . . . he hoped.

But damn, it was a long way from the second bump to the third! Todd figured he would have to jump farther than he had ever jumped on downhill skis if he was going to make it. In the starting gate, Todd thought: camels. As he made the first couple of turns and tucked across the flats, he thought: camels. He went off a big jump just above the camels and thought: camels. Tucking toward the camels he thought: camels.

Camels, camels, camels.

And then he was there. He sucked up the first bump and aimed himself at the crest of the second. (I'm not going to jump the camels today. I'm not.) When he hit the takeoff point he extended his legs like a Nordic ski jumper and took flight. Get tight, he told himself. Get tight in the air. Todd pulled up his knees and tried to keep his arms low, but he couldn't: They flew crazily over his head. The racer looked down. The snow seemed impossibly far away; it was like looking down at the clouds from a 747. Todd wasn't just jumping. He was . . . flying! The coaches and course workers below looked like ants. He was a bird, a big, round, redheaded bird with skis for wings. He was going to make it!

Suspended in the thin mountain air over Italy, sailing over the up-turned, admiring faces of mortal men, Todd Kelly looked down at the earth and screamed in ecstasy. He landed softly just beyond the crest of the third jump and skied away alive—more alive than ever.

*   *   *

Ueli Luthi watched the second training run from the camel bumps. He was always easy to find on the hill: He wore ugly pink ski boots, boots most other people on the tour wouldn't have worn even as a joke. Bill Egan and Jim Tracy gave him a lot of grief about the boots, but he didn't care. They felt good on his feet. Ueli didn't converse much with the other coaches during the training run. He preferred to stand by himself, busily making notes on the back of a list of the day's racers. Ueli seemed happiest when he was watching ski racing. Every time a racer came by, he clomped a few feet up the hill, as if to greet him. He squatted as the racer went by, the better to analyze the guy's technique. Then he slid back down the hill, following the athlete as he disappeared around the corner. Finally, Ueli took out his pencil and scribbled until the next racer came along. The other coaches and athletes on the American team knew Ueli could be infuriatingly stubborn and argumentative. They also knew he was one of the best downhill coaches around.

Ueli loved standing on the camel bumps. It was exciting to watch the racers soar through the air, hilarious to hear them howl when they looked, bug-eyed, at the ground far below. But what the coach liked most about this section was that, in his opinion, it tested the racers' manhood. Ueli, a stoic, believed men should always strive to be macho, implacable, fearless. He had no time for sensitive, heartfelt discussions with the downhillers. They were men and they were supposed to behave like men. Ueli seemed to enjoy discovering who was a real man and who wasn't. As far as he was concerned, if you jumped the camels, you were a man. If you didn't, if you skied around the bumps, you were—this was the word he used—a "pussy." Except when he said "pussy," his accent made it come out "poosy." Some of the people who watched from the camels had a hard time deciding which was more fun—seeing hapless guys ski around the bumps or hearing Ueli call them "poosies."

Though Val Gardena was the Italians' home course, few of them jumped the camels. None of the forerunners did.

"Poosies," Ueli said.

Neither did Italian star Peter Runggaldier.

"Poosy."

Danilo Sbardelloto, yet another Italian, also skied around the camels. "Poosy," Ueli said, cackling.

The Hotel Laurin, where the Americans stayed, was crawling that week with ski-racing groupies—racer chasers, in the vernacular. These were women who followed the tour in hopes of meeting, or doing whatever with, the international ski studs. Among the racer chasers in Val Gardena were two thirtyish women in tight ski pants and heavy eye makeup. They may or may not have been related, but the American racers, unimpressed with them, nonetheless called them the Grim Sisters, or sometimes just the Grimsters. That week the women seemed to have their eyes on Luxembourg's Marc Girardelli, who was also staying in the hotel, and who, as one of the greatest all-around skiers in history, shone much more brightly in the constellation of ski stars than any of the Americans. Also hovering around the hotel were the Garmisch Girls, a pair of racer chasers who looked a lot like the Grim Sisters. The Garmisch Girls apparently were German, but they had been chasing racers throughout Europe since the early 1980s.

The Americans wouldn't have anything to do with the likes of the Grimsters or the Garmisch Girls, whom they found unattractive. They preferred younger dates. Jeff Olson—handsome, charming, and, ever since his wedding had been canceled, extremely available—did well with the European women. He always had something witty to say to the waitresses and hotel chambermaids, and he usually got them to say something back. Once in a while, the bantering landed him a brief but memorable date. AJ wasn't as successful, partly because he didn't try as hard to seduce women as Jeff did, and partly because he lacked Jeff's dimples and his gee-whiz delivery. Even so, he had his share of dates, but only on off-nights. (None of the downhillers had the time or inclination to chase women until after race day.) The rest of the guys lived like monks when they were on the road. Kyle was married, and Reggie, Tommy, and Steve had steady girlfriends. And quite a few European women had been disappointed to learn that Bill Hudson was spoken for.

And yet Val Gardena was the setting for a pretty good story involving

Hudson. In the late 1980s, before he began dating Kathrin Burkhart, Bill had gone out dancing with a very young local, a woman he later described as "a little Italian girl." Tommy Moe, also unattached at the time, escorted the young woman's friend. The double date took place on a Saturday night, after the race. Bill and his date had an excellent time— so completely, unexpectedly, mutually excellent that the athlete gave the woman his racing bib to commemorate the occasion. When they parted, he figured he would never see her again. But he did. The next day, the woman appeared at Bill's hotel room. Bill and AJ, his roommate, were packing their bags when she showed up. "I just came to say good-bye," she told Bill. And then she said, "Look." She raised her ski sweater. Underneath, she wore Bill's tight-fitting racing bib, and nothing else.

The woman was known thereafter as The Bib Girl.

AJ won the final training run. It didn't mean much to him. He knew he was skiing well, but he also knew a lot of other guys, including Franz Heinzer, had slowed down before they reached the finish line so nobody would know exactly how fast they had skied. AJ always got a small confidence boost when he won a training run, but he knew racing was a different matter entirely.

In Val Gardena, reporters were confined to a small pen near the finish line. After AJ caught his breath and collected his thoughts, he walked over to meet the press. The stringer for *USA Today* wanted to know if it was "just good luck" that the American downhillers were starting to do well. AJ, a little offended, said he thought not. A guy from Austrian radio said, "You can win tomorrow perhaps?" AJ said he thought maybe. One reporter asked a question the racer had not heard before. "What do you fear most?" Perhaps the reporter expected AJ to say that he feared catching an edge in the finish schuss, or landing on the wrong hump in the camels, or blowing out a knee. AJ paused for a second. Then he said, "Getting a cold and not being able to race." A few minutes later, a journalist asked if he could meet AJ at the hotel later that night for an interview. "I don't do any interviews the night before a race. But I'll talk to you right now if you want," AJ said. And then he stood and questions until the reporter ran out of them. Was this the same AJ who had snapped at the reporter in Aspen a few months earlier? Yes, it was, but the situation was different. In Aspen, AJ had skied badly, and the reporter had accosted him while he was still out of breath from his run. Here, AJ had skied well, and he had not had to face the pack until he was ready. He could be gracious and helpful to reporters, but he wanted to do it on his own terms.

While AJ was being treated like a star, one of his teammates was confronting failure and disappointment. Steve Porino's time as a ski racer, the most challenging and exciting time he had ever known, seemed almost over.

His troubles had begun months earlier. After his mediocre 1990–91 season, his ski supplier, Head, did not renew his contract, and Porino was forced to go begging for a new sponsor. After several rejections he made a deal with Volkl, a German ski company. (Volkl had an unintentionally hilarious English-language slogan: "If all sports you can, then you are a Volkl fan.") Steve was crazy about the skis—they ran great—but the deal they'd given him was pretty meager. The company agreed to give him free skis . . . and nothing else. It did not pay him a retainer to use the skis, the way Head did. Nor did the Volkl technician travel with the American team the way the Rossignol and Head and Dynastar reps did. Steve's technician traveled with the German team. Every day, Steve had to drive his skis to the guy's hotel, then go pick them up when they were ready. The Volkl rep was a nice guy, but he spoke very little English, so Steve was never sure if the fellow understood him. The Volkl deal was humiliating, in a way. Everybody who saw Steve that year could see that Head had dumped him, and that Volkl didn't consider him a star.

Early that season, Porino realized he had lost some of his enthusiasm for ski racing. In past years, the mere thought of seeing a movie on the flight to Europe had been enough to get him excited. Not anymore. Travel was a hassle now; it was tiresome, and it took him away from his girlfriend, Kristina, in Salt Lake City. He didn't enjoy being with his teammates as much as he used to, either. The never-ending competition among them—competition over anything, from a game of basketball to a woman to a dinner roll—used to amuse him. Now it pissed him off. Which also bothered him; he didn't like to feel that way about his friends.

The place Porino was most frustrated was on the race hill. He simply was not going fast. In the race at Val d'Isère he had finished fifty-fourth, almost four seconds behind AJ. In Val Gardena he was eightieth in the first training run, forty-sixth in the second, and fifty-sixth in the third. Those results wouldn't have been bad for a young kid just starting on the World Cup circuit, but Porino was no kid. He had turned twenty-five that spring. He felt he should be among the best in the world, but he wasn't. He wasn't close. He wasn't even among the stars of the American team. Steve had been the fourth- or fifth-best guy on the team for a long time, and he was getting tired of it. He felt the coaches were getting tired of him, too. It seemed to Steve the coaches paid a lot of attention to AJ and Tommy and some of the other guys whether they needed attention or not. But when he needed it, Bill and Ueli were too busy. That was how he saw it, at least. Steve was beginning to wonder why he tried anymore.

But if he didn't ski race, what would he do? The question haunted him. He had no college degree and no goals, except to win ski races. He didn't even have a home. Chicago wasn't home anymore. His parents were building a house in Vail, Colorado, but that wasn't home, either. His relationship with Kristina was young; who knew where that would lead?

For now, Steve had nowhere to go and nothing to do when he got there.

Some of the American athletes got together before the team meeting the night before the race to watch themselves on video. (Coach Jim Tracy had set up the video monitor in one of the upstairs lobbies at the beginning of the week.) Everybody enjoyed the footage of Todd Kelly. Tim "Swampy" LaMarche, an assistant coach, had shot video of Todd as he made the first turn in the course, a long, very steep right-hander. The trick to this turn was to set the edge of the left ski and ride that edge all the way around the bend. On the videotape, Todd could be heard telling his ski, "Come on, baby. Come around." Swampy could also be heard cracking up. Todd was probably the only athlete on the tour who engaged in conversation with his skis while racing.

Ueli Luthi arrived a few minutes later for the team meeting. He told AJ that he would be starting twelfth in the race.

"What number is Heinzer?" AJ said.

"Two," Ueli said.

"Good. He'll have the slow track." AJ knew the forerunners and snow seeds would not ski a perfect line down the hill. Heinzer would have to find the line for himself.

The coaches made their speeches brief. Ueli said, "We are not worse than anybody else on that hill." He never would have said the Americans were better than anybody on the hill. For optimism, "not worse" was the best he could do. Ueli also urged the racers to keep a low, aerodynamic profile in the air. "If you stand up," he said, his arms and legs outstretched, "you hang out your whole laundry." Bill Egan said, "We've got it all together. Be confident. Be confident. Maybe you had a bad training run or two. Fuck it. Forget it. Just go out there and do what you can do." And then the athletes went downstairs for dinner.

Later that night, Steve Porino was playing backgammon and drinking cappuccino in the hotel lobby when he heard someone laughing just around the corner. It was a distinctive laugh, a slow, nasal cackle. Eh-heh. Eh-heh. Eh-heh. It could be only one person.

"That's Billy D.!" Porino said. "Hey, Billy D.!"

Yes, it was he—Bill Johnson, the 1984 Olympic downhill champion, Billy D., the legend. Bill and Steve had been teammates on the U.S. Ski Team a couple of years earlier. Johnson came over, cackled a couple of times, shook Steve's hand, picked up Porino's now-empty cappuccino cup, a fine piece of hotel china, and spat tobacco juice into it. Johnson's day as a media star had passed, but he still knew how to make an entrance.

Steve was a little surprised to see Johnson in Europe. Only a few weeks earlier, Bill's young son had fallen into a hot tub and drowned. Everyone on the ski team had heard about the tragedy.

"I was really sorry to hear about what happened," Steve said.

"Yeah, thanks," Johnson said. Eager to turn to a less painful subject, he mentioned that his wife was pregnant again. "Time to start over."

"That's great. Good luck," Steve said. Then he asked, "So what are you doing here?"

Johnson had come to Val Gardena on a whim. He earned his living as the resident celebrity for the Crested Butte ski resort in Colorado. His job was to pose for photographs, take VIPs skiing, and so on. Earlier that week, he had flown to London to give away a trip to Crested Butte. He had decided, at the last minute, to zip over to Val Gardena. He was planning to bill his ski supplier, Atomic, for the trip. Steve, who had little chance of becoming a ski celebrity, couldn't help being envious. But he didn't resent Johnson's success; he felt Johnson deserved everything he had.

"So you came over just to see the race?" Steve said.

"Yeah. I came to watch AJ win," Johnson said. Eh-heh. Eh-heh.

AJ had gone to bed early, as he always did the night before a race. Johnson, the last great American downhiller, would have to wait until morning to see the man who might be the next one.

Race day was overcast and bitterly cold. On the hill, the coaches' toes went numb in their boots. In the finish, ten thousand Italian downhill fans huddled around the huge corral, hopping in place and clapping their gloved hands for warmth. From the top of the course to the bottom, people jockeyed for position in hopes of getting a clear view. They also wanted to be ready to take part in an insane and hilarious Val Gardena tradition. Each year, Italian ski fans, mistaking themselves for real downhillers, poured onto the course after the last racer went by and rocketed full speed to the bottom. Seeing this from the finish area was like watching the beginning of the New York Marathon, except in this case the racers were going forty miles an hour and didn't know what they were doing. It was chaos. People elbowed each other, whacked their helmetless heads on gates, crashed into the woods, and generally had a marvelous time.

At 12:30 P.M., Franz Klammer, Austria's 1976 Olympic downhill champion, skied through the finish wearing a fresh haircut, mirror sunglasses, a fancy jacket, and bright orange skis. Klammer enjoyed his status as a celebrity. Besides, he made his living endorsing products. He was in the habit of cruising into the finish corral before the start of every World Cup downhill, just so people could see what he was wearing and what brand of skis he was using. Now the race could begin.

Germany's Berni Huber raced first, finishing in 2:01.30. Franz Heinzer, number two, skied flawlessly and came in more than a second ahead of Huber. Apparently somebody forgot to tell Franz he had the slow track.

Heinzer was still in first place when racer number twelve, AJ Kitt, left the starting gate. As usual, AJ didn't know who was leading the race, or what the best time was. His own performance was his only concern. He skied well on the top of the course, the easiest part, and sprang joyfully over the camels—Jack out of his box. Fifteen seconds from the finish, AJ snagged his left ski pole on a turning gate. His body kept shooting forward, but his left hand, the one with the pole strap around it, got jerked behind him, hard. The force ripped the ski pole out of his hand. AJ was thrown off balance, but he found his feet and kept going. Damn! he thought. It felt strange to ski with one pole. AJ thought for a second about tossing away the right pole too, but decided not to. It would take too much time. Besides, all he had to do was tuck down the finish schuss. He didn't need poles for that. He flew off the finish jump, his single ski pole splayed out to the side, and skied beneath the banner. His time was 2:00.78. Fourth place. Nobody would beat Heinzer today.

When AJ saw the result on the scoreboard, he pumped his fist and hoisted one of his skis. He stood at the top of the finish corral for a moment, savoring the feeling. The fourth-place finish was tied for the second-best result of his career. And he had achieved that finish even though he had cut too close to a gate and had had his pole ripped out of his hand. Fourth place? He'd take it. He had finished out of the prize money, but he would still collect a few grand in bonuses from his sponsors. Yeah, he would definitely take that. As he glided toward the athletes' finish area, AJ saw Bill Johnson standing alongside the corral. It was the first time he had seen Johnson since the Olympic champion had come to town.

"Hey," Johnson said. "I came to see you win, not come in fourth!" Eh-heh. Eh-heh. Eh-heh.

AJ wasn't insulted. He knew exactly what Johnson meant. Fourth place had never been good enough for Bill Johnson, and Johnson obviously knew it wasn't good enough for AJ either. The two men had raced together for about a year when AJ was starting his career and Johnson was ending his. While they had never been close friends—neither was capable of really being buddies with his competitors—they liked and respected each other. It made AJ feel good to see Johnson in Val Gardena. To him, it was as if a former Wimbledon champion had come to see his fellow countryman compete in the U.S. Open.

None of AJ's teammates came away feeling as happy as he did. Tommy Moe was twenty-seventh, a disappointment after his thirteenth-place finish in Val d'Isère. Kyle Rasmussen was thirty-eighth, Jeff Olson thirty-ninth. (Jeff's finish was disappointing because he had won a Europa Cup super G race immediately after the Val d'Isère downhill. He was hoping the result would change his luck in downhill, but it didn't.) Steve Porino finished forty-seventh, which only intensified his sense that he should think about doing something else with his life. Reggie Crist had an unusually bad day. After nearly crashing on the finish jump, he came in sixty-seventh.

Todd Kelly, the rookie, also had a hard day. His troubles had begun early that morning when he was filing the edge of his ski in the basement of the Hotel Laurin. He was chatting with Curtis Bacca, the Head ski rep, when the file slipped out of his hand. He lost his balance and ran his palm against the sharp metal edge of the ski. The cut was deep. While Todd gripped his wrist and cursed, Bacca got his radio and called Courtney Brown, the doctor assigned to the race. Brown shot Novocain into the racer's hand and stitched the wound.

By the time he got into the starting gate, Todd had forgotten about the cut. He skied poorly on the top, a little better in the middle, and horribly on the last pitch. He was in a good aerodynamic position in the finish schuss, shoulders low, hands in front. But something went wrong when he got to the finish jump. His teammates, who watched from the finish, would say later that he seemed to fall asleep on the jump; instead of sucking up the bump he just stood there and let the hill throw him. Todd fiercely denied that. He said he made a move, just not a very good one. That was for sure. He almost tipped over backward in the air, but somehow managed to make his skis touch the snow before his back did. As soon as he made contact with the snow he caught an edge and rocket-shipped into the padded fence on the right side of the course.

There was a loud thud. Skis flew. The public-address announcer said, "Ay, ay, ay, ay, ay." The crowd got quiet. And then Todd got up, walked a few feet down the hill to the finish line, kicked his foot over the finish line and thrust his poles over his head in mock victory. Ta-da! The Italians went bonkers. Todd, hearing their cheers, thought, God, this is like being in a football game, it's so loud.

He collected his skis and walked off the course. That was when he started to feel the pain. When he put weight on his left leg he wanted to scream. He felt sure it was broken, but he later found out it wasn't. While looking at his leg he noticed something odd about his ski boots.

The soles were missing. Holy shit, he thought. That's incredible. The impact of the crash had blown the soles right off his boots.

He took off his gloves. His right hand was covered in blood. The crash had also exploded Courtney Brown's stitches.

"Fuck that, man," Todd muttered. "What a shitty day."

Bill Hudson was the last American to race. He moved into the starting gate as soon as the guy ahead of him was gone. The goggles man cleaned his goggles. Curtis Bacca wiped the bottoms of his skis. Gary Myers, the physical therapist, rubbed his thighs, back, and upper arms. Bill was focused now; he thought of nothing but the camels and the meadows and the finish schuss. He didn't feel afraid; he was pretty sure he had gotten his fear out of the way in Val d'Isère. Besides, he knew skiing scared could get him seriously hurt. Now he was eager, sharp, ready to go. This was the mental state every athlete strove to achieve right before the big competition. Ten seconds before he was supposed to leave the gate, something, some odd impulse, made Bill glance at the side of the course, where the spectators stood two- or three-deep. He allowed himself only a peek, but that was enough.

There she was: The Bib Girl!

Suddenly the facts of their relationship flashed through his mind like a film played at high speed—the double date, the highly excellent evening, his gift of the bib, her memorable goodbye. Whoa! Bill thought. Get it together! You have a race to run! This kind of lapse in concentration was disastrous for a downhiller, especially one coming back from an injury. To become competitive again, Bill needed to focus all his attention on the course. He had to envision himself finding the right line and following it safely and quickly to the finish. This was no time to reminisce about his adventures with women. Then the clock beeped and Bill pushed off, leaving the summit and The Bib Girl behind. He skied distractedly and finished fifty-seventh. Bill was still in the finish area when the last racer skied under the banner, followed by several thousand wild-eyed, whooping Italians.

The racers left Val Gardena that Monday, which left them with two days to kill before the beginning of downhill training Wednesday in St. Anton, Austria. (The St. Anton race was eventually snowed out.) For Bill

Egan, finding ways to fill the time between races was always a challenge. Usually he found a hill where the racers could train or, even better, looked for a small super G or even giant slalom race for them to compete in. Finding a race wasn't easy. The event had to fit perfectly into the Americans' schedule, and it had to be in a place the team could reach quickly. You couldn't compete in a downhill in Italy one day and expect to make it to a super G in France the next.

This time, Egan got lucky. According to his Fédération Internationale de Ski handbook, the Italian village of Pampeago, just over the mountain pass from Val Gardena, had a giant slalom race scheduled for that Tuesday. Perfect. Whenever Egan wanted his racers to work on their skiing technique, he entered them in a giant slalom race or set up a giant slalom course on the training hill. In giant slalom, the downhillers could work on their turns without sacrificing too much speed. Indeed, a lot of people in the ski world believed that a racer who did well in giant slalom could be competitive in any event. Egan sent a fax saying the team was coming, the guys all got their giant slalom skis ready, somebody found Pampeago on a map, and the whole caravan rolled over there.

When the racers got to the village of Pampeago, there was no snow. None. There was plenty of yellow-brown grass and lots of spry green trees and abundant dirt, but no snow. It looked like springtime in Italy. But hey, that didn't mean there was no snow up on the mountain. So the racers drove up the hill to the ski resort. When the van pulled up to the base of the hill, the athletes could see a single, narrow trail covered with man-made snow. And on the trail itself, stuck in the snow like candy canes, were . . . slalom gates. Pampeago was having a slalom, not a giant slalom.

The race organizers told Bill they had notified each national ski federation of the change, but curiously, only the Italians seemed to be aware of it. The Germans, for example, had no slalom skis whatsoever; they would have to race on their longer, less maneuverable giant slalom skis. The change surprised the American downhillers, too. They didn't mind competing in giant slalom, but being downhillers, they condescended to run slalom only when absolutely necessary—that is, only when the slalom was part of a combined downhill. (In combined downhill, racers competed in a downhill one day and a slalom the next. Whoever skied the best overall was the winner.) Most of the American downhillers were miserable, just miserable, on slalom courses. Because they rarely competed in the event, their world rankings were poor. And because their rankings were poor, they usually got three-digit starting numbers. By the time they got to race there would be holes in the course the size of Subarus. This would not be fun. When Todd Kelly saw the slalom gates he said, "Let's go to St. Anton, now." His shins still hurt from the crash Saturday afternoon, and he didn't think smacking them against slalom gates would make them feel any better. Tim "Swampy" LaMarche, an assistant coach and a devotee of the downhill cult, stuck a sign in the window of his van: "Just say no to slalom."

But Egan insisted on staying, so they stayed. He figured it wouldn't hurt the racers to work on their turns, even if they had to do it in a slalom. Besides, they didn't have anywhere else to go; the team wasn't supposed to arrive in St. Anton for another day.

The race committee sent the team to a nice hotel—or what was certain to be a nice hotel as soon as it was finished. To get through the lobby, the racers had to step over the carpenters who were busy sawing wood for the dining room. Upstairs, workers were still pouring cement floors. That afternoon, the sound of the racers' boom boxes was overwhelmed by the whine of a circular saw.

At dinner, Egan passed out the racing bibs. Tommy Moe would start fifty-fourth, and his number was the lowest among the Americans. Reggie Crist had number one hundred sixteen, AJ one hundred thirty. There were one hundred forty guys in the race.

Inspection was held early the next morning. Because of the shortage of snow, and because this was hardly a major race, the course was only forty seconds long (a typical World Cup slalom run took about a minute). That is, it was forty seconds long for the fastest guys. For the American downhillers, who hadn't been getting much slalom training, it was closer to forty-five or fifty. Nobody had a good day, but Kyle Rasmussen came close. He didn't like the way his Head skis felt in the first run, so he kicked them off and put on Steve Porino's Volkls. (If all sports you can, then you are a Volkl fan.) In the second run he did much better, and finished in the top forty—not a horrible result, considering the size of the field.

AJ had a decent day, too. His starting number was so high that it wasn't important for him to get out of bed early. So while the other racers ate breakfast, he slept. While they trudged up to the hill, he ate. While they inspected the course, he watched a movie on the video player in his room. He walked up to the race hill about fifteen minutes before he was supposed to start. On the way up the chair lift he inspected the course—glanced at it, really. "You don't need to inspect a highway to know how to drive," he said. AJ didn't expect much from this race. The course would be so full of craters by the time he skied that he knew he had a better chance of getting seriously hurt than he did of winning. Still, he had something to gain by competing. AJ, ranked in the top five in the world in downhill, was three thousandth in slalom, mainly because he hadn't competed in the event in more than a year. All he had to do was finish this race to improve his ranking by a couple thousand places. If he improved his ranking he would get better starting numbers in the future, and he would heighten his chances of doing well in combined downhill events. Finally AJ made his two runs, skiing well enough to beat half the field. In doing so, he improved his slalom ranking to three hundredth in the world. Alberto Tomba, the Italian slalom superstar, had nothing to fear, but AJ was still pleased.

Soon after the race ended, Bill Egan and Jim Tracy put some bags and skis into the cargo truck and drove it out of town. Thirty minutes later, the downhillers also got ready to leave Pampeago. When they had finished loading their van, they realized they had too many bags with them; they wouldn't be comfortable during the day-long ride to St. Anton. They decided to catch up to the cargo truck so they could get rid of some stuff. Bill Hudson was driving, and he punched it. Hudson's racing motto was controlled aggression, but there was nothing controlled about the way he drove. The van screamed downhill toward the valley, the engine whining and the tires hollering in the turns. Steve Porino, sitting next to Bill in the front seat, had to clutch the dashboard to keep from being thrown out the passenger window. The van caught up with Egan and Tracy at a gas station in the valley. When Hudson got out of the van, he saw thick white smoke billowing from the overheated front brakes. And then he laughed and said, "Nice!"

After a day of slalom racing, Bill had enjoyed getting back to downhill—even if he'd had to do it on a narrow mountain road, in a white Volkswagen van.

11

Getting Weird in Garmisch

The Christmas vacation passed in a blur. The downhillers spent ten joyous days at home, and then packed their clothes and their ski gear for another long stay in creaky old Europe. In previous years, they had prolonged the break as long as possible and had flown back to Europe just in time for the start of downhill training in Garmisch, Germany, site of the Kandahar race. But it had never really worked very well. Bill Egan felt jet lag was one reason his kids had skied poorly in Garmisch in 1991. (Another obvious reason was that they had been allowed only one training run on the grimy, snowless course.) This year, Bill told the athletes to fly into Zurich, the team's traditional European meeting place, a few days early. The racers hated the idea of cutting short their vacation, but they knew Bill was right and didn't argue with him. Leaving home early was hardest on Kyle Rasmussen: When he got into the car to go to the airport, his son, Anthony, not quite two years old, stood in the doorway and cried. About that time, television started airing the commercial Kyle had made for Visa, the credit card company. Seeing the commercial, Anthony would toddle to the TV, touch the screen, and say, "Da-da." Kyle always felt guilty when Linda told him things like that.

A couple of days into the new year, the racers warmed up by competing in two Europa Cup super G races in Switzerland. By the time they drove into Garmisch, the site of the first World Cup downhill race of 1992, they had recovered completely from jet lag. It was a good thing, too:

Right on the Edge of Crazy

The 1992 Winter Olympics were only a month away. In December, the Albertville games had seemed far away, and the athletes had not thought or said much about them. But that was changing. More and more, the athletes were fantasizing about competing in the Olympic downhill, the opening event of the games. Only four members of the U.S. Ski Team would get to race. So far, AJ Kitt and Tommy Moe were the only two had qualified for the downhill team. They had done this by finishing in the top fifteen in at least one World Cup downhill race. That left two slots open. If any of the other guys finished in the top fifteen in a World Cup downhill race, he also would qualify automatically. If nobody did, the coaches would examine the racers' overall results and make a choice that way. For Kyle, Bill Hudson, Jeff Olson, and the rest, every race in January would be a new chance to make the Olympic team. And the race in Garmisch, on a relatively easy course, would be the greatest opportunity of all.

But on Wednesday, the first day of training in Garmisch, it seemed that nobody would take advantage of the opportunity. AJ, still skiing well, finished eighth, but none of the others did any better than thirty-fourth. Even the guy who came in thirty-fourth, Jeff Olson, had a rough time. As he steamed toward the finish, he caught his inside edge and nearly crashed.

At Wednesday's team meeting, Ueli Luthi announced that he had invited a promising young technical racer, Paul Casey Puckett, to take one of the four American slots in Sunday's super G race. That meant the slot would not go to a downhiller.

"You guys have had a lot of chances to do something in super G," Ueli said. "I think Paul Casey deserves a chance."

Bill Hudson and Kyle Rasmussen were furious. Yes, Paul Casey had beaten some people in Nor-Am competition in December. But he didn't have any World Cup super G experience. Bill and Kyle didn't think he could beat any of the downhillers head-to-head, and they said so.

"Well, that is the decision," Ueli said. Bill Egan said he supported Ueli.

"That's bullshit," Bill Hudson said.

"It's not bullshit," Ueli snapped.

Hudson was angry that Egan had lined up against him. That seemed to be happening a lot lately. He and Egan had gotten into a similar argument in late December, during their brief stay in St. Anton, Austria. That time, Egan had announced that he had chosen somebody else to take Hudson's slot in the combined downhill. Again Hudson was steamed, and he argued bitterly. Egan, who rarely raised his voice, had found himself literally screaming at his friend. Hudson and his teammates were horrified at the outburst. The coach felt sorry about it too: Later, over drinks in the hotel bar, he muttered, "I must be going out of my mind." The controversy died when the races in St. Anton were snowed out. And yet Hudson and Egan had never patched things up. This new argument had only made things worse. Both men could sense that their friendship was deteriorating. It it hadn't been the same since Hudson's crash in Kitzbühel almost a year earlier. But neither seemed to know how to make things better.

In the end, the argument over the Garmisch super G was also for nothing: Paul Casey Puckett decided not to enter the race, and Tommy Moe, not Hudson or Rasmussen, got his slot.

It was warm that week. In downtown Garmisch, tourists strolled without gloves and hats, and taxi drivers worked in their shirtsleeves. Brown patches showed through the snow on the Alpspitze. During Thursday's inspection, racers were asked not to ski between the gates, lest they wipe away the thin sheet of snow.

AJ Kitt and Kyle Rasmussen skied well that day, but the others seemed to be dragging, as if their minds were somewhere else. Bill Egan speculated that Jeff Olson had been frightened by his near-crash on Wednesday, but Jeff said he simply wasn't feeling well. That night at dinner, Bill Hudson said, "I beat two Slovenians and a Japanese." Unfortunately, they were the only people he had beaten. Egan was most concerned about Tommy Moe, who seemed to be going through the motions. "He has no fire at all. He's skiing like he's just here for the free meals," the coach said privately. Egan, who as a football player had few gifts but lots of fire, felt that losing your fire was the worst possible failing. He couldn't believe Tommy was slacking off already. The downhillers had just returned from a rest; they should have been more fired up than ever. But if somebody needed to be kicked in the ass, Egan was willing to kick him. At the team meeting that night, his remarks seemed to be aimed mostly at Tommy.

"Be competetive," he said. "Don't be a guy who gives up on it. Be competitive. That's why you're here. So don't give up. It's only the first week of January. You're not here to see the sights or screw around with your buddies. You're ski racers. So give it all you've got. You guys ski too well and you pay too big a price to take this lightly now."

Every night after the team meeting, physical therapist Gary Myers set up a folding table in an upstairs lobby and rubbed the kinks out of the athletes' muscles. Kyle needed a rubdown every night to soothe the pain in his back; the congenital defect in his spine was likely to make him sore as long as he kept skiing. Most of the other guys required only an occasional tune-up. Jim Tracy had plugged in the team's video equipment in the same lobby, so the racers took advantage of the opportunity to watch videos while Myers worked. A visitor from the United States had given the athletes videotapes of several recent National Football League playoff games; the grateful racers watched the games several times, fast-forwarding through the commercials. Another night, somebody plugged in the movie *The Silence of the Lambs*; nobody moved until it was over.

The athletes always managed to find lots of ways to pass their free time at races. In Garmisch, Bill Hudson and Steve Porino played backgammon on a tiny, portable board. Whenever Bill had a lucky roll of the dice, he rubbed it in by looking at Steve and saying, "Oh, that's unfortunate." Todd Kelly spent hours and hours with his audio equipment, making cassette tapes for his girlfriend back in the states, whom he called "my woman." Most of the racers tried to make time to send postcards to friends and relatives. AJ was particularly good about it: You could often find him sitting at a desk in his room, scribbling notes and crossing off names in his address book. He sent dozens of cards at a time. One afternoon, a bunch of guys drove to the U.S. Army base in Garmisch to shop at the PX. The racers found they could buy all kinds of great stuff. Somebody bought a copy of *Playboy* magazine. Somebody else bought an electrical adaptor suitable for European current. You needed an adaptor to fit American appliances into European plugs. AJ bought a big box of Froot Loops. He was thrilled. In all his years on the team, he had never found Froot Loops anywhere in Europe. Those Euros just didn't appreciate excellent breakfast food.

The downhillers also played a lot of basketball that week. The Army base had a gymnasium, and the American skiers and coaches played full-court pickup games there almost every afternoon. Jeff Olson, the best basketball player and best all-around athlete, was so aggressive that the other guys often yelled at him to get his elbows down. Todd Kelly, who played backcourt, was all dribble and bluster; he was so serious it was funny. Todd liked to pretend he was Tim Hardaway, his favorite professional player, but he didn't have Hardaway's ball-handling skills: The other guys called him Throwaway. Predictably, Kyle Rasmussen never said a word. He just muscled people out of the way and scored from under the basket. (Few shots were taken from the outside; the object of these games was to bull your way in for the layup.) Bill Hudson, who had springs in his legs, was the best rebounder and fastest runner. Once, Hudson was driving toward the basket when Jeff Olson stepped in and fouled him, hard. Bill crashed to the floor, his knees and elbows slamming loudly against the wood. The rest of the downhillers froze, and the gym went silent.

"You OK?" Bill Egan said.

Hudson got up slowly, but nodded yes. Everyone watched him closely, wondering if he would throw a punch at Jeff, but he didn't. Hudson never even looked at him. Instead, he wiped the dust off his hands and called for the ball so he could take it out at midcourt.

The downhillers' games were always rough. For them, basketball was a contact sport, like hockey or lacrosse. They played the game for aerobic exercise. But they also went to the gym to settle all the grudges that built up after living for a few days or weeks together on the road. Jeff hadn't really meant to hurt Bill. But he was so competitive, and his relationship with Hudson was so strained, that he was always willing to do just about anything to keep Bill from scoring. In a way, this sort of thing was therapeutic. Playing basketball gave the downhillers a chance to run into each other without necessarily starting a fistfight.

The game continued. Tommy Moe, the Golden Child, launched several unmakable shots—and made them. Steve Porino was a solid player, but not a star. Reggie Crist had a sore knee and didn't play much. Bill

Right on the Edge of Crazy

Egan, a five-foot-seven-inch guard who played like five-nine, preferred to pass instead of shoot. And AJ Kitt made up for his lack of skill with determination. Like most of his teammates, he played like he skied.

On Friday, the final day of training, AJ finished second, behind Switzerland's Daniel Mahrer. Soon after AJ's run, the unpredictable Garmisch weather got strange again. First, a chill wind pushed all the warm air over the top of the Alpspitze. Then a fine mist began to form at ground level, like smoke generated by a Hollywood special-effects machine. Within minutes the mist rose to eye level and thickened into fog. Still, the race organizers went ahead with the training run. The fog was thickest at the Troglhang, the steep, turny pitch near the top of the course. Several racers skied through it standing straight up. The fog was so damp that the athletes came out wet, like dogs climbing out of a pond. The snow was slushy, too. Finally, an Italian racer named Luigi Colturi got lost in the soup and crashed. A helicopter picked him up and disappeared into the gray sky. Two more racers were permitted to leave the starting gate before the organizers called it a day. Bill Hudson never got to take his training run that day, and he wasn't sorry. He wasn't interested in skiing in those conditions.

The bad weather came at an inopportune time for Garmisch. The village had recently applied to host the 1997 Alpine World Championships, the next best thing to the Olympics. Putting on a successful World Cup race would enhance its chances of being selected. The Fédération Internationale de Ski was scheduled meet in June to choose among Garmisch and the other applicants— Chamonix, France; Sestriere, Italy; and Laax, Switzerland. The winning village would likely earn big money on hotel bookings, lift tickets, and so on. Beyond that, television would expose the venue to skiers and other tourists around the world. It would be a publicity bonanza, and Garmisch wanted it.

The village had wanted it for a long time: Garmisch had applied for the next two, in 1993 and 1995, but had lost first to Japan, and then, in a close decision, to Spain. But perky, proud, stubborn Garmisch wouldn't take no for an answer. Since 1990 its application committee had been working full-time to woo the Fédération Internationale de Ski. In a glossy promotional magazine published by the German ski federation, the chairman of the committee made Garmisch's feelings clear: "In our opinion it is Germany's turn again."

There was merit to that argument. The village had a lot to recommend it as a site for the World Championships. For one thing, it had history on its side: Garmisch had been the site of the 1936 Winter Olympic Games, a fact that was noted in every tourism brochure. It had also hosted the 1978 Alpine World Championships. The Kandahar course was a proven site for the premier event of the championships, the men's downhill. The village's location, close to Munich and Innsbruck, Austria, was ideal. And Garmisch was uniquely suited to host such a big event. For a European ski town, it was unusually large—easily large enough to accommodate all the athletes, coaches, and press who would show up. Everyone agreed it was a handsome place, full of tony boutiques and bakeries and bright architecture. What more could you ask for?

The glossy promotional magazine included an interview with Klaus Mayr, an official of the German ski federation.

"Mr. Mayr," the interviewer asked, "what experiences have the contestants had until now with Garmisch-Partenkirchen?"

"To put it briefly, the very best," Mayr replied. "The slopes in Garmisch are marvelously well suited for every demand of Alpine competition. Since the last World Championship in Garmisch in 1978, we have had very good experience there and have registered many successes."

Huh? In 1988, 1989, and 1990 the Garmisch downhill had been canceled because of a lack of snow. In 1991 the organizers had gotten the race off, but blades of grass were showing through the ice. No new snow had fallen this week, either. The snow cover in January 1992 was as thin as the glossy paper in that promotional magazine. Sure, the slopes in Garmisch were marvelously well suited for the World Championships. Except they hardly ever had any snow on them.

Saturday was suddenly and strangely cold, the sort that pricks the toes and fingers. The freezing air had made everything hard—the snow, the trees, the frosted mud on the side of the course. In the morning, a cloud of gray-white fog lingered near the top of the hill. Even the festive race decorations looked sad. In the finish, hot-air balloons bloomed like gaudy flowers and the snow sculptures looked old and decayed. Everything seemed wrong, off kilter. The crowd was restive, as if waiting for something bad to happen. Weird and mystical forces were at work. It was a terrible day for a ski race.

Things started to go wrong right away. Berni Huber of Germany, the third racer, made a bad mistake and caught his skis on a gate at the top of the Troglhang pitch. He spun around backward, launched into the air, and landed hard on the base of his spine. Then he tumbled into a fence. It was an unlikely mistake because this was Huber's home course. In the finish, the German crowd watched silently as the hideous crash was shown again and again on the big TV screen. Soon a helicopter fluttered up the hill to collect the injured racer. It took more than twenty minutes to evacuate Huber. He had broken a vertebra in his back, pulled a thigh muscle, and severely wrenched an ankle.

As soon as the race was restarted things got weird again. The next racer, Hannes Zehentner, another German, missed a gate, further blackening the crowd's mood. Leonhard Stock's boot came unbuckled near the top of the course; the Austrian tried to fasten it as he speeded through the flats below the Troglhang, but it was no use. He had to pull off. Switzerland's Daniel Mahrer, the 1991 winner, left the starting gate without battening down the lens on his goggles. When he got up to speed the wind in his eyes nearly blinded him, so he couldn't find the line he had wanted to take down the hill. In the finish he found he was about a second behind the leader, Patrick Ortlieb. He yanked off the glasses and spiked them at the feet of a television cameraman, no doubt making his eyewear sponsor as miserable as he was. Only eight of the top racers had skied, and already four were out of it. What was going on here? It was the craziest World Cup race of the season, maybe of any season.

Things got worse. The Garmisch downhill was Rob Boyd's first since undergoing back surgery in the off-season. The Canadian star, who had finished third in Kitzbühel a year earlier, had skied tentatively in training, but that didn't surprise anyone: After an injury, racers needed time to get comfortable with the speed of downhill. But Boyd, number twelve, never had a chance to get used to it. On race day he caught his right edge as he sliced through the last turn. He seemed to regain his balance, but then his left ski snagged in the snow and blew off. Boyd went airborne—he flew right past coach Jim Tracy, who was standing in the turn—and tumbled into the hay bales, blowing out his right knee. End of season. It took another fifteen minutes to load him on the helicopter.

Norway's Atle Skaardal, racer fourteen, was the next victim. He went down where Boyd did, only harder. It was as if gremlins were crouching in the turn, waiting to grab racers by the ankles as they passed. As Skaardal entered the turn he caught an inside edge and his legs suddenly shot apart. He pitched forward between his skis, landing mostly on his face. Then he bounced high into the air, like a football someone had spiked in the end zone. Skaardal broke through the hay bales on the side of the course and toppled a dozen spectators like bowling pins. Arms, legs, and skis flew everywhere. Nobody in the crowd was hurt as badly as the racer was. He was bleeding from the forehead and his legs hurt. The doctor on course patched the cut and Skaardal, more or less conscious, managed to stand. After twenty minutes Skaardal put on his skis and slid nervously into the finish. A helicopter awaited. Skaardal had hoped the injuries weren't bad, but by the next day he was on a plane back to Norway. He had torn the ligaments in his left foot and stretched the ones in his right knee. Season over. By now, some of the coaches in the finish were afraid to have their racers ski down. Things were out of control.

As Skaardal hobbled off and the course workers replaced the hay bales, racer fourteen, AJ Kitt, stood in the starting shack, shivering in the cold. AJ never sought out information on how his competitors were doing in a race, so he had no way of knowing exactly what had happened to Huber, Boyd, and Skaardal. But it was clear from the long delays that something was terribly wrong on the course. AJ tried not to let it bother him. Downhill was a dangerous sport; people got hurt. He couldn't do anything about that. It helped, too, that he didn't know exactly how bad things were. He didn't fantasize about crashes as he stood there in the starting gate. For AJ, the real challenge was just to keep his concentration. He was only partly successful. For the first few minutes of the Skaardal delay he was eager, ready to go. But as the time dragged on he got bored. Instead of thinking about the course and how to attack it, he started to think about when he would finally get to race, and then, as he became more frustrated, about whether he would ever get to race. Gary Myers, who took care of the racers at the start, tried to keep AJ loose and warm, but there wasn't much Myers could do for his concentration.

Right on the Edge of Crazy

Finally AJ was allowed to race. Not surprisingly, he felt ragged at first, as if he had just stepped out of bed and into his bindings. He flew a long way off the middle jump—farther, really, than he wanted to—and found he often couldn't hold an edge because the snow was so slick. To the coaches' relief he skied through the last turn without crashing. Still, the turn cost him: He skied too wide and lost time. He finished in 1:51.69, fifth place at the moment. He would end up eighth.

AJ, still wheezing, grabbed a radio and gave a course report to his teammates at the top of the hill. Don't set the edges too hard in the tops of the turns, he said; they won't hold. Just maintain a good body position and make disciplined turns. Oh, and one other thing.

"Be aggressive," he said. "Don't hold back at all. Just grit your teeth and be aggressive."

And then the demons took over again. A moment after AJ finished his report, Frenchman Luc Alphand, one of the most aggressive—some would say least careful—skiers on the circuit, did the splits in Jim Tracy's turn and crashed into the hay bales, deepening the dents made there by Atle Skaardal and Rob Boyd. Alphand was lucky, if a person who severely strains his groin and stomach muscles can be considered lucky.

For Tommy Moe, racer thirty-three, Garmisch was a special challenge. The course gave him the willies, mostly because of his terrifying ass-plant off the finish jump the year before. What Bill Egan had interpreted as lack of effort was mostly just nervousness. Now, as Tommy waited in the start, racers were dropping as if there were snipers in the woods. And it was happening while the course was still in reasonably good shape. This, clearly, was a scary situation. Tommy had a right to be freaked out now.

But after a few seconds on the course, he forgot his fears. That bleak day in Garmisch, Tommy got into the sort of groove all athletes search for, a place where they can do what they do without fear or even thought. Damn the accidents! On the top part of the course he skied as well as he ever had; he was thirteenth fastest at the first split and eleventh at the second. At the third checkpoint, which came more than halfway into the run, he was sixteenth. Tommy was cruising, and he knew it. He couldn't tell exactly how well he was doing, of course, but he knew he was having a great race, knew he was flying.

And then things got screwy again. Tommy was streaking into Hell, the fastest part of the course, a place where people hit eighty miles an hour, when suddenly, impossibly, his skis turned sideways. Tommy's first impulse was to save himself. He was sure he would be thrown sideways out of his bindings. He was already bracing for a tremendous crash when, somehow, he managed to point his skis back down the hill. He was alive! But all his speed was gone. He was crawling. Tommy thought, What the hell . . . ? It was the feeling people get when they're driving along a country road, mellowing out, and the next thing they know the car's in a ditch and deer guts are in the radiator. Damn! Tommy thought. All he could figure was that he had hit a snow snake—an S-shaped pile of snow kicked up by other skiers. Whatever the reason, Moe's great run was over. He trickled under the finish banner in 1:53.69, twenty-seventh place. Not bad at all! But oh, what it could have been!

"I was cooking, and the next thing I knew I was sideways, man," Tommy said in the finish. "I would have been top ten, I think, if I hadn't made that mistake."

Top ten! That would have been the best World Cup finish of his career, the kind of finish that would have given him confidence for the rest of the season, and for the Olympics. But suddenly that finish was gone, poof. One minute Tommy had been in an amazing groove, and the next minute he was out of it. It was galling. The worst part was he didn't know how he had found that groove to begin with. It was one of the mysteries of the day.

Tommy tried to make his way to the clothing bag now, but it wasn't easy: The place was teeming with journalists interviewing the apparent winner, Patrick Ortlieb. Ortlieb, whose beefy build seemed more suited to rugby than downhill, was popular among the American racers: He knew English, had a wry sense of humor, and liked to party. One after another, the journalists elicited a four-sentence version of his life story, as they had done with AJ in Val d'Isère; and as they had done then, they all planned to write glowing things about this new Austrian star, this challenger to Franz Heinzer. The German fans, though, were glum: Their heroes, their countrymen, had lost. Worse, they had lost to . . . an Austrian.

But wait! Today, nothing was certain. As Ortlieb stood in the finish, shaking hands and posing for the cameras and waving his long Head racing skis in the air, Markus Wasmeier, racer thirty-eight, a German, flashed down the hill and won the race. Swiped it, just like that. He beat

Ortlieb by six hundredths of a second. The Austrian looked stricken, as if someone had poked him in the stomach with the butt end of a rifle. Wasmeier thrust his arms in the air and polkaed around the finish in his downhill skis. The Germans went ga-ga. Everyone knew Wasmeier was capable of great things—he had won the Wengen downhill in 1987 and placed second there in 1988, and was known as one of the most elegant skiers in the world. But a bad crash in Japan had set him back, and he had never quite regained his form. Well, what a time to make a comeback!

It was a shocker, all right. Austrian TV had discontinued its broadcast of the event after about the thirtieth racer. Congratulations to Patrick Ortlieb, the commentators had said. Congratulations to Austria. So long. When Wasmeier finished, the announcers had to go back on the air and say, in effect, Oops. Sorry we got you all excited. Wasmeier's victory was the ultimate stroke of weirdness, the impossible becoming real.

For the rest of the American team, there would be no finish-line polkas. Reggie Crist started thirty-fifth and finished thirty-sixth. It was an improvement over the year before, when he had been fifty-seventh at Garmisch, but not as much of an improvement as he would have liked. In what he would call "the worst race of my life," Kyle Rasmussen finished sixty-ninth. He also had problems with his equipment. The ice on the course burned the bottoms of his skis so badly that the edges wouldn't hold; he had to get rid of that pair after the race. Steve Porino, who finished sixty-second, couldn't blame his equipment. "My skis were holding really well," he said, "I just skied like shit." Steve had viewed the race as a way to slow down his free-fall toward retirement, but things hadn't worked out. His career was still slipping away from him. Todd Kelly was fiftieth. Bill Hudson, still skiing technically well, but slowly, came in sixty-fourth. He was inclined to throw a fit in the finish—spike his helmet or yell an ugly word or something—but some of his girlfriend's relatives had come to see him, so he didn't think he should. Maybe some other time.

Jeff Olson had another disastrous day. About four gates into the race, he tipped over and slid a few yards on his hip. He sprang up and kept going. Bill Egan, who saw the fall, radioed down to Ueli Luthi, "I don't think Jeff is going to make it down to you. I hope he can find a safe place to pull off." Jeff, furious with himself, considered quitting, but he figured he had to get to the bottom somehow, so he might as well ski between the gates. Besides, his parents were in town for the race; they'd be expecting him. At the first split Jeff was more than two seconds behind Markus Wasmeier. The American's time on the top section was the slowest of the day. He was "DFL"—racer slang for "dead fucking last."

He skied badly the rest of the way, too, finishing in 1:56.06, sixty-sixth place. (Kyle Rasmussen's feelings of humiliation deepened: Even with a fall at the top of the course, Jeff had beaten him by a second.) In the finish, Jeff made one last dramatic mistake. He ducked under the banner, threw his skis sideways, and went down hard on his side, just as Kyle had done in Garmisch the year before. Like Kyle, Jeff seemed to pick up speed as his stiff body skipped toward the padded fence at the end of the corral. He hit it skis first. Pow! He was luckier than Kyle had been: The fence opened up and let him through. Jeff, stunned but unhurt, found himself in the crowd, next to a table where a woman was selling wieners. Weird. He cleared his mind for a minute, then went to join his teammates. Later, he wished he had smiled, introduced himself to the wiener lady, and ordered a couple of hot dogs to go.

The Americans skied poorly in the super G, as usual. After a downhill, the racers couldn't get excited about a super G. Even the usually intense AJ seemed only half interested in racing. Afterwards, the athletes and coaches had some decisions to make. The next weekend, two downhill races would be held on the devilish and horrifying course in Kitzbühel, Austria. The athletes could go there or they could drive to Wengen, Switzerland, for a couple of Europa Cup downhills. In two weeks, the whole team would gather in Wengen for the World Cup race.

For some, the choice was easy. AJ definitely would go to Kitzbühel to challenge Franz Heinzer. Tommy Moe definitely would not. Tommy felt ski racing should be fun, and Kitzbühel had not been fun the year before. He had spent the whole week scared out of his gourd. Well, to hell with that. This year, he wasn't going. (Tommy ended up not racing in the Europa Cup downhills, either; instead, he went off by himself to compete in some technical races). For others, the decision was more complicated. Todd Kelly, Kyle Rasmussen, and Steve Porino wanted to ski Kitzbühel (well, Steve sort of wanted to), but it didn't make any sense for them to do so. If they hoped to make the Olympic team, they needed to go someplace where they could win a race, or at least come close. In Kitzbühel, the most they could hope for would be to get to the finish without losing consciousness. No, they had to go to Wengen. Bill Hudson did too. Never mind that he wasn't sure he wanted to leap off the ledge of the Mausefalle again. And never mind that the thought of his doing so made Bill Egan groan in his sleep. The plain truth was that Hudson wasn't skiing well enough to go to Kitzbühel. He just wasn't ready. Egan felt differently about Jeff Olson. Jeff had had a bad race in Garmisch, but he was one of the few guys on the team whose skiing seemed to be improving as the season went on. Also, Jeff had a lot of experience in Kitzbühel. So what if most of it was painful? He knew the course, knew what it took to get to the bottom standing up. Besides, he really wanted to go. Egan couldn't say no.

Reggie Crist agonized over the decision for a long time. On one hand, he really liked the way he was skiing. Over the Christmas break, Reggie had gone home to Sun Valley, Idaho, and skied his brains out. But he didn't ski any gates. Instead, he put on his favorite headband, waxed his giant slalom boards, and had a wild time. The toughest run at Sun Valley was called Exhibition, or, if you were a local, Exy. Exy was a long, narrow, almost vertical pitch with moguls the size of Volkswagens. (If Sun Valley had wanted to be honest, it would have named the slope Severe Cartilage Injury.) A lot of people who considered themselves expert skiers looked like stumbling drunks on this run. Reggie spent much of his vacation shredding Exy at full speed, the sleeves of his jacket flap-flap-flapping like sails smacking at the wind. As he blasted down the hill, kicking up clouds of snow behind him, skiers on the chair lift whooped and hollered and cheered for this white-haired snow god, this dancer in Head skis. When he heard them cheer, Reggie, not normally overburdened with self-confidence, allowed himself to think, Damn, I'm good. Well, he still felt that way when he had gotten to Garmisch. Thirty-sixth place was less than he had hoped for, but at least he had gone for it. At least he had punched it. Still, he wasn't sure he should go to Kitzbühel. He wanted to ski the course known as the Streif, but not if it would endanger his chances of making the Olympic team. After the Garmisch super G, Reggie went to Ueli Luthi's hotel room and asked for his advice.

"It's up to you," Ueli said. "Probably you can get a good result in Wengen. I also think you can handle Kitzbühel."

And Reggie thought: You're right. I can. Reggie had skied the Streif several times in training the year before; he had fought the dragon before, and had survived. The more he thought about it, the less interested he was in going to Wengen. Who needs a Europa Cup race? Fuck that, Reggie thought. The Hahnenkamm is the Super Bowl of downhill ski racing. I'm going.

On Tuesday, the downhillers split up into two groups. One group drove off to Wengen for the Europa Cup races. Reggie, Jeff, and AJ climbed into the Passat for the drive to Kitzbühel. It was dark when they reached the city limits.

"It's amazing how your blood pressure goes up when you get to this place," Reggie said.

"Yep," said Jeff, who had been quiet—sleeping, or just thinking—during the two-hour ride from Garmisch. "This is my wake-up call."

AJ was riding in the back seat, looking out the window at the brightly illuminated downhill course, a flat white snake wriggling up the mountainside. "There it is," he said. "The Streif. God, I'm so psyched."

Then he addressed the mountain directly.

"I'm going to kick your ass."

12

Bill Egan's
Vertical Children

On Wednesday, the team's first morning in Kitzbühel, Bill Egan rode the cable car up the hill for the first of two training runs. He was nervous. To the racers, two runs meant two opportunities to overcome their fear and learn the course. But to Bill, it meant two chances for disaster. After the 1991 race—in which two guys, Bill Hudson and Kyle Rasmussen, were seriously hurt, and a third, Eric Keck, would have been if he hadn't been so large and faithful—Egan couldn't help being edgy. In all his years of coaching, that week was the worst. All he could think of was Hudson going over the fence and . . . not getting up. Just not getting up. Egan remembered looking across the course, pleading for the racer to stand up, but of course it didn't happen. Sometimes, Egan considered how close Hudson had come to being killed, and it made him feel ill. It also made him feel protective. When he discussed the accident, Egan tended to refer to the racer as "one of my best friends," even though their friendship had faltered since the accident. Calling Hudson a close friend was Egan's way of explaining how badly the injury had affected him, Egan. If he ever had to endure another week like that, he told himself, that would be it. He would take his teaching certificate and become a history instructor somewhere.

When Egan skied slowly down the course that Wednesday morning, he found the Mausefalle jump—the setting of his nightmares—substantially changed from the year before. For one thing, the course was wider. If you crash-landed you would slide for a while, losing speed all the way, before you creamed something. For another thing, the nets had been extended up the hill, making it impossible for someone to ski over the fence, as Keck and Hudson had done. Curtis Christian, a Canadian who coached the British downhillers, called the new net the Keck Catcher. (Probably Hudson deserved to be immortalized, too, but he wasn't.)

But the most significant change was in the jump itself: It was a lot smaller. The lip had been shaved down so the racer would have a clear view of where he was going, which would improve his chances of landing safely.

Egan liked the refinements in the course, except he thought it would make the section faster than ever. With the smaller jump and the wider landing, most guys would feel free to really punch it. They'd carry a lot of speed into the carousel turn at the bottom of the hill, and into the Steilhang—the harrowing right turn where Brian Stemmle had almost been killed in 1989.

As always, a lot of racers were scared off by the Streif. On the first day of training in Val d'Isère back in December (to cite one example), one hundred one had gone down the course. Now, in Kitzbühel, only sixty-three guys showed up for the first run. That meant thirty-eight guys—tough, sleek, fearless characters—had made other plans for the week. A lot of them were in Wengen, competing against the rest of the Americans in the Europa Cup races.

The first training run began at 11 A.M. Normally, a World Cup race has four to six forerunners, or human sacrifices. In Kitzbühel, the race organizers scheduled eight forerunners, none of whom was really up to the challenge. The first guy flew so far off the Mausefalle that the sight made Egan gasp. Another kid smacked into the net just below the carousel turn, bounced off, and kept going. These guys looked like twelve-year-olds trying to drive Indy cars. But somehow they all made it to the finish standing up.

AJ Kitt had drawn number one. Bill Egan liked his chances at Kitzbühel. In recent weeks, AJ had started turning slightly better to the right than to the left. It wasn't anything AJ could explain, but it was lucky for him that the three hardest turns at Kitzbühel—the carousel, the Steilhang, and the turn before the Hausberg—were all right turns. The course was made for AJ.

Still, when AJ got into the gate that Wednesday morning for the first training run, Bill had the willies. A few seconds before AJ started down the hill, the coach began to talk to himself. "All right, come on now. Come on, AJ, make a good move off that jump, now," he said. AJ came into view just before he reached the Mausefalle jump. "Move!" Bill said, and AJ absorbed the jump nicely. He made a smooth landing and raced toward the compression. "Now get your ass up, get your ass up!" the coach yelled. AJ, who could not possibly have heard Bill, got his ass up. When he set the edge of his left ski to make the carousel turn, Bill shouted, "Get on that fucking thing! Get on it!" AJ made the turn cleanly, then disappeared toward the Steilhang. Mr. Control skied the rest of the course the usual way, and ended up twenty-fifth for the training run. At one point during the two-minute run, AJ was clocked at sixty-six miles an hour. Bill, meanwhile, had stood in place. The whole thing had been much harder on Bill.

And AJ was the least of his worries. Reggie Crist and Jeff Olson were still to come. Egan tried to tell himself not to worry about Reggie. "Reggie will be just fine," he said at one point, mostly to himself. It became sort of a mantra: Reggie will be just fine. Reggie will be just fine. Bill didn't really know that, but he had to believe it. Last year, Bill had allowed Eric Keck to train at Kitzbühel, and Keck had thanked him by taking a high-speed hike in the woods. Now Bill had taken a chance on another racer, and he had to believe Reggie would prove the decision to be sound.

But Reggie had a bad habit: He tended to dive into turns. That's what Bill called it, anyway—diving in. One of the turns in this course was called the carousel. It was like a wheel, with the gate at the hub. To make the turn well, a racer had to ski halfway around the wheel, making a nice, round turn before zipping off toward the Steilhang. If you dove in, that meant that you started at the top of the wheel, then made a beeline toward the hub, cutting off part of the circle. That was the wrong thing to do. If you skied straight toward the gate, you would have to turn extremely hard at the bottom of the wheel, which would cost you speed. And if you really dove in, really took a lot of speed toward the gate, pow! You'd ski right through the bottom of the wheel and land in the net.

On the radio, Bill gave Reggie a warning. "Don't dive into this puppy today," he said. Bill called a lot of things "puppy." "Don't be in a hurry to make the turn."

Soon after, a French racer named Christophe Fivel—people called him Fish—flew into the carousel and . . . dove in. He had to slam on the brakes to keep from whacking the net. Bill cringed. He didn't want Fivel to go on. "Fuck, Fish," he said. "Pull off. Pull off, man."

It was the sort of thing Bill didn't need to see just then. It only heightened his anxiety about Reggie and Jeff. To make things worse, the first twenty skiers had scraped off most of the snow in the carousel, so Reggie would have to turn on what amounted to slippery concrete. The course workers could have softened the snow by sideslipping the turn— skiing down it sideways—but they just stood there, watching. They didn't seem to think it needed it as much as Bill did.

"Fuck," said Bill, who cursed this much only when he was nervous, "I'd like to go out and sideslip that fucker before he comes, because I know he's going to dive in. He always dives into everything."

At the top of the hill, the tones sounded and Reggie dropped into the course. He skied so rigidly off the Mausefalle jump that Bill could only snort and shake his head. Then Reggie approached the carousel. "Come on, Reggie, just don't dive into this fucking thing today," Bill said.

He didn't. He made a sweeping turn—not a perfect one, but a safe one—and moved down the course.

Reggie was just fine.

"That'll do," Bill said. "He was good."

Two down, one to go. Bill loved to watch Jeff Olson ski . . . sometimes. The trouble was, Bill never knew which Jeff Olson would come down the hill—the great athlete or the utterly confused kid. Indeed, Jeff was one of the few racers on the World Cup circuit who seemed capable of winning a race, finishing DFL—dead fucking last—or anything in between. He was so gifted athletically, and so unpredictable emotionally, that almost everything he did was some kind of surprise. Bill never knew what Jeff was going to do, and that scared him. What scared him more was his sense that Jeff didn't know, either.

Jeff had a bad history at Kitzbühel. One year he could see that he was going to crash into the net in the Steilhang, so to minimize injury he had leaped into it head-first. It turned out to be a good idea: He wasn't hurt at all. In 1990, he crash-landed off the Hausberg jump and broke his collarbone. Now, as Bill thought of all that had happened to Jeff on the Streif, he was beginning to regret bringing him here.

"OK, Olie," Bill said on the radio. "Make a good move off that first jump. Reggie, when he came through here, looked like he had a stick right up his butt. He didn't do anything."

Jeff skied over the jump a minute later, and he didn't do anything, either. As he moved through the air, his body was completely erect, more or less in the position of a Gumby doll. It was not an aerodynamic pose. But he landed cleanly and made the carousel turn competently. He finished thirtieth, which was exactly halfway between winning and being DFL.

That afternoon, all three Americans improved their times, and AJ finished third. Egan and his colleagues were just happy they'd made it through the first day.

"Today was pretty good," Ueli Luthi said at that night's team meeting. "In Kitzbühel, it's always good if everyone is still walking in the evening."

Egan celebrated with a schnapps at the bar.

Jeff Olson began his training run the next morning with a mistake: After making a good move off the Mausefalle jump, his first good move of the week, he nearly packed it in when he caught an edge in the compression. OK, he told himself. You're all right. He skied well through the middle third of the course. He had a lot of speed as he crossed the traverse. The snow was hard—"bulletproof," he would say later—with ridges so pronounced you could climb them like stairs. His eyeballs shivered and his bones jangled as he approached the Zielschuss, the freefall to the finish. For sheer terror, the Zielschuss was hard to beat: It made the world's best skiers stiffen up like beginners taking their first lesson.

A moment before Jeff got to the Zielschuss his right ski blew off. Just came off his foot. He never figured out whether it was because he caught an edge, or just because the ski gods were angry with him that month. But there it went—*poof*. He hit the jump at seventy miles an hour, on one ski.

Olson's mind played at fast-forward.

He thought, Shit.

Maybe I can pull this off on one ski.

No way can I do this on one ski.

That's it. Season's over.

This isn't going to feel good.

It didn't. When he got into the air, his right leg kicked out to one side, and for that moment he was part downhiller and part Rockette. He landed on his left foot—the one with the ski on it—and then on his ass, and then on his back and shoulders. He slid to the bottom of the hill and lay there in a crucifixion pose. His right pole was gone. His left pole lay beneath his helmet. His left ski, more loyal than the right, was still on his foot. It had stayed with him all the way down the slope.

OK, Jeff told himself. Relax. He did an inventory of his body parts, as Eric Keck had done at Kitzbühel the year before. Yep. Everything's still here. Doesn't seem as if anything's broken. His ass hurt, that was all. Somewhere along the way, maybe when he was sliding, Jeff had coughed up a gob of goo. He sat up and spat—and the goo stuck in his face mask. What a day. Someone came to help him up. He slid and stepped to the side of the course. Within a few minutes the American coaches, all of whom were still on the hill, got word that he was all right.

During the car ride back to the hotel, he sighed and said, "Thank you, Lord."

That afternoon, Austrian television showed the crash twice, including once in slow motion, but Jeff didn't see the TV coverage. He saw the spill for the first time that evening, on a videotape made by one of the coaches. Jim Tracy had set up the team's video monitor in the dining room of the Schwarzer Adler. Before dinner, Jeff, AJ, and Reggie gathered there to watch themselves race. The tape of Jeff's crash was not clear because it was made at such a long distance. But when the downhillers played it in slow motion, they could clearly see Jeff's ski floating away from his foot, like a rocket booster separating from the space shuttle. They could also see him struggling to keep his balance as he disappeared off the Zielschuss jump. The racers replayed the tape several times. AJ and Reggie had a good laugh over it, but Jeff didn't laugh. He just watched, shaking his head slowly. This moment of stark terror was not easy for Jeff to witness. We all have scrapes with disaster, but few of us have to relive them later, on videotape. After dinner, Jeff's teammates had a good time playing backgammon and listening to music, but Jeff just lay on his bed, icing his bottom and reading *It Was on Fire When I Lay Down on It*, a book of inspirational tidbits by Robert Fulghum. He hardly spoke to anyone the rest of the evening. In a way, he was still frightened. In his opinion, the Zielschuss was about the worst place on the World Cup circuit to crash. Todd Brooker, the Canadian, had pretty much ended his career in a crash there; Jeff could have, too. Now he was feeling just a bit sorry for himself. He asked himself, Why did that have to happen to me? He had skied scared all last season because of the same kind of near-disaster. Why did it have to happen to him again? It had been a bad day, as bad as any Jeff could remember. He felt so depressed that he went to sleep without telling anyone on the team that it was his twenty-sixth birthday.

The starting order for Friday's race was drawn early Thursday evening, in the center of town, across from the Drop In Disco. The world's top fifteen downhillers were there, standing atop a trailer festooned with lights and banners. AJ Kitt was among them, of course. The event was shown live on European TV. Fourteen of the athletes wore their team uniform jackets. AJ had on a brown leather jacket with the Rossignol symbol, a red R, on the left breast. Own program.

The crowd packed in close to the trailer. In Europe, World Cup race organizers liked to draw the starting order in public: The TV cameras always showed up and provided some free publicity. Besides, the public draw gave people a chance to be near their racing heroes—closer, as a matter of fact, than sports fans in America could ever dream of getting to, say, football's Jerry Rice or baseball's Roger Clemens. In Europe, you could walk right up to a ski racer after the public draw and get his autograph. Then he walked back to his hotel and you walked back to yours.

The Austrian fans came to the Kitzbühel draw in the greatest numbers, but the Swiss supporters, especially the members of the Franz Heinzer Fan Club ("The Idiots," according to AJ), were the most vocal. Many had gotten drunk and painted the Swiss flag on their faces (or maybe it was the other way around). By now they were making quite a racket with their bells and chants and whoops. The event lasted awhile: The master of ceremonies spoke several languages, and a lot of each one. He interviewed the racers after their numbers were drawn. Leonhard Stock, whom AJ had beaten in Val d'Isère, drew number two. Then AJ drew and got number three. The announcer asked him, in English, if he liked the number.

"Yeah, sure," AJ said. "When I go after Stock, I ski fast." AJ smiled. Stock managed to smile back.

Friday morning was cloudy. The faraway sunlight cast a dull, silver-yellow light on the hill, like a daguerreotype. On the ground, it was the usual Kitzbühel scene: Thousands of people scaled the hill next to the Zielschuss and thousands more lined the finish corral. The public-address announcer—the same fellow who had emceed the public drawing the night before—jabbered incessantly for an hour leading up to the race. It didn't matter, because few people tried to carry on conversations: Most communication was done in the form of hooting and screaming and singing "Olé, olé, olé, olé," by far the most-often-heard song in Kitzbühel that week. The members of the Franz Heinzer Fan Club cracked their whips and rang their cowbells and wore their white caps. They planted a "Hopp Franz" sign near the finish. Other Swiss fans hung a sign for William Besse. The Austrian fans displayed a banner for the team in general.

Some young, sloshed Americans vacationing in Kitzbühel hung a sign for AJ Kitt just below the Mausefalle. The gang had met the American downhillers the night before at the Schwarzer Adler. Their banner bore a slogan that Bill Egan had suggested.

"AJ is best," it said. "Fuck the rest." It was in plain view of the TV cameras.

AJ felt good that morning, felt ready. He went out of the gate feeling confident, unafraid of the Streif, and then he screwed up. He skied too low in the carousel turn and ended up near the net. He had to cut back up the hill to get to the next gate, at the entrance to the Steilhang. He knew he had made a mistake, but he thought he could overcome it. He made a lot of small, technical errors after that. In the traverse, for example, he skied up the side of the hill instead of letting the skis run across it. And he leaned back as he went over the finish jump, which wasn't something he usually did. Normally, AJ was a good jumper. Then he shot under the banner, looked up, and found himself in third place after three racers. Skiing behind Leonhard Stock hadn't helped him. At the bottom of the corral, AJ cocked his right ski pole and used it to smack the fence.

Right on the Edge of Crazy

What had gone wrong? All AJ could say was that he didn't have "that edge"—the competetive edge that helps you win. He had learned that you could be in great condition and have a sunny attitude and feel as if you were born with skis for feet . . . and still not win, or even come close. Worse, you could think you had the edge when you didn't have it, and you wouldn't find out until you got to the finish and found yourself third in a field of three. After he smacked the fence, AJ stood alone and smoldered for several minutes. He was pissed. Fortunately, he told himself before he left the finish area, I'll get another chance tomorrow.

Franz Heinzer, racer number fifteen, was like a trapped animal in the starting gate, twitching and snorting, his eyes unblinking. He looked as if he would bite someone if he didn't get out soon. Then the beast burst out of the cage. Later, when Bill Egan saw Heinzer's run on videotape, he marveled at how aggressively the racer had poled out of the start. The first slope on the Streif was so steep that most racers were content to drop out of the starting shack and fall quickly into a tuck. Heinzer shoved himself downhill as if something were after him. He skied so smartly over the Mausefalle jump that he was able to land in his tuck, which helped him to build speed for the carousel turn. He skied it effortlessly, and went on to handle the Steilhang the same way. At each World Cup downhill race, timing devices were placed in several spots on the course so fans could get a sense of how the racers were doing relative to the rest of the field. In the finish, the scoreboard flashed Heinzer's first intermediate time—32.81 seconds, the fastest yet. He was on his way.

Heinzer's run was a beautiful thing, and rare. He had the grace and strength and sense of purpose of a ballet dancer. No downhiller ever looks exactly like a dancer, of course: The mountain will not permit it. For the dancer, the stage is still and flat, a blank space that waits to be colored with movement. But for the skier, the stage keeps rising and dipping, changing shape and texture, dealing surprises. The course, especially one like the Streif, determines when the racer moves, and how. And yet in their best moments, downhillers move as if to music, skiing with the rhythm and power and confidence of Nureyev. Franz Heinzer skied that way on Friday in Kitzbühel. The run seemed choreographed, with Heinzer performing the dance brilliantly.

Heinzer stayed in a low tuck throughout his run, even when he was going into a sharp a turn. This was a man seeking speed, a man doing his best to be a bullet. At every moment, he projected his lean, muscular body down the hill, toward the finish. Imagine a man getting out of an armchair. He throws forward his shoulders first, then extends his arms out front to pull himself up. Heinzer looked that way throughout his run—shoulders forward, elbows in front of the knees, a man going some-where. The racer who skis slowly, who is unsure or afraid, leans subtly backward, pulling his elbows in and sitting back. He takes a seat in his armchair.

The Swiss star beat teammate Daniel Mahrer by a little less than two tenths of a second. Swiss racers also placed third and fifth. Later, the American downhillers came up with a new name for the Kitzbühel race. They called it the Swiss National Championships.

A light fog crept up the hill before Reggie Crist left the gate. Bill Egan didn't want it to upset him.

"That fog isn't going to screw you up at all," he said into the radio. "You're fine, OK?"

Yes, he was just fine. Reggie skied pretty well to the traverse, where he got sideways and almost, as the racers liked to say, biffed it. He dumped a lot of speed and came in at 2:00.50, forty-second place. In the finish area, he hit himself in the forehead—he had forgotten to ski well, apparently—and then put his hands on his hips and gently shook his head. With Reggie, you never got bursts of emotion—he didn't spike his helmet or holler foul words. He just stood there looking bereft.

There was one consolation for Reggie: According to the downhillers' tradition, he was no longer a rookie. He had finished the race at Kitz-bühel.

Jeff Olson skied solidly on the top of the course. But in the turn just below the Hausberg, the one where he had broken his collarbone two years earlier, he skied too low and had to slice back up the side of the hill to get to the Zielschuss. (That turn was beginning to do to Jeff Olson what the Collombin jump had done to Roland Collombin.) Jeff skied the Zielschuss bravely, finishing in 1:59.59, thirty-fifth place. Jeff also shook his head when he finished. He wasn't much for tantrums, either.

When the race was over, AJ was in fifteenth place, same as last year. That afternoon, he watched Franz Heinzer's run on videotape. He was impressed. Heinzer had skied beautifully; he had deserved to win. For all the time they spent together on the hill, AJ and Franz didn't know much about each other. They occasionally rode a chair lift together, but because of the language barrier, their conversations didn't go far. "He speaks English gibberish and I speak German gibberish," AJ said. Besides, the two men were too busy being competitors to become good friends. To AJ, Heinzer was a mythical figure, a powerful and fearsome beast who had to be subdued. But on this day, the beast had won.

At the team meeting, Ueli summed up the race. "Today was ... a good day," he said. "It could have been a little bit better. We have a guy in the top fifteen. Olson breaks the two-minute mark, and after your fall that's something to be proud of."

Bill Egan also congratulated Jeff for having the guts to ski the Zielschuss after crashing there in training.

Luthi then turned to Reggie and delivered what was, for the unsentimental Swiss, a great compliment.

"And Reggie, you'll do better tomorrow. You didn't suck."

The American tourists who had made the "AJ is best" banner showed up at the Schwarzer Adler that night, during dinner. They were hammered again, or maybe they had never sobered up.

As it happened, Ueli had arranged a big dinner party that evening. All the downhillers and coaches were there, along with some guests— television commentator and World Cup founder Bob Beattie, former Kitzbühel slalom champion Chuck Ferries, AJ Kitt's mom, Nancy, and AJ's agent, Jon Franklin. AJ's mom and his agent had flown in at the last minute; Nancy Kitt had never seen AJ compete in a European World Cup race.

The drunks arrived about the same time dessert did. They wanted autographs, they said, and then they'd leave. The coaches and racers, flattered by the attention, signed jackets, hats, pieces of paper, and so on. One woman, who probably would not remember any of it the next day, even had some of the racers sign her belly.

Then she walked over to Reggie Crist and said, "Can I have your autograph?"

"Sure," he said, taking her pen.

"Left or right?" she said.

Reggie looked at her legs. "Uh, left," he said.

The woman raised her sweater and showed him her left breast. "Here," she said.

Crist looked surprised for a moment. And then he signed it.

On Saturday morning, the day of the second race at Kitzbühel (this one was considered the official Hahnenkamm race), Reggie and Jeff feasted on a breakfast buffet of cheese, fruit, yogurt, several kinds of bread, corn flakes, granola, juice, and coffee. AJ ate Froot Loops and frosted cherry Pop Tarts he'd bought in Garmisch.

During inspection, Bill Egan showed his athletes a new way to make the carousel turn. On Friday, they had skied up the hillside and then swooped down to the gate, like glider pilots making a gentle arc across the sky. Today, Bill had a different idea. He told them to take a more direct route toward the gate, then make a sharper, more aggressive turn around the wheel. Essentially, he wanted them to dive in just a little bit. They might seem to lose speed, but at least they wouldn't slide all the way to the net, as AJ had done on Friday. Egan believed this would put them in a better position as they entered the Steilhang. The racers said they'd try it.

At the public draw Friday night, Franz Heinzer had drawn number six, AJ eight. AJ liked that: Heinzer would reach the finish first, and then sweat it out until he got there.

In the starting gate on Saturday, Heinzer reflected on his win the day before, and on his victory at Kitzbühel in 1991, and thought of how happy he would be to make it three wins in a row on the Streif. Only the great Franz Klammer had won Kitzbühel three times in a row. In the first part of his run, it seemed a sure thing that Heinzer would reach his goal. But when he reached the turn below the Hausberg jump, the turn that had always baffled Jeff Olson, he made a mistake and slid way down the hill, losing time. Then he tipped back as he went off the finish jump. He showed the bottoms of his skis to the crowd and windmilled his arms, but managed to land on his feet instead of his back. He came through the finish in 1:56.04, breaking his day-old course record and taking over first place.

Right on the Edge of Crazy

AJ glided into the starting gate about the time Heinzer finished, but he didn't listen for Heinzer's time, or even think of how he might have done. Instead, he thought about the course, especially the carousel turn. The Streif had gotten the best of him on Friday, and he was angry. He wanted to get even. And of course, he also wanted to beat Heinzer.

He pushed hard out of the starting gate, as hard as Heinzer had the day before. AJ handled the Mausefalle without trouble, then followed Bill Egan's new line through the carousel. When he finished the turn, he knew he had a good run going. Bill, watching from the side of the course, knew it too. The line had worked. AJ skied into the Steilhang much more quickly and gracefully than he had the day before. AJ's mom, Nancy, who was standing at the bottom of the hill, saw his first intermediate time on the scoreboard and shrieked. AJ had skied the top part of the course in 32.84, almost three tenths of a second faster than Heinzer had.

AJ was a different racer today. He was forceful, aggressive, almost mean. To him, skiing the Streif was like beating up the person he hated most in the world—not that he actually had someone in mind. He thought of the race as a fight: The course had provoked him, poked him in the chest, and now he was swinging back, and landing the punches. He was kicking its ass. It was a significant change in him, not just from the day before, but also from the year before. In the 1991 race, AJ had not tried to ski the course so much as survive it. The idea, especially after Bill Hudson's crash, had been to get to the bottom—quickly if possible, but anyway to get there. Now things were different. Now AJ was confident enough to actually race in Kitzbühel. He had grown as a racer, and as a person. The Streif would never bully him again. After this, what would he have left to fear?

His second intermediate time was 48.53, nine hundredths faster than Heinzer's.

He flew so far off the steep Zielschuss jump that it looked as if he had jumped from the window of a fifth-floor apartment. It didn't matter. He knew the landing was clean. He got a lot of air off the finish jump, too, and loved it. Then he skied under the finish banner, the one that said Kitzbühel in bold black letters, and threw his skis sideways to stop.

The scoreboard flashed a number: 2.

AJ, holding his poles, pumped both fists, just as he had done in Val d'Isère. And then he jumped out of his skis and held them over his head as the man holding the TV camera bore down on him and the photographers with their long, cannon-like lenses fired away, their motor drives whirring. The Swiss cheered AJ happily: He had skied well, but thankfully not quite well enough to beat Heinzer. The sun lighted up the finish area while AJ posed for pictures. Above, a big, yellow hot-air balloon hovered like a gumdrop.

Soon, AJ got on the radio and told Reggie, "It isn't real tough." Then, having reached unbelievable speeds, he added, "The speed isn't anything unbelievable."

A man with a video camera approached him and asked, "What made you go so fast today?"

"Yesterday," AJ said.

Racer number twenty, Peter Rzehak of Austria, crashed in the Mausefalle and wrecked his knee. The race was delayed for several minutes while Bill Egan and some other coaches helped him off the course. Then Bill got on the radio to reassure Reggie, number twenty-seven.

"No big deal. No big deal," the coach said. "He just made a bad move."

Actually, Reggie wasn't thinking about Rzehak. He wasn't even thinking about skiing. Reggie had the sort of mind that liked to take long walks in the woods, even when his body was preparing to do something near-crazy. That morning, Reggie was thinking about signing that woman's breast. When he thought of it, he laughed out loud. It had definitely been a first. In the few times he had stood in the start at Kitzbühel, he'd had a hard time thinking of anything funny. Reggie wasn't the sort of guy who laughed at danger, at least not before it had passed. Indeed, while a lot of downhillers got scared at times, he actually owned up to it. So it meant something that he was laughing now, ten minutes before he was to drop over the Mausefalle. It meant that he wasn't scared anymore, or at least not as scared as he used to be.

Reggie was as confident on his skis that day as he had ever been. He skied well in the section just before the Hausberg—so well that he would later say, "I fucking railed it." That was unusual, too: Reggie wasn't in the habit of boasting even when he had something to boast about. He also skied much better in the turn below the Hausberg. When he finished he was in twentieth place, but some other racers skied well and moved him back. Jeff Olson was one of them. He screwed up the Hausberg turn, as usual, but still managed to finish ahead of his teammate by four hundredths of a second. Jeff was thirty-second, Reggie thirty-third.

Even so, Reggie was pleased. That was nine places higher than he had finished the day before. It wasn't great, but it wasn't bad, either. He hadn't made much of an impression on the racing world today, but he was beginning to feel that he would, and soon. It was a new feeling, and a nice one.

When Reggie left the finish area, a young woman appeared before him and asked for an autograph.

He gave it to her. In her autograph book.

When all the racers were in, AJ was still in second place. He couldn't believe it. Second in Kitzbühel. Second. Later that day, Reggie Crist would ask his teammate whether it was more exciting to win in Val d'Isère or finish second in Kitzbühel, and AJ would say it was pretty nearly the same feeling. "A total personal achievement," he would call it. And a singular one. Once he had left the gate, nobody had told him when to turn or when to tuck. He'd had to face fear on his own—not just face it, but stare it down, overcome it. He hadn't thought much about staring down fear when he was in Val d'Isère, but he had thought of it today. The Streif had a way of making young men think about things they usually didn't think about.

Tommy Moe watched the race from his room in the Schwarzer Adler. He was finished with his technical races, and had come to Kitzbühel to watch his teammates compete.

On TV, the Kitzbühel course looked fine—soft, white, fast. Beautiful, even. It surprised him. Last year, when he had run it, the snow had been grimy and bumpy, more like gravel than snow. But now the Streif looked . . . well, as the guys liked to say, buffed. So buffed that Moe began to wish he were out there racing instead of sitting in the hotel, watching. It made him angry at himself. What a fool! What could he have been thinking when he decided not to race here? Downhillers were supposed to go out and tame the mountain, not kick back and peer glassy-eyed at the tube. That was how he felt about it. He really wished he could have that decision back! AJ was going to entertain everyone at lunch that afternoon with war stories about the 'Bühel, and Tommy would have to sit there and listen, like some kind of wide-eyed groupie. But AJ wouldn't be the only one telling stories. Jeff and Reggie would have theirs as well. That would make it worse. They were good racers, but no better than Tommy was. Not even as good, a lot of the time. Still, they were running the Hahnenkamm today and he wasn't. There was no denying that. People would respect Jeff and Reggie, admire their daring . . . and they wouldn't pay any attention to Tommy at all. What a mistake!

Well, he wouldn't make it again. He made himself that promise right there. Next year he would run Kitzbühel, period. After last year's race, he had told himself he wouldn't put himself through anything like that again. Well, to hell with that.

Moe had decided he would rather go through that than go through this.

The race organizers staged the awards ceremony at 5:30 that evening, in the center of town. It was a way of getting live TV coverage. The Kitzbühel race organizers seemed to prize live TV coverage above everything else, including live spectators. Most World Cup races were the same way. Television, as everyone knew, drew millions of viewers. To get their attention, advertisers sponsored ski races, and then congratulated themselves for doing it by putting their names all over everyone and everything. The Hahnenkamm wasn't just the Hahnenkamm; it was the Toyota Hahnenkamm. Every racer's bib had the car company's name emblazoned on it, so people could see it on TV. The tube made itself conspicuous in other ways, too. When a racer finished his run on the Streif that Saturday, he could expect a fellow with a TV camera to stomp over to him and put the lens within a couple of inches of his face—or his ass, if he happened to lean over to unbuckle his boots. The TV guy got these proctoscopic shots at will, but the newspaper and magazine photographers couldn't get nearly as close. They put on their long lenses and tried for shots from inside the press pen, where they were obliged to stand so they wouldn't get in the way of the TV people. And when the athletes walked through the archway to the coaches' area—an archway decorated with the logo of the Sergio Tacchini clothing company, an important sponsor—they could expect to be caught in the cross hairs of more TV cameras. (The newspaper and magazine people weren't allowed in the coaches' area, either.) Finally, at the awards ceremony, the TV people crowded onto the stage alongside the athletes, so that many of the people who were actually present could see nothing but the sturdy backs and sagging slacks of TV camera people. It made no sense to invite thousands of people to an awards presentation that they couldn't hope to see, but so what? The event was shown on TV, and that was what counted.

The ceremony was brief. The talkative Kitzbühel master of ceremonies had scarcely mentioned Franz Heinzer's name when the Swiss—there were thousands—began singing and cheering and clanging their cowbells. AJ, wearing his leather jacket again, was introduced next, and got polite applause. He thanked everyone for coming and then left the stage with a pewter stein and a check for 4,800 Swiss francs. His mom, who had arrived early enough to get next to the stage, saw the whole thing. Her son was a star.

Indeed, if AJ thought about it, he probably could look back on that day, January 18, 1992, as the day he became a real celebrity. It was funny. AJ had never dreamed of being famous; he had wanted only to win ski races. About the only thing he liked about fame was that it helped him make money. Still, he was learning that being kind to the press and the fans was part of his job. As it turned out, he got far more attention for placing second in Kitzbühel than he did for winning in Val d'Isère. He had signed a few autographs in Val d'Isère, sure, but in Kitzbühel he was mobbed. The moment he stepped off the stage that evening, he was surrounded by people pushing pens at him. Many were kids, but just as many weren't. Quite a few were adult men who asked him to sign ticket stubs or ski jackets or just scraps of paper. They struggled hard to get close enough to get his signature, but it was clear they weren't as interested in watching him write his name as they were in simply getting close. By skiing fast, AJ had turned himself into an idol, someone who lived out the fantasies of thousands of lesser men. Now some of those men wanted to be near him, to pat him on the back, as if the stuff that made him fast and daring might come off on them.

And after they got his signature, they showed it off to their friends as if it were a twenty-dollar bill they'd found in the street.

And how did AJ respond to all these people, these demanding strangers? By signing his name as fast as he could. He signed for everyone—men, women, kids. Anyone would have signed; it was fun. But AJ did more than that, more than he had to do. He tried to oblige people in any way he could. He posed for snapshots in the center of town. He chatted with anyone who knew enough English to start a conversation. When he got back to the Schwarzer Adler, a man plopped his son on AJ's lap and motioned that he wanted to take a picture. It could have been an awkward moment: The guy had interrupted a conversation between AJ and his mother. But the racer just put his arm around the kid, smiled, and sent the pair away happy.

The athletes went to the Londoner that night, of course. AJ had sort of an entourage: His mom and his agent went along with him. The racers all got drenched in beer, inside and out. They danced on tables and chairs and stepped out of the way each time somebody keeled over in their direction. They drank several toasts with Lasse Arnesen of Norway and Daniel Mahrer of Switzerland. AJ's mom and his agent got soaked in beer and left early. Jeff Olson kissed the same waitress he'd smooched the year before. At 3 A.M., AJ walked a young woman home, then ran back to the hotel, his wiry, beer-soaked hair freezing solid in the chill air. Ueli Luthi mentioned the next day that he was glad other ski towns didn't have places like the Londoner. If they did, he said, he would never know where his athletes were.

Bill Egan and Jim Tracy rambled out of Kitzbühel on Monday morning, in the cargo van. They were leaving the athletes with the Passat. As the big blue van left town, Bill thought about the horrifying week he had spent in Kitzbühel a year earlier, and about the thrilling week that had just ended. This year, thank God, his kids were OK. He laughed and said, "Oh, man, is it great to be leaving this town with vertical children."

13

Making It

The downhill team was reunited in Wengen, Switzerland, on Monday. In any other year, the Americans would have been excited about the Lauberhorn downhill just because the course was so long and challenging and the crowd so large and zany. But this year, those things didn't make a bit of difference. In 1992, most of the American racers cared about the race for just one reason—because it was their last clear opportunity to make the Olympic downhill team. The Lauberhorn was the final World Cup downhill race before the games, one last chance for the Americans to prove they could compete against the best in the world. The pressure was immense. As the team settled down for a late dinner Monday night at the Park Hotel, AJ Kitt and Tommy Moe were still the only racers who knew they had made the team. Six others—Jeff Olson, Todd Kelly, Kyle Rasmussen, Steve Porino, Bill Hudson, and Reggie Crist—were sweating it out. For them, the Lauberhorn was not an end in itself, but a means to an end. Yes, a guy could have a rotten race in Wengen and still be selected for the Olympic team on the basis of earlier results. But nobody wanted to take that chance. The downhillers knew the only sure way to get to Albertville was to ski fast through Wengen.

Steve Porino and Bill Hudson weren't confident they could do that. They had skied badly in Wengen's two Europa Cup downhills. One day Steve had made such a bad turn that he had screamed right in the middle of his run; fortunately, attendance for these minor-league races was so low that nobody had been around to hear him. And Bill couldn't figure out how to go fast anymore. He had been so angry with himself after one race that he had started trembling on the chair lift. But he soon regained his sense of humor. A couple of weeks earlier, several of the Americans had begun to grow goatees, just for something to do. Bill shaved off his facial hair after the second race, explaining that he would rather be handsome and slow than ugly and slow. Todd Kelly didn't distinguish himself in Wengen either, but at least he kept his goatee.

Among the Americans, only Kyle Rasmussen had skied really well in the Europa Cup races, finishing second and third. But even those results weren't enough to assure him of a place on the Olympic downhill team. Anybody who skied well in the Lauberhorn race—held on the same course as the Europa Cup events—could swipe Kyle's slot on the team.

The week got off to a slow start. Wednesday's training run was canceled because of bad weather. On Thursday, the athletes and coaches took Wengen's rickety trolleys up the hill for inspection, but again the weather was grim. A fierce wind blew snow sideways across the course like dust across the plain; far in the distance, the racers could see small avalanches spilling like fluffy waterfalls off the three peaks—the Eiger, the Jungfrau, and the Mönch. At first the race organizers said the training run would begin at the top of the mountain, where it normally started. Then they moved it thirty seconds down the hill, to a jump called the Hundschopf. Late that morning, they called the whole thing off until Friday.

While he was still on the hill that morning, Bill Egan was presented with an interesting offer. He was standing a few hundred feet above the finish when he heard someone yell, "Bill Egan! Bill Egan!"

It was Silvain DaoLena, a coach with the French ski team. He was a short distance down the hill, herringbone-stepping toward Bill. Like all the French coaches, DaoLena wore a hat bearing the logo of GMF Assistance, a company that sponsored the team. The American coaches didn't know what GMF stood for, but they liked to say it meant, "Go, motherfucker."

At last DaoLena reached Bill. "Bill Egan," he said, looking around to make sure no one else was listening, "we make a deal." A few weeks earlier, Bill had been chosen, in a drawing of World Cup coaches, to set the Olympic super G course. That meant it would be up to him to decide where the racers would turn and where they would go straight. DaoLena wanted to take advantage of that. Bill wasn't scheduled to place the gates in the snow until the games were under way, but DaoLena asked him to come to Val d'Isère right after the Lauberhorn and set the course early. That way, he said, the French racers—and any athletes Bill might like to bring—could train on it for a few days before the World Cup super G in Megève, France, the following weekend. DaoLena assured Bill that he could reserve the race hill for the days they would need it.

"What do you think?" DaoLena said.

Bill thought a lot of things. He had already made plans for after the Lauberhorn: He was going to take his racers to Serre Chevalier, a vast French ski resort. They were going to stay in a hotel owned by the family of French downhiller Luc Alphand, a friend of the American team. He wasn't sure he could change his plans on such short notice. But DaoLena's offer intrigued him. He was excited, and a little nervous, about setting the Olympic course, and he wanted to do it well. If he went to Val d'Isère early, he could learn the dips and rolls in the hill. He'd be able to set a better run. This was a great opportunity for him.

It was a rare opportunity for his racers, too. The reason was simple. In super G, skiers didn't get to train on the course immediately before the race, the way they did in downhill. The rules said they could only inspect it. So when the time came to race, they had to fly down the hill with only a vague idea of what might be the fastest line to the finish. Racing in a super G was something like driving fast down a mountain road at night: You never knew what might be around the next corner, and you probably wouldn't have time to react when you saw it. The rule against practicing on the course was one of the things that made super G so difficult and exciting. But DaoLena had found a loophole. True, the racers couldn't practice on the Olympic course once it was set. But there was nothing in the rules that said they couldn't go to the hill a couple of weeks early and practice on a course *much like* the one that would be used in competition. That was exactly what DaoLena wanted the French and American teams to do. But if Egan didn't agree to the deal, there wouldn't be a course to practice on.

DaoLena could see that Bill was turning it over in his mind. "You think about it," the Frenchman said. "I'll talk to you later."

Bill didn't have to think about it for long. He decided later that day that to go to Val d'Isère from Wengen.

* * *

The racers all had television sets in their hotel rooms. The local television station repeatedly aired a story about the improvements that had been made to the Lauberhorn course in response to the death of Gernot Reinstadler. Safety experts had designed special, reinforced fences for several sections of the course, including the place where Reinstadler had crashed. A racer's ski could no longer penetrate the fences the way the Austrian's had. The announcer described the new safety features in a firm, reassuring way, alluding only infrequently to Reinstadler. That was how it was in Wengen that week. Everyone thought about Gernot Reinstadler, but no one wanted to mention his name. There was no reason to. After his death, the racers—not just the Americans, but all of them—had two choices: They could hold onto their faith in their own skill and good fortune or they could quit racing. The Lauberhorn race organizers had been expected to rebuild the fences, and it was appropriate to say they had done so. After that, nothing was left to do but hold the race.

The first few nights of that week, the downhillers held their nightly meeting in the hotel dining room. Ueli Luthi eventually saw that he needed to find a better place. The athletes were more interested in their dinner rolls and soft drinks than they were in what he was saying. On Thursday night Ueli said, "Tomorrow night we'll have the meeting downstairs in the conference room."

Naturally, Todd Kelly had something to say about the decision. Todd could always be counted on to add his two cents, especially when Ueli Luthi was giving a speech. Todd liked to kid Luthi by calling him "Lucy."

"Yeah, right," Todd said under his breath. "You'll be the only one there."

Ueli turned on him and snapped, "What?" Except it came out, "Vat?"

"I said, 'I'll see you there.' "

Everybody cracked up.

After dinner, Ueli and Bill Egan met with Alpine Program Director Dennis Agee, who was in Wengen for the race. The purpose of the meeting was to make a list of athletes who should be considered for the men's alpine Olympic team. This was the beginning of a momentous process, a process that would fulfill some dreams and shatter some others.

Anyone included on the coaches' list would still have a chance to go to Albertville, and those excluded would not. The downhillers didn't have a chance to lobby the coaches ahead of time because they didn't know there was going to be a meeting. The coaches had kept it a secret to avoid that sort of thing. As it turned out, there was no need for lobbying, at least not by the downhillers. After talking for thirty minutes, Egan, Luthi, and Agee agreed on a list of fifteen racers. It included seven members of the technical team—and all eight downhillers. As of that night, everybody on the U.S. Crazy-Ass Get-Out-of-My-Way Downhill Maniac Team still had a chance to go to the Big Show.

America's popular press ignored ski racing most of the time. That changed drastically when the Olympics rolled around. The coverage sprouted two or three months before the Olympic games, blossomed on the weekend of the opening ceremonies, and withered as soon as the slalom, the final alpine event, was over. After that, most publications abruptly resumed ignoring the sport. For this reason, a lot of people naturally assumed that after the games were over, America's ski racers went home and sat around drinking beer and eating peanuts until the next Olympiad. But during the Olympics, well, the press went all out. The nation's sports writers tended to fulfill their obligation to ski racing the same way every four years. First, they attempted to explain the sport to their readers, with mixed results. In an Olympic preview article, the *Modesto Bee*, published near Kyle Rasmussen's home in California, incorrectly described the combined downhill and slalom event as a mixture of downhill and *super* G. The *Calaveras Ledger Dispatch* did even worse. It said the combined "consists of three competitions: downhill, which consists of nothing more than a slope; giant slalom, which is a technical course with plenty of turns, and super G, which has bigger, more sweeping turns."

Second, the sports journalists wrote articles saying the U.S. Ski Team was a Big Disappointment because it didn't have as many great skiers as dinky foreign countries like Switzerland and Austria. Every publication ran a Big Disappointment story because it was easy to write; all you had to do was look at the results of a few World Cup races and search the thesaurus for synonyms for "abysmal." Third, despite the trashing, the press went looking for someone to love, an American ski racer whose picture could be displayed beneath a big bold headline saying something like "America's Hope," as if the United States might as well fold up the flag and merge with Mexico if this person didn't win.

In 1992, America's Hope was AJ Kitt. About the time the downhillers were in Wengen, several major magazines published features on him. His favorite by far was the one in *Sports Illustrated*. The magazine had put his picture on the cover (the photograph showed him pushing out of the start in Val d'Isère in December). Getting his picture on the cover of *Sports Illustrated* had been one of AJ's career goals, almost as important to him as winning the overall World Cup downhill title. (Another career goal was to be interviewed in *Playboy*.) The headline on the *Sports Illustrated* article said, "The Whole Kitt and Caboodle," and the line just beneath that said, "U.S. medal hopes in skiing rest almost solely on AJ Kitt." The magazine's angle on AJ was that he was a Good Person. It called him "a well-behaved, hard-working young man" and speculated that his "hard-earned success" could mean that "nice guys are going to start finishing first—at last." By contrast, 1984 Olympic medal winner Bill Johnson was branded "a redoubtable loudmouth," a "motor-mouth," and "a chronic misfit and troublemaker." He was Goofus to AJ Kitt's Gallant. AJ disagreed with the characterization of Johnson, whom he knew as a pretty nice guy. But he also knew the press could never resist cooking up a story. Of course, AJ was much more complicated and interesting than someone who is merely "nice," and Bill Johnson often was charming and gracious, but so what? The *Sports Illustrated* story did what it set out to do—hype the Olympics and advance the America's Hope theme.

AJ got equally good ink in *The New York Times Magazine*, which ran a cover picture of him slicing through the air in Val d'Isère, the trees behind him a green-brown blur. The *Times* called him a "stand-tall, no-excuses competitor" and "exceedingly polite." The writer had interviewed AJ in the bar at the Hotel Post in St. Anton, where AJ was waiting out the late-December blizzard that eventually caused the race to be canceled. "Throughout the conversation," the article said, "he has a difficult time not being distracted by the attractive waitress, who pays him inordinate attention." America's paper of record didn't mention that AJ later took the waitress on a date, and that she went home that night with another guy. Indeed, the *Times* story stripped off AJ's Superman suit for only one clause, calling him "cocky when it fits." His teammates weren't treated as kindly. The 1988 Olympic team, which included Bill Hudson and Jeff Olson, "was made up of a couple of has-beens and a bunch of nobodies," the article said, brutally. When it was done bemoaning how bad the U.S. Ski Team was, the story returned to AJ, who, it said, would go to the Olympics with an enormous weight on "his young, broad shoulders." The implication was that the Atlas of the slopes could handle it.

A *Rolling Stone* article trashed the ski team and extended the America's Hope motif in a single sentence. AJ, it said, was "the best hope for a medal on the U.S. alpine ski team, which has perennially fallen on its face in world competition." AJ was photographed in a Calvin Klein sweater and the sort of Ray-Bans you might expect a Colorado state trooper to wear. He wore a grim expression and clutched a pair of slalom skis, which might have explained the expression.

All this attention, all these expectations, did not seem to affect AJ at all. He was flattered, but that was about it. As far as he was concerned, the only burden he had to bear was the weight of his own expectations. As for being America's Hope, well, he simply didn't think of himself that way, no matter how many times the media tried to make him. *Sports Illustrated* and *Rolling Stone* and the American public could hope for anything they wanted; that wasn't his problem. He didn't care. Some people might have said he was arrogant to think that way. He didn't care about that, either. On race day in Val d'Isère he would be skiing to please himself, not to fulfill the premises of magazine articles. Indeed, when the *Rolling Stone* article came out, AJ probably had a right to be fed up with all the America's Hope stuff, but he wasn't. He understood that the press had to sell that sort of junk.

Besides, the magazine had given him a really neat gray *Rolling Stone* sweatshirt, which he frequently wore on his young, broad shoulders.

On Friday, the weather broke. To make up for lost time, the race organizers decided to hold two training runs, one right after the other. This worried Bill Egan. He feared the extra run on the long Lauberhorn course would wear the guys out, which would increase the chance of accidents. During inspection, he warned each athlete to be careful. Then he radioed up to Gary Myers, the physical therapist, and told him to be ready to give a lot of rubdowns after dinner. "These guys are going to have some sore legs," Bill said.

Something strange happened during inspection. A few Swiss and Austrian racers decided they didn't like the placement of one of the gates near the top of the course. In their opinion, the way the gate was set would make them carry too much speed into the Hundschopf jump. They talked it over for a while. And then Austria's Patrick Ortlieb, who had finished a heartbreaking second in the Garmisch downhill, just picked up the gate and moved it, setting it in a place that would slow down the skiers. Bill Egan couldn't believe what he was seeing. What Ortlieb had done was equivalent to Michael Jordan strolling onto a basketball court and painting a new foul line a few feet closer to the basket. Bill was upset mostly because AJ and two or three other guys had already inspected the top part of the course. It would not be difficult for them to find their way around the new gate, but still . . . it wasn't fair. Bill complained to the race officials, but they didn't listen. The gate would stay where Ortlieb had put it. (Ortlieb did well as a coursesetter: He finished fifth in the morning training run and third in the afternoon one.)

For most of the Americans, the training was routine. AJ, who was still learning the course, made what amounted to two fast inspections, finishing fortieth and twenty-third. Todd Kelly made such a poor turn around Ortlieb's gate that he could be heard laughing at himself on the videotape. Only Reggie Crist had an unusual day. Reggie felt that Kyle, Steve, Bill, and Todd had an advantage over him because they had skied the Lauberhorn course in the Europa Cup races. He had a lot of catching up to do. So, in the first training run, the second run of his life on this hill, he went out of the gate as if it were race day. He punched it all the way down. The results were comical. Reggie missed a gate about thirty seconds from the finish, then whizzed past another one right before the finish jump. Oops! He was a nearsighted tourist driving too fast on unfamiliar streets. The standings showed that he finished forty-third in the first training run, but if it had been a race he would have been disqualified for missing a gate. Maybe, he thought after the run, I should have ridden the brakes a little bit.

When he got into the starting gate for the second run, Reggie was furious. It was too late to pump the brakes now. He had to go for it. That first run was bullshit, he told himself. You can't miss gates at this level of competition. You just can't. Reggie was really getting worked up now. In Sun Valley, he had had a coach who told him, "You have to be an asshole to win." Reggie, who always tried to be a nice, laid-back guy, was beginning to understand what the man had meant. Reggie felt that AJ fit his coach's description. He didn't think AJ was a bad person, not at all. But he could see that AJ was able to cop the kind of attitude he needed to win. Reggie admired the asshole, he really did. And Reggie and his teammates certainly felt AJ deserved the attention he was getting from the press. Now Reggie was going to be a raging butthead himself, or at least try. He blasted out of the starting gate and lunged down the hill. Hey, if he could punch it in Kitzbühel, he could punch it here. The run passed in a blur.

Reggie railed a few turns and screwed up a few. But always he leaned forward, projected his shoulders down the hill. He also made all the gates. He hopped off the finish jump, skied under the banner, turned, and found he was . . . eighteenth! Reggie's elfin cheeks went red. He pumped his fist. All right! Well, this was an exciting development. Maybe he was Olympic material after all. If he could ski that way in the race tomorrow, he might just win himself a ticket to Albertville. Making the Olympic downhill team meant everything in the world to Reggie. Being a World Cup racer was great, but in his opinion, getting to the Olympics was the ultimate achievement. It was the whole point, really. Besides, all the important people in his life—his parents, his brother and sister, his girlfriend, the gang back in Sun Valley—were holding their breath, waiting for word on whether he would make the team. Suddenly he felt closer than ever to making it. Oh, it felt sweet.

Reggie felt even better when he looked at the scoreboard. On the list of finishers, AJ's name was five places below his. He had beaten AJ for the first time since . . . well, since Reggie didn't know when. Now, that was sweet.

On the morning of the race, AJ again had Froot Loops for breakfast. According to an advertisement on the package, the box contained an action figure from the Tale Spin cartoon series. The names of the figures were Baloo, Molly, Kit, and the dangerous Don Karnage. Kitt got Kit.

As he ate, AJ told his teammates about a dream he'd had the night before. He dreamed that he, Tommy Moe, Kyle Rasmussen, and Edi Waldburger, the Rossignol man, were in a field behind AJ's boyhood home in Rochester. As a kid, AJ used to dig holes in the ground and use them as forts. In the dream he was surprised to find the holes still there. One of the holes had water in it. A fish several feet long, partly white and partly spotted, wriggled around in the pond. For some reason everyone thought it was a striper. Then Tommy dove in and wrestled the fish to shore, using only his hands.

That was all AJ remembered. He had no idea what the dream meant. If it was in any way related to today's race, nobody could figure out how.

The story started a long conversation about sleep and dreams. Steve Porino said he hadn't slept much at all the night before the race. Steve was the kind of guy who sometimes lay in bed and worried about silly things. The night before the Wengen downhill, he worried about his briefcase. Someone had stolen it from the hotel lobby in Garmisch, and for several days he had been without his passport, his plane ticket, and some other important things. But then someone from the hotel in Garmisch had called to say that the case had been found. Only a tape player and Swiss Army knife were missing, but the passport and plane ticket were still inside. The hotel was sending the briefcase to Wengen right away. Steve was delighted. But that night, he kept himself awake wondering if the plane ticket was the right plane ticket, his plane ticket. He had a strong hunch that he wasn't going to make the Olympic team, and he wanted to be able to get home if he didn't.

At one point, Steve accidentally bumped something off his nightstand. Hearing the noise, his roommate, Todd Kelly, turned to Steve, held out his hand, and said, inexplicably, "Hand it over, Mook." His eyes were closed.

Todd, a guy who always had something to say, was not likely to stop talking just because he was asleep. At one race, he roomed with a young guy named Craig Thrasher. The two men were sharing a bed with a large light fixture hanging over it. In the middle of the night, Todd crawled to the end of the bed and began reaching for the light. When Craig woke up, Kelly, still asleep, pointed at the light and shouted, "Get it, Thrasher! Get it!" It spooked the hell out of Craig.

But Todd's best sleep-talking story, one he told that morning in Wengen, involved his mother. Once, when Todd was twelve years old, his mother went into the room where he was sleeping and began to vacuum the floor. Normally, Todd wouldn't have minded the noise. But that day he did. As his mom was pushing the vacuum, Todd sat up, looked straight at her, and said, "What the fuck are you doing?" Then he lay down again and closed his eyes.

When they finished telling their stories, the athletes went back to their rooms and put on their downhill suits. They had a race to run.

The race wasn't scheduled to begin until 12:30 P.M., but the Swiss fans began cracking their whips and clanging their cowbells right after breakfast. There was no automobile traffic in Wengen, so the fans took the trolley to the village and then walked along a narrow road, through the woods, to the finish area. They moved in a great, slow, hooting mass, a bobbing sea of faces painted in the red and white of the Swiss flag. The Lauberhorn race was the Swiss team's biggest home game, and also one of the community's greatest events. The Swiss were like American college football fans on an autumn Saturday—joyful, inebriated, and unabashedly partisan.

Just before the race started, the raucous crowd briefly quieted down. The public-address announcer said, "In memory of Gernot Reinstadler, who had a fatal accident during last year's training runs, we kindly ask you to respect this moment of silence." For a moment the world was still. Many in the crowd bowed their heads, as if to look away from the fence where Reinstadler died. Two minutes and thirty seconds later, Swiss hero Daniel Mahrer, racer number one, skied through the finish and gave the fans a reason to cheer. Patrick Ortlieb, the self-appointed coursesetter, came down next. He beat Mahrer by almost a second. Franz Heinzer, number three, then turned in one of the most powerful performances of his career. He flung himself down the hill and finished in 2:28.33, more than two seconds faster than Ortlieb. There was no way to beat that time. After Heinzer finished, everyone else was skiing for second place. Germany's Markus Wasmeier, the surprise winner in Garmisch, eventually took the second spot. Heinzer's margin of victory over Wasmeier, 1.6 seconds, was by far the largest of the year on the World Cup tour.

AJ, number fourteen, skied conservatively, making approximately the same number of mistakes he expected to make, considering how little he knew about the course. He was in fourteenth place after fourteen racers. It was warm and sunny in the finish area. AJ took off his gloves, put on his Ray-Bans, and schmoozed the other racers. He had not won, but he was satisfied.

Reggie Crist knew halfway through his run that he wasn't skiing as well as he had the day before. But he had to keep going, had to search for speed. He had a chance to go to the Olympics; it was time to punch it. He would show them he wasn't just some mellow surfer kid. Ueli Luthi always thought that Reggie didn't "lay it on the line"—that he was never one who would take the chances you had to take to be a great downhiller. Well, today he was laying it on the line, letting the skis run. Let them run, he told himself. Ride these rocket ships. He rode the skis fast into the S-turns. He made the first turn all right, but started the second one late. Suddenly he found himself below the last gate, the one at the crest of the finish jump. He skidded uphill to get there, but it was too late. He broadsided the gate, fell sideways in the snow, and slid into the fence. Reggie lay still for a moment. Then he stood, skied limply down the Zielschuss, and stopped in the middle of the finish corral, a tragic character at center stage. He crouched and buried his face in his hands, as if he couldn't stand to look at his crumbled world. It could not have been an easy thing for the crowd in the finish to see: Reggie was, in a sense, making a scene by standing in the middle of the corral. He stayed there for a long time, suffering alone while an audience watched. Finally he stood and let his skis carry him to the athletes' finish area, a dead man riding a funeral cart.

All that day and the previous night, Reggie had fantasized about victory, about turning and seeing that he was twelfth or third or first— that he was great. And in his fantasies he howled and pumped his fists and thrust his Head downhill skis to the sky as if God Himself were up there cheering. That was his dream of glory, the sort of dream all young athletes, maybe all young people, have for themselves. But maybe he had prepared himself for the wrong thing. Anybody can win, or rather, can be a winner: You just thank your mother and smile for the cameras.

Losing is harder, and more common. This was the moment he really had to be ready for, a moment that called for . . . grace. Downhillers lose most of the time, and they do so in public, inside red fences.

Soon Reggie moved off to one side, to suffer more privately. And then Michael Mair, the Italian racer, raced through the finish and sprayed snow all over the crowd, and all over Reggie. This cold baptism brought Reggie alive, and he smiled and laughed. He gathered his things and moved into the coaches' area, where a TV camera crew was waiting to speak to him. He was still breathing hard when the interviewer asked him how he felt.

How did he feel? Disappointed. Devastated. And yet. . . .

And yet he had gone for it, hadn't he? He had done what he said he would do. For Reggie, ski racing was not mostly about winning or losing. It was a matter of conscience: If he did the best he could, he could live with himself. Whether he finished first or fiftieth, his conscience would be clear. Today he had made some ugly turns, sawed off a gate with his skis, and very possibly blown his last chance to make the Olympic team. But he could live with it because he had done his best.

On Monday, January 27, the downhillers caught a train from Wengen to the village below. The team was splitting up now. Bill Hudson, Steve Porino, and Reggie Crist were headed to Les Orres, France, for two more Europa Cup downhills. The Olympic team would be named on February 2. Bill Hudson had been thinking about the Albertville games— dreaming about them, really— ever since he had skied off the course in the 1988 Olympics in Calgary. This was going to be his Olympic downhill, his moment of greatness. Now he was certain he wouldn't be going. He was so disappointed he couldn't possibly talk about it, or about anything else. Steve knew he wasn't going either, but he took it better, possibly because he hadn't really expected to make it. When he said goodbye to AJ and the others, he gripped their hands a little more firmly than usual, as if to acknowledge he wouldn't be seeing them for a while.

Reggie was going to Les Orres without really knowing where he stood. He could probably guarantee himself a place on the team by winning the downhills in Les Orres, but that wasn't likely to happen. No, he would have to stand on his results so far, and hope that the coaches liked them. For the next few days he would simply have to wait.

After their equipment was loaded into the vans, Bill Egan, Gary Myers, and the rest of the downhillers drove to Val d'Isère, France, to participate in Silvain DaoLena's super G training scheme. The scheme did not work perfectly. No matter how easy Bill tried to make the course, the racers gained so much speed on the slick, steep Face de Bellevarde that they kept missing gates. Bill experimented so much with the layout that, in two days of training, the racers never really got to practice on a completed Olympic super G course. Bill would have to tinker still more when he returned to Val d'Isère for the Olympics. Still, the week wasn't a total loss. Bill felt that AJ, Tommy, Jeff, and Kyle were the four athletes most likely to be named to the Olympic super G team, and he was pleased that they had gotten to know the hill.

After a couple of days on the Face de Bellevarde, the racers climbed into the van and drove to the tony ski resort of Megève, France, for the final World Cup super G race before the Olympics. Todd Kelly, who had also trained in Val d'Isère, still had an outside chance of making the Olympic super G team.

It all depended on how well he did in Megève.

Megève was glorious that week. The sun shined, the wind stilled. And the view was magnificent. The downhillers stayed in a mountainside hotel overlooking Mont Blanc, the awesome, white-capped French peak; afternoons, AJ, Jeff, and their teammates lounged on a sun deck in their T-shirts and sunglasses, drinking sparkling water, eating fresh bread, and taking in the view. From where they sat they could see the tanned, relaxed European vacationers coasting down the last gentle slope to the base of the hill. Once in a while a local dog would lope over to their tables and woof for a piece of bread; the racers always obliged. Evenings, the downhillers retired to the hotel lounge for a game of backgammon or Monopoly and a glass of wine. Sometimes—just sometimes—this European travel thing wasn't bad at all.

The temperature fell on the day of the super G, making the snow good and hard. Jeff Olson, number twenty-nine, was the first American to race. He skied badly. Of the twenty-eight racers who went before him, twenty-four finished. Jeff beat two of them. When he saw his time, he just shook his head. The run had been so poor, apparently, that it wasn't worth getting really upset about. He picked up a radio and gave a brief course report.

"Tell those guys to get after it," he said. "It's really easy." Kyle Rasmussen, who had not heard Olson's time, said later that he could tell just from the tired sound of his teammate's voice that he had not done well.

Tommy Moe was the next American. In the days before the race, he had fantasized about coming from the back of the field to win the race, as Markus Wasmeier had done in the downhill in Garmisch. And why not? He was confident and healthy. He felt certain he could become the first American man ever to finish in the top fifteen in a World Cup super G. The morning of the race, he studied the course carefully, and believed he knew where he wanted to go.

But shortly after he left the start he skied through a deep rut and was thrown off line. He made a few mistakes after that, and by the time the run was half over he knew he wouldn't have a fast time. He beat Jeff Olson by four hundredths of a second, which he did not consider a great achievement. In the coaches' area, he planted his poles in the snow and propped his helmet on top of them. Then he yelled "Fuck!" and pounded his fist on the helmet. It bounced off the poles and landed near his feet. Later, Tommy blamed Jeff for giving a poor course report. The way he saw it, if Jeff had given him better information, he never would have skied into that rut.

As AJ Kitt was skiing into the starting gate, the race organizers halted the race to smooth out the ruts and bumps in the course. For AJ, it was a lucky break: the smoother the track, the better his chances of doing well. He stood in the gate for at least ten minutes while the repairs were made. Finally, he was allowed to start. He skied well on the top of the course: His intermediate time was only eight tenths behind that of Switzerland's Paul Accola, the leader. AJ had a chance to finish in the top twenty, maybe the top fifteen, if he kept it up. He didn't. He was skiing across the flats near the bottom of the course when he caught an edge and went down hard. *Fwap!* He landed head-first, then wiped out a couple of gates and slid into the fence. He lay still for a moment. Ueli Luthi, just uphill from the crash, began to put on his skis, but before he could get them on AJ picked himself up and skied away. The racer unfastened his chin strap as he coasted into the finish. Just before he stopped, he ripped the helmet off and spiked it into the snow as if he were trying to kill it. It took one big bounce and then rolled away. The fans in the finish murmured, but AJ didn't seem to notice. He pulled off his gloves so fiercely it seemed he would rip his fingers off with them.

Kyle Rasmussen, racer number forty-nine, arrived in the finish a moment later, unaware of what had happened, and asked AJ how he had done.

"I fucking crashed," AJ snapped, and then stormed away. Kyle hadn't done much better. His time was only slightly faster than Jeff's and Tommy's.

Todd Kelly wore number fifty-two. This was it: His last chance to make the Olympic team. He knew he would not be selected to compete in the downhill—clearly, he was not among the four best Americans in that event—but he might get to race in the super G, if he could just ski fast today. Kelly liked to think he had realistic expectations for himself as an Olympian. He hoped to make the team in 1992, ski as well as he could, and accept whatever happened at the games. Then, at the 1994 Olympics in Norway, he was going to go like crazy for the medals. Lately, he had been thinking about something Italian downhiller Michael Mair told him in Wengen: "When it comes to the Olympics," Mair had said, "the important thing is to be there." Todd agreed. He just wanted to be there.

Before he left the gate, he heard Ueli's voice on the radio. "The course is in excellent condition. It's as if you're running number one," the coach said.

But the course wasn't in excellent condition, not in Todd's opinion. He had a rough ride. The hole near the top had been smoothed over, but the rest of the course was still hard and rutted. He might as well have been driving a fast car through a field of potholes. As he skied, he got angrier and angrier. Was Ueli out of his mind? The ride was loosening Todd's teeth. He finished in 1:31.60, behind Jeff, Tommy, and Kyle. As soon as he got his helmet off, Todd began to gripe. As always, he relied on overstatement to make his point.

"That was the worst course report I've ever heard," he said. "I'm never listening to another course report again. Never."

And then, all at once, he calmed down. That was the thing about Todd: One moment he might seem to be really pissed off, and the next moment he'd smile and laugh, as if the whole outburst had been a performance he had staged just for you. A few minutes after he finished the race, Todd gathered up his gear and headed for the car, talking all the way about whether he would fly home in coach or pay for an upgrade to first class. He was definitely on his way home after that run; he knew he had not made the Olympic team. He was disappointed, but he wasn't the type to sulk or pitch fits.

Todd Kelly was twenty-two years old; he would get other chances to compete in the Olympics. There was nothing he could do now but pack his bags and make sure he had a comfortable seat on the plane.

Bill Egan was disappointed, too, but he was not going to get over it so quickly. When he got to the finish he was grim-faced; his jaw looked like it had been wired shut. Someone from the press stopped him and asked if he had a comment about the race. Bill was silent for a moment. He looked as if he had a half-dozen words in him and was trying to decide whether he should part with them. Finally he choked out, "It wasn't a very good race." He turned and clomped toward the car, carrying his skis over his shoulder. Then the bubbling pot boiled over: Suddenly, he stopped walking and slammed the skis to the pavement. They didn't bounce as well as AJ's helmet had.

What a disaster. For weeks Bill had been trying to get the guys psyched up about super G. He had told them they were skiing the event too carefully, as if they merely wanted to finish when they should be trying to win. Well, just finishing wouldn't do anymore. The day before the Megève super G, Bill had told the racers to "get after it" and "lay it on the line." Getting after it and laying it on the line were phrases Bill had often used in his football days, but he felt they applied equally well to ski racing. If people were going to compete, by God, they should get after it and lay it on the line. So what had his athletes done? They had skied like . . . well, like scared little boys. They had not gotten after it. They had not laid it on the line. OK, maybe AJ had. Bill was not unhappy with his performance, even though AJ had left a little Kitt-shaped dent in the snow. And a young American named Toni Standteiner had done well, considering it was his first World Cup super G. As for Jeff, Kyle, and Tommy . . . well, Bill couldn't even talk about them. If this was the best they could do in a World Cup super G with a few thousand people watching, how were they going to accomplish anything in the Olympics, with the whole world tuned in?

Later that afternoon, Ueli, Bill, and technical coach Thor Kallerud met in the hotel lounge to select the men's alpine ski team for the 1992 Winter Olympics. Their task was to name eleven skiers to compete in five events—slalom, giant slalom, super G, downhill, and the combined event (a downhill followed, the next day, by two slalom runs). Only four athletes could compete in each event. Some would come from Bill's squad of downhillers, the rest from the technical team. These three coaches often got together for a glass of wine and a few laughs, but today they were tense and businesslike. Ueli—who, because he was the head coach, would make the final decisions—feared that Bill and Thor would argue so strenuously for their own athletes that things might get unpleasant.

"We should try to be as fair as possible," Ueli began. "We don't want to yell at each other. We have to make a decision. We have to choose eleven guys."

As it happened, most of the choices were simple. For the slalom, everyone agreed that technical racers Matt Grosjean, Joe Levins, Paul Casey Puckett, and Kyle Wieche were the best skiers available. For the giant slalom, Ueli suggested Grosjean, Puckett, his brother Chris Puckett, and Rob Parisien. Bill did not argue. None of his kids had better results in these events than the technical racers did. Just like that, six of eleven places on the team were taken.

For the super G, the coaches chose Jeff Olson, who had won a minor race in Obereggen, Italy, and Tommy Moe, who hadn't won anything but had skied pretty well in super G most of the season. "These are positions who will not be changed again," Ueli said. That left two slots open in that event. The coaches agreed that Kyle Rasmussen and AJ Kitt should get them, almost by default. They had not done much in super G, but the other downhillers and technical racers had done even less. Jeremy Nobis, the star of the technical team, probably would have made the super G team, but he had wrecked his knee in a giant slalom race in late December and was out for the season. Ten of eleven team members had been chosen.

Next came the glamour event, the downhill. AJ and Tommy had qualified for the Olympic team by finishing in the top fifteen in at least one World Cup race each—AJ had several top-fifteen finishes, and Tommy had placed thirteenth in Val d'Isère. For the third slot, Ueli recommended Kyle, mostly on the basis of his second- and third-place finishes at the Europa Cup races in Wengen, Switzerland. Fine, the other coaches said.

That left one slot open in downhill. At that point, the meeting became as interesting for what was not said as for what was. No one even mentioned Steve Porino or Todd Kelly: There was nothing to say. In the four World Cup downhills they had competed in that season, Steve's best finish was forty-sixth and Todd's was thirty-third, both in Wengen. That was not good enough to make the team. The coaches didn't talk about Bill Hudson either. He had skied bravely all season, but Ueli and Bill and Thor weren't there to salute bravery. They were there to reward people's achievements, and Hudson had not achieved much. If anything, he had only become more and more frustrated as the season had gone on. As much as all the coaches admired him for overcoming his injuries, they could not name him to the Olympic team.

That left Reggie Crist and Jeff Olson, both of whom desperately wanted to ski in the Olympic downhill. This would be the coaches' first really difficult decision. The reason was complicated. The Fédération Internationale de Ski, the sport's governing body, ranked racers according to a system of points. The idea was to keep the number of points you had as low as possible. The system rewarded racers for skiing well against good competition. Generally speaking, you could lower your points more quickly by placing fourth or fifth against the best racers in the world than you could by beating a bunch of nobodies.

The coaches used this system to help them choose between Jeff and Reggie. When they looked at the points one way, Jeff seemed to be a better downhiller than Reggie: The average of his two best results that season was better than the average of Reggie's two best. But it was a close call, so they checked to see who had the best overall ranking. Reggie did, by a long shot. He had the third-best ranking on the downhill team, behind AJ and Tommy. Jeff was way down in seventh place, ahead of only Bill Hudson. And yet Reggie might not have achieved that ranking if not for his good fortune the year before. In December 1990, the Fédération Internationale de Ski decided to award lower-than-usual points to anyone who skied well in a Nor-Am or Europa Cup race. At the time, Reggie was competing on the Nor-Am circuit, and he made the most of the opportunity. He skied well, and his ranking improved much faster than it would have under normal circumstances. Jeff, who was skiing on the World Cup circuit at the time, did not get the same kind of break. Ueli and Bill could have argued that Reggie had not achieved his excellent ranking legitimately, and that he was really no better than Jeff.

But they did not argue that. Instead, they went ahead and named Reggie to the team. They did it partly because Jeff had already been selected to race in the super G. If they also named Jeff to the downhill team, Reggie wouldn't have the opportunity to go to the Olympics. Besides, naming Reggie rounded out the team at eleven athletes. In addition, Ueli and Bill didn't have much confidence in Jeff as a downhiller just then, and they knew he didn't have a lot of confidence in himself either. Reggie wasn't a great racer, but he had improved while Jeff was stagnating. So Reggie it was.

"I think," Ueli told Bill and Thor, "that we can go and look people in the eye and say this is the way we did it."

The coaches had one last bit of business to tend to. They had to select four guys for the combined event. AJ and Jeff qualified automatically because they had both finished in the top fifteen in at least one World Cup combined. For the other two slots, Ueli suggested Tommy Moe and Kyle Rasmussen. At that point, Thor Kallerud decided to speak up on behalf of his racers.

"Aren't we overlooking some technical guys?" he said. After all, technical skill would be needed for the slalom portion of the event. Thor felt that Kyle Wieche, a skinny, gutsy skier from Connecticut, might do well in the event.

But Ueli and Bill wouldn't hear of it. Any skier who wanted to compete in the slalom part of the event first had to survive the downhill part.

"We didn't properly prepare your guys for this," Ueli told Thor.

"If Wieche gets hurt," Bill said, "we'll catch big shit for putting some-one like that on a downhill course."

Kyle Rasmussen got the last slot in the combined.

A couple of hours later, at the team meeting, Ueli Luthi announced who had made the team. AJ, Tommy, Kyle, and the guys from the technical team applauded themselves heartily. After the meeting, Kyle called Linda in California to give her the news.

"Hello?" Linda groaned. It was still early morning in California, and the call had awakened her.

"Guess what? I'm an Olympian!" Kyle said.

Then Kyle called his mother and said the same thing. She was so excited that she made an announcement on the loudspeaker at Bear Valley, where she ran a ski apparel store.

Jeff Olson eventually called his family too, but he didn't feel good about what he had to tell them. He couldn't understand why the coaches named Reggie to the downhill team instead of him. He didn't have anything against Reg; it was just that the downhill was the biggest event of the games and he felt he had earned the opportunity to be in it. He begged Ueli and Bill to reconsider, but they wouldn't listen. The decision had been hard; they weren't about to reverse it. Jeff was still upset when he went to dinner.

Bill Hudson did not ski well in the Europa Cup races in Les Orres. After Saturday's race, he ventured off by himself to compete in some giant slalom races elsewhere in France. He could have gone to see Kathrin back in Utah, or to see his mother in California, but he chose not to, at least not right away. He was afraid they would say how sorry they were that he had not made the Olympic team, and he didn't want to hear that. He didn't want to think about the Olympics at all. Better, he thought, to go race somewhere else than to face the disappointment.

On Saturday afternoon, Steve Porino, Reggie Crist, and a couple of younger American racers left Les Orres in the team van. They were scheduled to meet Bill Egan at a restaurant outside Megève that evening.

Steve, who was behind the wheel, knew he was not going to the Olympics; he was just thinking about going home.

However, Reggie still did not know if he had made the team. He had skied pretty well in Les Orres—he was the top American in both downhills—but by no means had he clinched an Olympic berth. Only when he saw Egan would he learn his fate.

As the van rolled toward Megève, Reggie's mind raced. He was too nervous to help Steve with the driving, too jittery even to listen to music. The van crossed over miles of beautiful country, past green hills and frosted mountains, but Reggie hardly noticed. He looked out the windows but didn't fix his gaze on anything. His mind was stuck on the Olymics. AJ and Tommy had made the team; everyone knew that. But what about Jeff? What about Kyle? What about him? The downhill was Reggie's only chance; he hadn't accomplished much in super G, and he wasn't skilled enough in slalom to race in the combined. So had he made the team or hadn't he? The question haunted him. God, that ride frayed his nerves. He couldn't sit still. He just wanted the answer. A lot of other people did, too. Reggie's father, Roger, was planning to come to Val d'Isère for the downhill. So was his mom, Diane. They had already bought their tickets. Reggie's girlfriend, Liz, had bought hers too, and it was too late to get a refund. He had spoken to her by phone a few days earlier and said, "Well, you might as well just buy the ticket and come." Now he wasn't sure it was the right decision. What if she showed up in France and he wasn't even on the team? What would they do then? Where would they stay? He had no idea. A part of him—the part that was like his mother—wondered if he had created bad karma by telling Liz to buy the plane ticket. Maybe the angry downhill gods, or other unseeable forces, would repay him for his arrogance by keeping him off the team. These things really went through his mind.

At last the van pulled into the restaurant parking lot. Bill Egan was there waiting. He walked up to Reggie and shook his hand. "Come on," Bill said. "You're coming with me."

Reggie lit up. He went into a daze right there and didn't come out of it for a week. No need to cancel those reservations, thank you. When he got to the hotel in Megève, the other downhillers shook his hand and told him congratulations. Then he got on the phone to Sun Valley and told everybody the news. In the morning, he would load his gear into the van for the ride to Talloires, France, the site of the United States Olympic Committee's operations center. From there, it would be on to Val d'Isère, and the Big Show.

The next day, Reggie's parents spread the news around Sun Valley. By mid-morning, the lift operators had posted signs in honor of their blond hero: "Reggie made it!"

14

Congratulations, You're a Big Deal

The sun was shining and warm when the downhillers arrived at the United States Olympic Committee's offices in Talloires, France, twenty kilometers from the host city of Albertville. They had come here to be clothed, lectured, photographed, probed, tutored, briefed, wined, dined, and patted on the back. The people of Oz did something like this to Dorothy and her gang before they let them see the Wizard.

As soon as they walked into their hotel, Alpine Program Director Dennis Agee told them to read and sign several pieces of paper. One document asked them to promise that they would behave themselves during the Olympics. If they didn't, they were told, the Olympic Committee could take away their uniforms, confine them to their rooms, make them apologize, or even send them home. In their first experience as Olympians, the downhillers were being treated like children: Every seventh-grader in America receives the same gloomy warnings just before the spring field trip to the planetarium. But they signed anyway, on the theory that it was best just to get these things over with.

After that, the athletes walked a couple of blocks to the Olympic Commitee offices to get their uniforms. It quickly became clear that the committee people took their work seriously, and themselves too. The highest-ranking ones carried two-way radios everywhere they went; the racers saw a couple of them on the way to the offices. Everyone with a radio also had a code name: Greg Harney, the man in charge, called himself Silver Thunderbird, after a Marc Cohn song he liked. A woman named Caren Black was Care Bear. Cheeseball and Night Light also frequently communicated by radio. This wasn't casual banter, either. You could tell from their radio conversations that a lot of the USOC people had been in the military. They said "negative" when they meant no, and "affirmative" instead of yes. When they wanted to find someone they would squeeze the transmitter button and say, "Thunderbird, Thunderbird, this is Care Bear. What's your twenty?" It cracked up the ski team people, whose own radio communications generally went something like this:

"Ueli!"

"Vat?"

"Where are you?"

"Vat do you mean?"

"Don't be a dick. Where are you?"

If anybody had ever said "affirmative" on a ski team radio, he would have been laughed off the mountain.

For its offices, the Olympic Comittee had rented Tufts University's European Center, a nine-hundred-fifty-year-old building on the rim of glimmering Lake Annecy. The building, designated as a historic monument in France, once had been a priory, the residence of the chief Benedictine monk. What was happening there now was much more material than spiritual: The place was jammed with goodies for the athletes. Room after room overflowed with official team clothing, most of it embroidered or emblazoned with the word Head, the name of the company that had paid for it. The athletes were given a checklist at the door. At Station One they received a duffel bag (they'd need it to carry the rest of the haul), two pairs of long underwear, gloves, a ski hat, and a headband. At Station Two, they were fitted with blue jeans, cotton pants, undershorts, and dress pants for the opening ceremonies. At Station Three, the racers got a cotton pullover, a red turtleneck, a red polo shirt, a couple of T-shirts, sweaters (heavy and light), and a red rugby shirt. Jeff Olson had a great time bantering with the Olympic Committee volunteers who handed out the stuff. Everytime he got something new he said, "All right!" or "Cool!" or (his favorite saying at the time) "Right on!"

There was more. At Station Four they got ski pants, a jeans jacket with the American flag on the back, a fleece jacket and pants, and stuff for the awards ceremonies, should they find themselves on a podium: a heavy top, a light top, and pants. They got their clothes for the opening ceremonies at Station Five; Tommy Moe looked dapper in the maroon fedora. Station Six was a fun one: They got a fresh pair of Reebok training shoes, leisure boots, parade boots, flip-flops, parade socks, two pairs of insulated socks, three pairs of crew socks, Ray-Ban sunglasses (AJ already had a lot of Ray-Ban stuff because the company was one of his sponsors, but he was happy to have the glasses anyway), a fanny pack, a portable tape player, a calculator, a Kodak disposable camera, and a Canon Sure Shot camera. But Station Seven was by far their favorite: There, they were fitted for a fourteen-karat gold ring imprinted with the Olympic rings (market value: God knows), and a black leather jacket with the Olympic rings embroidered on the back and the athletes' names printed on the inside. "I can't believe how nice that jacket is," Reggie said.

The downhillers carried their stuff out of the priory looking dazed and happy, like kids who had gotten everything they wanted for Christmas, and some things they hadn't even known they wanted. What a bonanza! They couldn't possibly use all those things (they already had most of the items already), and indeed some were already trying to estimate how much people would pay for some of them. But who cared if they didn't actually need the stuff? That wasn't the point. The point was that it identified them as Olympians, and made them feel like Big Deals. They could see now that this wouldn't be just another ski race. The Olympic games were a big to-do, a Busby Berkeley production on snow. And what happened at the priory was only the first of many fusses that people were going to make over the athletes.

Reggie thought he was in a dream. He had always fantasized about going to the Olympics, but he had never imagined he would be treated like this. AJ and Jeff and Bill Hudson had talked about how much fun they'd had at the Calgary games in 1988, how special they had felt, but somehow it hadn't sunk in. Well, it was sinking in now. Guys like Steve Porino had sometimes talked about the Olympic downhill as if it were just another race, and maybe he was right. But Reggie was sure of one thing: Being at a World Cup race was nothing like being at the Olympics. Nothing at all like it.

Herschel Walker, the professional football player, arrived in Talloires about the time the downhillers finished lunch. This was just what was needed to take the racers' minds off material things. AJ, a big Vikings fan (the Kitts had family in Minnesota), was especially interested in having the football player around. Walker had qualified to represent the U.S. in the two- and four-man bobsled competitions: He was going to push the little rocket ship across the starting line and then jump in and duck his head. When the football star walked into the hotel, the downhillers were getting ready to go to a lakeside park for a game of touch football. Jeff Olson asked Herschel if he'd like to play. "No, man, I'm going to have lunch," he said, and thus Jeff's team lost a serious ringer. AJ eventually caught up with him and had him autograph his Vikings cap.

After a lavish French dinner (wine was served, and drunk), the athletes—not just the downhillers, but also the figure skaters, bobsledders, freestyle skiers, biathletes, and lugers—were herded back to the priory for orientation, which turned out to be a series of long speeches. Greg Harney, Mr. Silver Thunderbird, began by introducing Chuck Foster, the Olympic Committee official who had the fancy title of *chef de mission.* "No matter what you do in the future, this will be a memory that you'll never forget," Foster said. Then he referred to the athletes as "the class of '92."

Harney's remarks were less sentimental. When he took the floor again, he noted that a lot of athletes had worn their red, white, and blue team jackets to the meeting. "Hang on to those. Don't sell them yet, or trade them," he said. No doubt he had read some of the Olympians' minds: Those jackets would be worth a fortune on the open market.

Next, the athletes heard from David Joyner, the Olympic Committee's chief physician. He urged them to have a good time, but not a foolish time. "The AIDS virus has not gone away and is not going away. Behave with the maturity and common sense that's necessary in our world today," he said.

The doctor spent considerably more time on the issue of drug use. There will be some drug testing at the games, he said, so be careful. Joyner offered some advice: At the doping control centers, don't let anybody handle your urine bottles; take your team doctor or some other team representative with you to the testing center; don't eat or drink anything on the way to drug testing if you don't know where it came from. Also, Joyner said, don't drink too much caffeinated Coke: The official soft drink of the 1992 Winter Olympic Games could cost you a medal. In their orientation packets, the athletes found a small card listing some of the products and substances that were illegal under International Olympic Committee rules. Among them were Primatene Mist, prednisone, Sudafed, Dimetapp, CoAdvil, CoTylenol, Alka Seltzer Plus (plop plop, fizz fizz, you're off the team), Contac, and Nyquil. The good news? Well, if worrying about the doping rules gave you a headache and an upset stomach, you were allowed to take two aspirin and a spoonful of Pepto Bismol. Greg Harney closed the subject by advising the athletes not to drink French tap water. "You might not be used to it," he said. "You don't want to get the trots or the green-apple two-step."

Bill Egan, who had been traveling in Europe for years and had no use for any of this information, sighed heavily and laid his head on his arm.

The advice kept coming. Kathy Rex, one of the athlete liaisons, told the Olympians they would be allowed to bring cameras to the opening ceremonies. But she implored them not to munch on M&Ms or carry signs saying such things as "Hi Mom." She also urged them to march in an orderly fashion: "Don't fall back into another country." Harney added, "When the national anthem is played, remember what you were taught in the second or third grade." A sports psychologist handed out a pamphlet called "Staying Focused at the Olympic Games." It covered a lot of territory. "Your dreams may be very vivid, or you may hardly remember them," page two said. "Some athletes have the same dream over and over. And athletes dream about both great victories and sad losses. We have never found any relationship between the dreams you have and your performance. In other words, dreams are nothing to worry about. Dreams are another sign that this is an exciting time for you." Egan, sitting in the back row, did not hear the psychologist's remarks. He was asleep.

A guy from the State Department got up to speak next. "We are aware of no specific terrorist threats," he said. "Having said that, I must tell you that governments have not been particularly good at predicting terrorist incidents." Now, that perked people up. "If you see a rock holding open a door at the Olympic village," the security expert said, "kick it out." Next, a French-born Air Force captain named Suzanne Cook provided some tips on French culture. The French appreciate it when you try to speak their language, she said. However, it won't do to speak English with a French accent. She explained that the French word for hello is "*bonjour*," but the lesson didn't go beyond that. Athletes who really wanted to speak the language would have to refer to the Olympic handbook, which contained a long list of useful phrases. It even showed how to pronounce them: Bone-swar, mad-mwa-zel. Ko-men-tahl-ay-voo? Jeh sweez a-may-ree-can. Jeh nuh parl pah fraun-say. At last, Harney thanked the athletes and excused them.

The skiers and coaches celebrated the end of the meeting by pounding a few beers and eating some pizza at a restaurant near the priory. The evening wasn't very French, or very Olympian for that matter. But they all had a great time. Jeff and AJ closed the place.

The coaches held a brief meeting over breakfast the next morning. Upon reflection, they agreed that Jeff Olson had a point. He deserved at least a long-shot opportunity to compete in the Olympic downhill. So they created a challenge for him: To win the fourth spot from Reggie, Jeff would have to finish in the top ten in training the day before the Olympic downhill. He would also have to beat Reggie. The coaches were giving Jeff a chance, but not much of one. He had never finished in the top ten of a major downhill in his life, and it was unlikely he would do it under extreme pressure on the eve of the Olympics. Jeff knew the odds were against him, but he figured it was better to have a very slight chance than to have no chance at all. As for Reggie, he wasn't upset by the coaches' decision. He knew Jeff had practically no hope of placing in the top ten. Besides, he planned to put the issue to rest by skiing well in training and proving he belonged in the downhill.

After breakfast, the men's alpine team met in the hotel lobby. Present were the downhillers, technical racers, coaches, and Alpine Program Director Dennis Agee. The skiers all wore their new sneakers, sweat pants, and the white and blue jackets they were supposed to wear at the awards ceremonies, if they were fortunate enough to go to any. They all looked quite snazzy and pleased.

Ueli had an announcement to make—"one thing who is very important to us," as he put it. At the Olympics, he said, athletes would not be permitted to wear any advertising on their clothing. If they had their sponsors' names on their helmets (Reggie Crist, for example, had a sticker on his helmet that advertised the Sun Valley ski resort), they had to cover them up. They even had to put tape over the name of the company—Spyder—that manufactured their downhill suits. A few of the racers grumbled, but Ueli said they had no choice. It was an International Olympic Committee rule, and any athlete who broke it would be disqualified. This was not meant to keep the games free of commercialism, by the way. The International Olympic Committee didn't care if people got rich off the games, as long as they were the right people. Only companies that had paid large sums of money to the committee could promote themselves. It was fine for Visa and M&M Mars and Coca-Cola, major sponsors all, to push their products at the Olympics. The yellow M&M Mars flag hung just below the Olympic flag on the streets of Albertville. But under no circumstances would Reggie Crist, who after all depended on sponsorships for most of his livelihood, be allowed to pick up a few extra bucks displaying the Sun Valley logo. The executives relaxing in their reserved seats could expect to profit from the Olympics; the young kooks who faced serious bodily harm hurtling half out of control down the Face de Bellevarde could not.

Before the meeting ended, Dennis Agee gave a brief inspirational speech.

"Try to keep everything in perspective. This is a big deal and you guys have done well and you should be proud of that. But let's keep it at a level where you guys can handle it," he said. "And look, this is not the end of your careers. You have not arrived. You still have to go all out. When this is all over, you have to go back to work, just like before. I don't want to see anybody sitting on their ass this spring saying, 'I made the Olympics.' "

After the meeting, the athletes posed for a few quick pictures in their snazzy outfits, then climbed into their vans for the ride to Val d'Isère, where they would be staying during the games.

The next day, the downhillers' first full day in Val d'Isère, the world went blank. Snowflakes as thick and heavy as cotton balls fell all day. The high blue sky collapsed and turned gray, and the dirty black streets vanished under mounds of cold white powder. The downhillers skied for a while, but the snow fell so heavily they couldn't see more than a few feet ahead of them. Without sunlight, all the dips and moguls came as surprises. Hundreds of men and women went to work on the Olympic downhill course, sweeping and shoveling away the snow one flake at a time. Training for the downhill was scheduled to begin in two days, but already the French were worried. The forecast called for snow to continue.

The Americans spent most of Tuesday and Wednesday at the athletes' village, just hanging around. Instead of building new housing for the skiers, the Olympic organizers had arranged to borrow Val d'Isère's Club Med, a handsome and spacious building that was normally used as a meeting place for vacationing singles. To get into Club Med you had to have a credential—a big plastic card bearing your picture—attesting that you were a coach, athlete, or employee of the French organizing committee. People entering the village presented their credentials to the man at the front door, sent their bags, if they had any, through the X-ray machine, and then walked beneath the arch of a metal detector. You weren't supposed to go into the village just to hang around, as if it were . . . a Club Med or something. But a lot of people did, including a large number who, though they wore organizing committee jackets and credentials, didn't seem to be doing anything for the organizing committee. Many of them were women—personable young women who seemed to enjoy talking to Olympic ski racers. The women were always there. Their presence probably wasn't essential to the Olympic effort, but nobody complained.

The main floor was the center of activity at Club Med. Just inside the front doors were a reception desk where racers could pick up phone messages and faxes, a few public phones (there were phones in the rooms, but you could only receive calls on them), a gift shop that sold newspapers and Olympic trinkets, and a small computer terminal that could be used to transmit messages to athletes at other venues. Up a short flight of stairs was a long bar, where the athletes could get a drink, with alcohol or without, anytime they wanted one. Most people went easy on the booze, maybe because it was the only thing at Club Med that was not free. Near the bar were a bank of big-screen televisions and lots of overstuffed chairs. Just beyond the TV screens was an auditorium of perhaps three hundred seats. At night the athletes could catch a movie (Club Med had films in several languages), listen to a band, or see a juggling act. Gigantic buffet meals were served in a cafeteria below the game room. For dinner, the athletes could have pasta, steak, fish, pork, or, if they were really hungry, all of the above.

Despite its attractive points, the American downhillers weren't crazy about Club Med. For one thing, the rooms were way too small. Club Med had made them tiny to encourage people to get out and mingle, which was fine if you were a single tourist traveling with one suitcase and a pair of skis. But the American downhillers, with their enormous bags of clothing and suitcase-size boom boxes, found the rooms impossibly cramped. Reggie Crist and Jeff Olson, who roomed together, often had a hard time just getting through their door: It opened only halfway before it came up against a little mountain of clothing. Tommy Moe and Kyle Rasmussen had the same problem. Only AJ, who had lucked into his own room, had enough space for all of his stuff.

A more serious problem was that for the first few days of the games there was no prohibition against smoking in the building. That drove the Americans crazy. God, they hated the Euros sometimes. Only the suave, chain-smoking French would invite a few hundred athletes to a big international competition and then gas them half to death in the hotel lobby. When the racers complained, the French announced a ban on smoking in the club, but they didn't enforce it. The Americans could always count on inhaling secondhand smoke as they walked through the lobby.

The racers' main reason for disliking Club Med was that it housed only ski racers. In the past, Olympic organizers had always tried to house athletes in one huge village in the host city. But in France in 1992, the games were spread across the vast Savoie region. Figure skating and hockey were in Albertville, women's alpine events in Meribel, bobsledding in La Plagne, men's alpine events in Val d'Isère, and so on. Each venue had its own small Olympic village. AJ said one of the best things about the 1988 games in Calgary was getting to know athletes from many different sports. By contrast, the people housed in Club Med in Val d'Isère were, except for the two Hungarians and the odd Korean or Romanian, the same people the racers traveled with all winter. The

Olympics were supposed to be special, but the housing plan made the games feel like just another World Cup race. How boring! Within a day of the team's arrival, Tommy Moe started calling the place "Club Dread."

Reggie Crist's stay was made more pleasant by two faxes he received on Tuesday. The first was from his sister Danielle, who was attending college at the University of Colorado.

> For: Olympic Superstar Reggie Crist,
> CONGRATULATIONS!!!
> Yeah Reg! I'm so excited for you. It must feel good! All the ceremonies, press & equipment; I can't believe my own brother is so famous! I saw your interview from Wengen on ESPN w/all my roommates the other day. I was so proud. What a great, positive attitude you have. It sounds like your head's in the right place. You had a great air about you. It was good to see a big-time athlete with so much competence and intelligence and so little arrogance. (Especially when it's my brother!) You sound strong & confident, I hope it all comes out this weekend! I wish I could be there to watch with the rest of the gang, but I've got to stick with the college team out here. . . .
> Anyway, I'm praying & thinking about you and hoping you ski as well as you know how. You've got so much talent and energy—I hope it all comes together for you. Give my best to Tommy, AJ and Rat [a nickname for Kyle Rasmussen] as well. Go team U.S.A.! Kick ass! I can't even tell you how proud I am of you. I mean that.
> Blow doors! I love you & good luck!
> Your favorite & loving sister,
> Danielle

The other fax was from Reggie's cousin Scott in Palo Alto, California. It said:

> No nose pickers.
> Just ass kickers!

At the team meeting Wednesday night, Bill Egan announced the racers' schedule for the next day—downhill training in the morning, slalom and giant slalom training in the afternoon. Bill acknowledged that the downhill run might be canceled because of the weather, but he didn't want anybody to plan a day off and then find himself in the starting gate, unprepared. He told the guys to stay focused, just in case. As he spoke, AJ Kitt thumbed through a copy of *USA Today*. His picture was on the front of the sports page, and inside there was an article bearing the headline, "US men's skiing hopes rest with AJ Kitt."

Bill Egan delivered his speech to a sizeable audience. At World Cup races, only the coaches, the athletes, and physical therapist Gary Myers attended the team meetings. But that Wednesday at Club Med, the room was crowded with people the racers had never seen before, and, after the Olympics, might never see again. One was Whitey Willauer, the Olympic Committee's top official in Val d'Isère. Also present were an Olympic Committee physical therapist, a translator, and a few other Olympic Committee operatives. All these people were friendly and eager to help, but they didn't seem to have much to do. Nobody ever asked translator David Miller to translate anything—the downhillers had gotten by in Europe without translators for years—so he spent most of his time skiing and having fun. And the team already had Gary Myers, so physical therapist Kevin Moody didn't have any work, either. At the Olympics, it seemed, you always got more than you needed, and sometimes more than you wanted.

At times, the Olympic Committee people could be a distraction. When Bill Egan finished talking, Whitey Willauer took a moment to talk about the threat of terorrism at the games. His report: Don't worry about it. "Through my own contacts with CIA, FBI, and State, there are no problems that they know of," he said. "It's quiet here." Willauer, who seemed to enjoy saying he had contacts at the CIA, mentioned as an aside that there was "noise" in Barcelona, the site of the upcoming summer games. But he assured everyone that there was no noise in Albertville.

The downhillers glanced at each other and tried not to laugh. CIA? State? Was this guy serious? Terrorism was not a joke, but please. Noise?

AJ's parents showed up at Club Med after the meeting. The Kitts, who had arrived in Val d'Isère earlier that day, were not the sort of people who boasted about their successful and increasingly well known son—at least not when he was around. That night, Ross and Nancy went out to dinner with AJ and some of his friends. At the cramped restaurant, Nancy was seated near an elderly Frenchman who was dining alone. The man started a conversation by asking which events Nancy had come to see. AJ's mother stifled the urge to burble something about her daring wonderful boy the ski racer, who was sitting right there (the Frenchman apparently didn't recognize him). The Kitts didn't want to embarrass AJ any more than was absolutely necessary. Nancy told the gentleman she was interested mainly in the downhill, and left it at that.

But the Kitts didn't exactly try to be anonymous either. Ross had appeared at Club Med sporting a white baseball cap bearing the U.S. Ski Team logo and the words, "AJ Kitt Fan Club." He wore it throughout his stay in Val d'Isère. And the Kitts had also brought with them a few dozen AJ Kitt Fan Club sweatshirts (the shirts had a little picture of a mountain on the front and an American flag on the sleeve), which they gave to anyone who seemed interested in having one.

Nancy wore her sweatshirt everywhere she went. Late that night, she and Ross visited a dusty joint called Dick's T-bar. They were accompanied by Bill Egan, who, they could tell right away, was planning a wild evening. Bill did not drink all that often, but when he did, he drank joyfully, with great spirit, and he tended to involve a lot of people, whether they wanted to be involved or not. When drunk, the downhill coach often let loose a high-pitched mad cackle that could be heard over loud music and through thick walls. Beatrice Tempesta, the owner of Val d'Isère's Hotel La Becca, where the team stayed every winter, used a French phrase to describe the laugh. She said it sounded—this is a rough translation—"like a nut rolling downstairs." Nobody on the team was sure if she meant an acorn or a lunatic, but either way the description was apt.

The nuts were really tumbling that night at Dick's T-Bar. Late in the evening Bill asked Nancy to dance. AJ's mother, a cheerful but by no means wacky woman, didn't know what she was in for. She and Bill jiggled to the rock and roll for a few minutes, and then Bill, cackling, dropped to the floor, lay on his stomach, and began wiggling spastically around. He was "doing the gator," he said. Soon he tried to drag Nancy onto the floor with him. The mother of America's Hope for a Medal in Alpine Skiing had not drunk enough that night, probably never had drunk enough, to really appreciate Bill's dance artistry. But she got down there for a moment anyway, just to be a sport. The place went wild. When she got up, everyone congratulated her on doing such a fine gator. She became an instant celebrity.

But Nancy's fame was fleeting, which was fine with her. The next day, people in Val d'Isère stopped talking about her dancing—and began speculating about what her son could do.

15

The Olympic
Downhill

So much for weather worries: Thursday was warm and bright, an ideal day for downhill training. That morning, a CBS cameraman became the first—as well as the second—person to crash on the Face de Bellevarde. The first fall happened at the entrance to the rock tunnel, the section that had confused even the best racers in the world a year earlier. The fellow was toting a camera, trying to get pictures of the racers as they inspected the course. It was common for TV people to do this at big events, and also common for them to fall down doing it. The CBS guy was not a good enough skier to handle the steep pitch between the boulders. He lost his balance at the top of the pitch, tipped over, and slid to the bottom. When he got there he toppled Alfonse Gomis, one of two racers representing the snowless African nation of Senegal. Nobody was hurt. The cameraman collected himself and kept skiing shakily on. When he got to a fence that had been set up above the next part of the course, the cameraman tried to stop, but he tipped over again and slid beneath it. As he passed under it, he hooked his ski pole into the cloth netting and used it to stop himself from sliding any farther. He held on for dear life, like a would-be suicide who has changed his mind and is now dangling from a window ledge. Everyone watched for a moment, wondering what would happen next. Nothing did. The guy just lay there. He couldn't get up. Finally, satisfied that nothing else interesting would happen, a coach skied over and hoisted him to his feet.

Cameramen were having a bad day all around. The first forerunner, a young Frenchman named Carquex, skied down the course wearing a lightweight TV camera strapped to his leg and a heavy sack of video equipment on his back. The pictures he made while tucking down the hill were shown on a giant TV screen in a finish. But soon he got going a little too fast, caught an edge, and vaulted headfirst into the rock tunnel. He hit the padding hard. It took him a few minutes to unscramble his circuits and get off the course.

Ueli Luthi, who saw the biff from his perch higher up the hill, said into the radio, "Now they know the nets work."

Yes, the nets did work, and it was a good thing. A lot of guys had trouble with the net turn, the sharp right turn that emptied out onto a narrow road. Even more skied badly through the rock tunnel, where athletes had to throw their skis sideways to keep from crashing into the padding. Even Franz Heinzer got out of control. In the rock tunnel he began his turn too late. The only way he could make it through was to ski up the side of the fence like a stock car driver making a banked turn. Somehow he finished the turn and continued on. Indeed, most of the skiers who made what might have been disastrous mistakes somehow bounced off the fences and kept going.

Most, but not all. On the first day of training, the Canadian men's downhillers began what would be a nightmarish week of ineptitude and frustration. The Canadian coaches had decided to choose their downhill team by using the training runs as qualification races. Eight men would train, and the four who skied fastest would compete in the Olympics. Bill Egan grimaced when he heard about the plan. He didn't like qualification races because they forced the athletes to go harder in the early training runs than they should. If a guy wanted to punch it in the last run of the week, that was fine; by then he'd know the terrain. But going like crazy in the first run of the week, Bill felt, could get you hurt. This time he was right. Brian Stemmle, racer number seventeen, went too straight off the tunnel jump and hooked his ski tip on the gate below. His legs split apart and his shoulder smacked the snow. He slammed so hard into the fence below the jump that it took a few minutes for the course workers to fix it. Stemmle skied off with a sore shoulder. Fifteen minutes later, teammate Roman Torn leaned the wrong way as he went off the finish jump, flew way too far, and crash-landed more or less on his backside. He aggravated an ankle injury he had sustained while skiing the day before. The way the Canadians were skiing was a health hazard, and it would only get worse.

Only the French seemed to understand the course: In the first training run, four Frenchmen finished in the top ten. The headline in the next day's Olympic newspaper, *Le Quotidien des Jeux,* said, "Practice makes perfect for the French." Exactly. Franck Piccard and his teammates, desperate to do well in front of the home crowd, had been training on the course like crazy. It was against the rules to take practice runs on the course once training had begun. But there was nothing saying the French couldn't practice on their new course in the months before the games began.

AJ Kitt skied through the rock tunnel that day as if it were a great big pinball machine and he were a silver ball. Like Heinzer, he creamed the padding, but somehow kept his feet beneath him and wobbled through. Even with the mistake, his time was 1:54.62, which put him in eleventh place. The American coaches tried not to make much of training times, but that afternoon Jim Tracy couldn't help sounding upbeat. "I kind of like where AJ finished today," he said. "He's not that far out." AJ was satisfied, too. He liked his line, except when it led him into the fence. His plan now was simply to go faster—be more aggressive, have a more aerodynamic profile. The first run had been a fast inspection. Now, little by little, day by day, he would build up to race speed. And on race day, he would go for it.

AJ also had to admit he liked the course more than he had the year before—not because he had changed, but because it had. The net turn and the rock tunnel were still tough, but the other turns were gentler now. Last year he had been forced to slam on the brakes in every corner. Now he could pump the brakes and still make it. It still wasn't his idea of a great downhill course, not hardly, but at least you could ski it. When AJ finished his run, he got a radio and told his teammates, "OK, overall the course runs real good. It's got a lot better rhythm than it did last year." But he added, "It's real turny. There's not a lot of places to grab a tuck."

Then he had to repeat his assessment for the biggest media throng he had ever seen. The downhillers had always wished for more attention from the press. Well, they were going to get it now, in a big way. As soon as AJ got off the radio, CBS grabbed him for an interview. As usual, the TV people could get much closer to the athletes than the print reporters could. But their access was not unlimited. In Val d'Isère, the camera people were confined in small wooden pens next to the coaches' area. To get an interview, a CBS operative had to coax the athletes toward the camera crew.

On that first day, AJ went along with it. He talked into the camera lens for a few minutes and then turned to leave. Former U.S. Ski Team Coach Bob Beattie, who was working for CBS radio, was there waiting for him. They talked. After that, Kitt chatted with the BBC, the American cable network TNT, a Mexican broadcast outfit, and countless print reporters. He couldn't believe it. All this for a training run? "It was like I'd won a race," he said later. It took him an hour to get away from them.

Well, there would be no more of that. At the team meeting that night, Bill Egan asked Howard Peterson, the head of the U.S. Ski Team, to find AJ after the next day's training run and hustle him away. Bill believed strongly that his athletes should do everything they could to promote the sport, and themselves. But things were getting out of control. This was the Olympic downhill, and AJ had a real chance to do well. Bill didn't want anything to get in his way.

Kyle Rasmussen got a lot of attention too, and liked it. After his run— he skied cautiously and finished tied for thirty-first—he was interviewed by Hank Kashiwa of CBS and by lots of print and radio people. He would have chatted all afternoon if they had wanted him to. Kyle had a thing about publicity: He felt he didn't get enough of it. In a way, he understood why. The press was interested mostly in winners, and he hadn't won anything, at least not on the World Cup circuit. But it seemed to Kyle that the press knew even less about him than his performance warranted. One year GGP Sports, a California TV outfit, covered the downhill race in Val Gardena, Italy. When Kyle appeared on the screen, announcer Greg Lewis said, "Kyle's twenty-eight now, near the end of his career." Kyle was apoplectic. Twenty-eight? At the end of my career? He was in his early twenties at the time, and barely getting started. Clearly Kyle was turning anonymity into an art form. Ever since then, he had been looking for opportunities to tell people who he was. At the Olympic downhill race it was easy. All you had to do was make it to the bottom and a few dozen reporters would be waiting to make you famous.

* * *

Before the training run, Reggie Crist got another fax from his cousin:

Today's training run—think of it as the first time with your girl, getting to know all the bumps and harsh curves on the course. On race day, you'll know exactly how to attack her. But don't let your dick drag. Go for it all.

Scott

Reggie was fired up for the Olympics, probably as fired up as Bill Egan had ever seen him. When deciding which line to ski in a downhill, Reggie had always done whatever the coaches told him. He wasn't confident enough to try new things. But after inspection that morning in Val d'Isère, he told Egan that he planned to try a different line in the tower turn. And why not? If I can ski Kitzbühel, Reggie told himself, I can ski this, and do it my own way. But it wasn't just Kitzbühel that had given him confidence: Wengen had too, which made him one of the rare athletes who actually gained confidence from a race in which he crashed. In downhill, you had to find inspiration in anything you could.

In the starting gate that Thursday, Reggie's mind wandered, much as it had in Kitzbühel. This time, instead of thinking of autographing a woman's breast, he thought of one of Val d'Isère's parking lots. Reggie had left Curtis Bacca's car there and, as he was prone to do, had forgotten to tell him. Just before he was to begin his freefall down the Face de Bellevarde, Reggie said to Gary Myers, "Tell Curtis his car is in the Funival parking lot. I left the key on the left front tire."

And then he was gone. He finished twentieth.

Jeff Olson came in forty-fourth in that training run. But he wasn't concentrating on skiing either, not completely. Jeff was still upset about the way the downhill team was being put together. He didn't feel he should have to finish in the top ten on the last day of training in order to qualify. Neither he nor Reggie had had stellar results in World Cup downhill races. Nor had Kyle, for that matter. Jeff felt the three of them should compete for the last two spots in the downhill. The guys who finished first and second would race, and the one who came in third would not. Jeff couldn't stop thinking about this problem. He was completely stuck on it. He tried to get Ueli to go along with the plan, but Ueli was not willing to change the rules again. So Jeff fumed. Because he was a nice guy, he didn't take it out on Reggie, his roommate at Club Med. He understood that Reggie wanted to race as much as he did. The two men never really talked about the problem, but Reggie knew how Jeff felt. He knew how important the downhill was to Jeff. But being on the U.S. men's downhill team meant you constantly had to compete against your friends. This situation was nothing new or unusual. Jeff would have to cope with this problem alone. But instead of going out there and proving himself, Jeff hung his head and lamented the unfairness of it all.

AJ got some happy financial news at the Olympics. First, he learned that he would get a cash prize for having the second-best overall results in what were known as the Club 5 downhill races—Val d'Isère, Val Gardena, Garmisch, and the two races at Kitzbühel. AJ had been aware that the events referred to themselves as Club 5 races, but he hadn't known the top finishers would get prizes. Surprise! Franz Heinzer had come in first, and AJ was second. His reward was 15,000 Swiss francs, or about $10,000. Pennies from heaven. The Club 5 organizers had invited AJ to Liechtenstein after the ski season to collect the prize, but AJ declined.

"I have plans for the spring," he said. "They involve America, my dog, the beach, and a chick. Any chick."

There was more good news. Jon Franklin, AJ's agent, told AJ he had signed a new headgear sponsor: McDonald's. Kitt was to wear the golden arches on his helmet in the last three downhill races of the season—Morioka, Japan; Panorama, Canada; and Aspen, Colorado. The fast-food company had agreed to pay $25,000 for the publicity. McDonald's could renew the deal for the next season—for six figures. AJ couldn't believe his luck. The World Cup victory, and that *Sports Illustrated* cover, had really paid off. Twenty-five thousand dollars? To put a yellow M on his helmet and wear a McDonald's baseball cap in interviews? You betcha.

When Jeff Olson got dressed for the training runs that Friday morning, he knew he had a lot of work to do. If he was going to beat Reggie Crist, he had to start skiing a lot better than he had on Thursday. But things didn't seem to go his way in downhill anymore, and that Friday was a humiliating example. He skied fairly well on the top half of the course in his first run. But as he was approaching the tunnel jump he saw an official waving a big yellow flag—the sign for racers to stop. The racer before Jeff had fallen, and he and his skis were still strewn about the course. If this had been a race, Jeff could have taken the lift back to the top and started over. But in a training run, you couldn't go back. The only options were to continue the run from where you were flagged off or leave the course. Jeff kept going, but because his run wasn't timed, he wouldn't be able to tell how he compared to the other racers.

Things went even worse for him that afternoon. In the tower turn, he skied too close to the net, then turned sharply so he wouldn't hit it. His right ski blew off. Jeff went down on his right shoulder. It wasn't a serious crash. Bill Egan, who was shooting video there, thought Jeff just bailed out so he wouldn't get hurt. The racer slid on his side about fifty feet, then bounced up and stood on one ski, breathing hard and shaking his head. Jeff couldn't believe his lousy luck. As far as he was concerned, the crash in the tower turn wasn't his fault. That afternoon, he explained what happened by saying, "It was just a total pre-release." The term "pre-release" referred to the sudden and unexplained opening of a ski binding. A pre-release left you with only one ski, and as a result you usually crashed. (Jeff felt his crash in the Zielschuss at Kitzbühel had also been the result of a pre-release.) Racers didn't get flagged off very often, and bindings didn't pre-release all that often, either. And yet Jeff had suffered both curses in the same afternoon.

Bad luck, yes, but there might have been another reason for Jeff's problems in downhill. As coach Jim Tracy put it, "He just doesn't seem to have that edge anymore." Tracy was talking about that competitive edge, the mental sharpness that downhillers need. (AJ Kitt, remember, had admitted that he hadn't had that edge in the first of the two races in Kitzbühel in January.) If you have the edge, you don't make a mistake in the tower turn. Or if you do, you find a way to ski through the trouble. You believe in yourself, and you ski well. Jeff was a terrific skier, no question; he was easily the best super G skier on the team. But to be a downhiller, to curl into a tuck and mock gravity the way downhillers did, you needed that edge, and Jeff didn't seem to have it. He had lost it somewhere, maybe as he flew backward off that jump in Val d'Isère more than a year earlier, maybe not, but anyway he had lost it. If he wanted to ski in the Olympic downhill, he had to get that edge back in a hurry.

The other Americans had mixed results, too. In the first training run, AJ skied well enough to finish seventh, but he landed with a bang off the finish jump and wrenched his back. He didn't feel like racing in the afternoon, and it showed: He bounced off the fence in the tower turn, whacked a gate with his shoulder (the two-legged red gate bent over like a palm tree in a hurricane), kept going, made a few lousy turns, and pulled off the course. Enough was enough.

Tommy Moe finished thirty-second and—this felt nice—eleventh. Reggie Crist was forty-second and twenty-third. He actually missed a gate in the first run. He skied too low in the tower turn and wound up skiing between the gate and the fence instead of between the two gates. Kyle was thirty-ninth, thirty-first, and miserable.

The Crashing Canadians were also back on the hill that day, except for Brian Stemmle, whose shoulder was still sore from his spill the day before. Ed Podivinsky, number twenty-four, made a mistake coming into the rock tunnel and wound up sliding through the chute on his side. Roman Torn made it a little farther than that, but not as far as he had the day before. He was finishing a long left turn just below the rocks when he lost his edge, sat back, tipped over, and slid into a fence. But Torn was a tough kid. He scraped the snow off his lenses, hobbled over to the lift, and went back to the start for the day's second training run. He was going to finish the course if it killed him. It almost did: On his next run, he caught an edge in the finish schuss and just managed to get under the banner standing up.

Every show has a sideshow, an interesting and often freakish complement to the main event. At the 1992 Winter Olympics, the best sideshow involved Helmut Girardelli, Marc Girardelli's father, coach, and supreme leader. For the people in the ski world, witnessing Helmut Girardelli's antics was just plain fun, a welcome diversion from the excessive pomp and glitz of the games.

Helmut Girardelli was a great character, one of the few people on the

Right on the Edge of Crazy

World Cup circuit everyone knew. Girardelli was easy to spot: He was the fat guy standing in his skis on the side of the downhill course, his gray-black hair covered in a white cotton ski hat, the stub of a cigarette sticking out of his lips. Girardelli smoked his cigarettes down to the filter and then forgot about them; it was not unusual for him to take one from the pack, poke it into the corner of his mouth, and light it, never realizing he already had a butt stuck in the other corner. But he could not be written off simply as a comic character: A lot of coaches, including Bill Egan, respected Helmut because he always stood up for what was right at World Cup meetings, even if it didn't directly benefit Marc.

They were quite a pair, the Girardellis. Helmut, who seemed to like a fight as much as a cigarette, had gotten angry at the Austrian national ski organization years before—he didn't feel Marc was getting adequate coaching—and had stormed off to Luxembourg to start his own ski team. The team consisted of Marc. Helmut was the coach, and a demanding one. The American downhillers liked to tell about a time when Marc fell in a race. According to the story, Helmut rushed down the hill and started calling his son an idiot even before Marc stopped sliding. Marc probably called himself worse than that. Marc—whom the Americans called Hooter, for no particular reason—might have been the hardest-working athlete on the World Cup tour. On days when there were two downhill training runs, most guys dragged back to the hotel after the second run to catch a nap. Marc always went back to the hill to practice slalom turns until the lifts closed. He was Tommy Moe's hero, and not just because, like Tommy, he used Dynastar skis. By the start of the 1992 Olympics, Hooter, twenty-eight years old, had won more than three dozen World Cup races, four overall World Cup titles, and eight Alpine World Championship medals. As it happened, though, he had never won an Olympic medal. He had been disqualified from the 1984 Olympics in Sarajevo, Yugoslavia, because he was not yet a legal resident of Luxembourg. And he had competed in the 1988 games in Calgary, but injuries had kept him from doing any better than ninth in the downhill. Everybody figured he would win at least one medal in the Albertville games.

But things began badly for the Girardellis at the Olympics, and got worse. First, they had transportation problems: The authorities wouldn't let them land the family helicopter in Val d'Isère—the airspace was closed for security reasons—so they had to drive into the mountains like everyone else. Then, on the second day of training, Marc crashed right below the place where Helmut was standing. Helmut asked several people if Marc was all right. No one answered. He asked again, but still no one told him if his son was hurt. He put on his skis and started onto the course, but a security guard stopped him. According to the rules, coaches were not allowed to go on the course during a training run. Helmut didn't care. He shoved the security man out of the way and skied to Marc, who, it turned out, was not injured.

Helmut's relations with the security people, however, were. During inspection the next day, Helmut arrived at the rock tunnel to find that the course workers had built a temporary fence at the opening. Apparently the idea was to preserve the snow in the tunnel.

"What's this?" Helmut said.

"You can't go through the tunnel. You have to go around," the security man said.

"That's stupid. Of course we can go through," Helmut said. He began to remove the fence. The guard tried to stop him. Helmut shoved him away. The guard shoved back. Helmut threw a punch, but didn't connect. Then he grabbed the fellow's radio and threw it into a pile of snow. Everyone watching thought the whole scene was ridiculous and unnecessary, but also quite entertaining. For a while, the Olympic officials considered revoking Helmut's credential, which would have meant that the father and coach of perhaps the greatest ski racer in history would be forced to watch the Olympics on TV. That didn't happen. The next day, he was allowed back on the hill. Helmut Girardelli was not the sort of man who often lost a fight.

The main topic of discussion at Friday's team meeting was the opening ceremonies, which would be held Saturday evening in Albertville, down-valley from Val d'Isère. The downhillers naturally wanted to go. The ceremonies promised to be bright and showy, something to see. They were also going to be televised in the United States, which meant all the athletes would have a chance to wave at their friends and family back home. Besides, it would be the only chance they'd have to wear their parade uniforms—a long jacket, a scarf, a handsome pair of slacks, that maroon fedora. But the athletes competing in Val d'Isère faced serious logistical problems in getting to the ceremonies. The road between Val d'Isère and Albertville was winding and narrow, as tricky as the downhill course; with traffic, the trip could take hours each way. Downhill training was scheduled to begin about 12:15 P.M., and buses were leaving Val d'Isère about forty-five minutes later. Racers who wanted to go would have to change clothes in the bus. The biggest problem was that the Olympic downhill race would be held the next day. On the eve of their big event, the athletes might not get home until midnight.

Ueli Luthi told the athletes, "I don't want to be a spoiler or an asshole, but I give you an opinion. If you want to race on Sunday and you want to do well, you should stay here Saturday night. The trip to Albertville is going to be strenuous. I don't think it is the best of preparations." Still, he would leave the decision up to the athletes.

AJ said he definitely wasn't going to Albertville. Tommy, Kyle, and Reggie didn't think they'd go either. Jeff said, "If I don't get top ten tomorrow, I'm going."

AJ finished thirteenth on Saturday, the last day of training. He made one big mistake—he hit a bump about halfway through and got tossed off line—but he still felt he skied as well as he had all week. He was ready to race. "I feel confident I can make the top five or ten. And if I have an unreal run, if I'm really, really on, I can be top three. Nobody has an advantage tomorrow. This course is hard for everyone. I think there are fifteen people who can place in the top three tomorrow."

Jeff Olson went to the starting gate that day feeling doomed. He doubted he could finish in the top ten, not after the way things had gone earlier in the week. Hey, he'd be lucky to finish at all. That was how he felt, at least. Still, it wasn't over yet. Maybe, Jeff thought, something good will finally happen and I'll make the downhill team after all. Jeff had skied plenty of good downhill races before; who was to say he wouldn't do it again now? Punch it, he told himself. Be aggressive. Go for it. He thrust his wide shoulders out of the gate and sizzled down the first steep pitch. Jeff skied fairly well, if tentatively, through the net turn. But when he got to the sweeping turn just below that, things went wrong. Jeff snagged his ski on a rut or a stick or a snow gremlin or something, and poof, he got high-sided, thrown forward as if someone had shoved him from behind. He managed to land on his feet and skid sideways until he stopped. It was all over, and he hadn't even missed a gate. Basically, he had washed out for no reason. Jeff just wagged his head and laughed to himself. That's about how my luck has been going, he thought. Then he skied dejectedly to the bottom, finishing fifteen seconds behind the leader, Jan Einar Thorsen of Norway. What a disappointment for him. Two years earlier, it had seemed a sure thing that he would compete in the Olympic downhill in Val d'Isère. He was going to be the team leader, America's Hope for a Medal. Now somebody else had that title and Jeff wasn't even a contender. In the finish, he stepped out of his skis and shook his head again. It was over. He put away his equipment, changed his clothes, and climbed onto a bus. To heck with it. He was going to the opening ceremonies.

Tommy Moe was also feeling bewildered. He too had a poor last training run: He caught an edge near the last gate, almost crashed, and finished forty-fifth, six seconds behind Thorsen. Kyle Rasmussen tried an experiment that day. Instead of using his long downhill skis, he raced on his super G boards, a shorter pair. Paul Accola of Switzerland was racing on super G skis and having great luck; Kyle, who didn't feel he had skied well all week, figured he might as well give it a try. It didn't work out. He finished thirty-third, partly because the shorter skis tended to rattle at high speeds. Schussing down a steep pitch on super G skis was like doing one hundred miles an hour in a car with a loose wheel. "They were a little squirrelly," he said. He was going back to the long skis on race day.

Of the Americans, only Reggie was completely satisfied with his skiing. He placed nineteenth, only four tenths of a second behind AJ. He felt the way he did on the last day of training in Wengen—that he had the ability to do great things, or at least really good ones. But he resolved that the Olympic race would go better than the one in Wengen had gone.

Two more Canadians, Cary Mullen and Rob Crossan, biffed it that morning, but luckily they both got up. Ed Podivinsky fell again, and didn't. He was entering a high-speed turn near the top of the course when he twisted sideways and then vaulted forward, like a motorcyclist getting pitched over the handlebars. He lay for a long time on the side of the course. The big television screen in the finish showed him lying there, then showed the helicopter drifting up the mountainside to get him. Tommy Moe had to stand in the starting gate for fifteen minutes while they took the Canadian off.

The cheerful public-address announcer tried to lighten the mood. "Ed Podivinsky seems to have been slightly injured . . . nothing too drastic," she babbled. "As you can see, this course is extremely well protected . . . Probably he will be all right." A moment later, she announced that he "just has a slight problem with the ligaments in his knee." The slight problem was that the innards of his right knee had more or less exploded, and he was going to need major surgery and months of rehabilitation before he could even think of skiing again.

Tommy bumped into Podivinsky later that day at Club Med. The Canadian was on crutches, his knee wrapped to the point of mummification.

"Tough luck," Moe said.

"Yeah," Podivinsky said. "Sorry to keep you waiting up there."

Late Saturday afternoon, the downhillers met at Hotel La Becca to study the video of the day's training runs. This would be their last chance to see what they were doing well and not so well, and examine how other racers were handling the Face de Bellevarde. As usual, it was not a terribly serious occasion. The tape showed Hannes Zehentner, racer number three, crashing heavily in the net turn and blowing out his knee. The Americans howled. "Let's watch that again," AJ said, and they played it one more time. Bill Egan, who was afraid of heights, had shot the footage from atop a huge boulder.

"Great video," Kyle Rasmussen said.

"I was scared to death. It's a big event, or I'd never have gone up there," Bill said.

Bill spent a lot of time talking to the racers about the long, one-hundred-eighty-degree left turn just below the net turn. He considered it a crucial part of the course. The racers entered the turn going as fast as they went anywhere on the course. As they skated around its arc, they passed over several bumps, each one just large enough to throw them off line. In watching the racers from atop the big rock, Bill had noticed that Marc Girardelli had taken a wider line than anyone else, thereby skiing around some of the bumps. Girardelli was increasing the length of the arc, and it was paying off: He had placed second in the final training run. Bill urged his racers to find Girardelli's line and follow it.

"We've got to go for that tomorrow," he said. "Got to."

Kyle Rasmussen stayed at La Becca after the video session to have dinner with his wife, Linda, who had arrived from California earlier in the week. (Their son, Anthony, was staying with relatives.) When they finished eating, they put on their heavy jackets and got a ride to the bottom of the downhill course, where the opening ceremonies were being shown on a giant outdoor television screen. Kyle and Linda took a seat in the bleachers to watch. What Kyle saw that night made him feel more Olympian, more a part of this event, than anything else he'd experienced. The French put together a spectacular show, part parade, part circus, part ballet, part Broadway musical. The ceremonies began with the procession of athletes into the Olympic stadium. Jeff Olson, decked out in his scarf, long jacket, dress slacks, and snazzy maroon fedora, marched into the stadium with the American delegation, smiling and waving. A cityful of pigeons flocked skyward. The Olympic flag was hoisted and the Olympic torch carried into the stadium and passed from hand to hand. Finally, a little French boy touched the flame to a thin steel cable. The fire crept up the cable and ignited the huge Olympic bowl. Seeing the little boy, Kyle thought of Anthony and got choked up. Soon, hundreds of jugglers and dancers spilled out of giant cornucopias, and roller skaters formed the Olympic rings. It was beautiful, as grand as the games themselves.

AJ, who was also watching the big TV screen with his parents and friends, was dazzled. So was Jeff, down in Albertville. Everyone was. In the weeks leading to the Olympics, the downhillers had not thought much about the opening ceremonies. They had been focused on the race itself. But as they watched this marvelous display of color and unity and emotion, Kyle and AJ and Jeff couldn't help feeling they were part of something incredibly important. These young men had been dreaming of going to the Olympics since elementary school. Now they were here, and it was everything they had hoped it would be. This is the greatest thing I've ever seen, Jeff thought, the hair rising on his arms. Thank God I didn't miss it.

Kyle reluctantly left the ceremonies early to attend the last team meeting before the race. AJ, as always on his own program, didn't attend; he had told the coaches he wanted to spend the time with his family and friends. Ueli Luthi opened the meeting. He had two final pieces of advice for his athletes. First, be aggressive. Project your upper body down the hill as you ski. "Don't take the backseat," he said. Second, don't try too hard to stay on line. If you can follow the line you picked out during inspection, great. If you stray from it, don't trouble yourself about getting back to it. Let your skis run and you'll be all right.

Ueli said, "The training is over, eh? It's the biggest downhill race you can go into. There is nothing bigger. Even if we are not the top favorites, don't let that bother you. Go for your personal best. Don't worry about who the other guys are. Go and ski your race. Don't think you have to do anything special tomorrow because of us, the coaches, or for the people watching in the U.S. You do this for you." Ueli paused, then turned to Egan and said, "Billegan?"

"You guys are skiing good," Bill said. "Really good. I'm always proud of the way you guys perform, and you should be too. The only thing you have to do tomorrow is be able to look yourself in the mirror and say, 'I gave it my best.' Somebody's going to pop through tomorrow, and it might as well be you guys."

Kyle watched himself on video for a few minutes after the meeting. He hated what he saw. His feet and his legs seemed all right, if you didn't count the rattle of those squirrelly skis, but his upper body . . . well, he could hardly stand to look. He was skiing with his arms wide open, as if he were waiting for a hug. And he was upright, stiff, as if his backbone had turned to stone. Sure, his back had hurt, but not enough to make him ski like that. He didn't let it show as he watched the tape, but Kyle was embarrassed, and angry. Maybe I don't belong here after all, he thought. His brother Greg, a pretty good skier himself, had been ragging Kyle about his skiing all season. "Goddamnit," Greg would say, "what are you doing there? How can you let these guys beat you? How can you let AJ beat you? You can kick his ass, can't you?" Kyle used to think he could, but wasn't sure. He didn't know if he could beat anyone anymore. In four training runs, he had beaten Reggie Crist only once, and he wouldn't have outrun Tommy Moe at all if Tommy hadn't almost biffed it in the last turn. Kyle had wanted more than anything to make the Olympic team, but just being here wasn't enough anymore. He wanted to ski really well, or at least respectably. Watching himself on video, he wasn't sure he could manage it.

When he was through, he met Linda in the Club Med lobby and they got a ride back to Hotel La Becca, where they would spend the night. In their room, Linda showed Kyle some newspaper articles she had brought with her. A few of them made him laugh. The *Modesto Bee*, published near Kyle's home, had run a story about his selection to the Olympic team. The headline said, "Happy Trails to Albertville." One paragraph said, "Rasmussen's teammates began calling him 'The Cowboy Skier' when they learned that he spent his summers working cattle on his grandfather's ranch near Angels Camp." That cracked him up. So far as Kyle knew, no one had ever referred to him as the Cowboy Skier until the day that story was published. But OK, he thought. I'll be the Cowboy Skier if they want me to be. Just as long as they call me something. A couple of days after the "Happy Trails" article, the same paper had published a big Olympic preview section. On the sports page, along with another story about Kyle, it had printed a beautiful color picture . . . of Steve Porino. Oops.

But most of the articles weren't funny at all. They were, Kyle thought, really nice. The headline in one paper said, "Kyle Rasmussen represents U.S.A. in 1992 Winter Olympics." The *Calaveras Californian* ("Home of the Jumping Frog") said, "Rasmussen off to Albertville." "Local skier earns spot on U.S. Olympic team," another paper said. Even the *Modesto Bee* had done well by him, if you didn't count the little mistakes. Its headline said, "Mother Lode skier looks for Olympic gold." The paper even mentioned that Linda was the 1985 Homecoming Queen at Bret Harte High. Linda was embarrassed about that. She didn't think that sort of thing necessarily mattered now that she was in her twenties and had a son nearly two years old.

Along with the newspaper stories, Linda had also brought some things from the folks back home—cards, letters, banners, and so on. Kyle especially liked the construction-paper cards some first-graders made for him. Each one had a little message: "Go Kyle!" "Don't fall." "Good luck." "Love you." Some of the kids even wrote down their phone numbers, just in case Kyle wanted to call and talk. Reading all this stuff, Kyle began to feel that what he was doing might actually be important, that it really mattered to people, even people he didn't even know. The folks at home didn't really understand his job—they didn't know what the World Cup circuit was, and probably never would. But they knew about the Olympics; that was for sure. For the first time, Kyle began to see that a lot of people were going to be watching, and pulling for him, when he pushed out of the starting gate the next day. No, it wouldn't be enough just to ski respectably. People are counting on me, he thought. I don't want to let them down.

He and Linda were getting ready for bed when she said, "Are you nervous?"

"Not really," Kyle said. "I probably won't start to get nervous until I get into the starting gate tomorrow."

Then the Cowboy Skier lay down in bed and began reading a dog-eared paperback copy of *Lonesome Dove*, Larry McMurtry's epic novel of the American West. Kyle enjoyed reading about Lonesome Dove and its funny, fearsome, hard-drinking inhabitants. In one passage, McMurtry describes a sign that Gus McCrae painted to advertise his cattle and livery business. When Kyle got to that page he laughed and told Linda, "Hey, listen to this."

He read aloud: "For rent: Horses and rigs . . . For sale: Cattle and horses . . . Goats and donkeys neither bought nor sold . . . We don't rent pigs." He and Linda both got a kick out of that.

A few minutes later, Kyle turned off the light and fell quickly and easily asleep. He wasn't worrying about representing his country in the Olympics in the morning. Instead, he was still smiling about the idea of pig rentals.

AJ Kitt's alarm woke him up at 7:30 on the morning of the Olympic downhill. He didn't feel nervous, or even excited. Today was just another day at the office. He knew, of course, that several hundred million people would be watching what he did at the office, but it didn't concern him. He really didn't care. For breakfast he ate pancakes, French toast, and a bowl of Sugar Pops (he had found a box of the sweet cereal in a store in Val d'Isère). He didn't speak to anyone at the breakfast table—not because he was trying to concentrate, but simply because he tended to be a little grumpy in the morning. After breakfast he watched video with Bill Egan. They discussed technique for a while, and then AJ went to his room to get dressed for the race, as he would on any other day. He wore the same things he always wore, with one exception: AJ's aunt had sent him a pair of white cotton underwear on which she had written the number thirteen, his lucky number, and the words, "Kick some butt." The shorts were a little too big, but AJ wore them anyway.

AJ skied from the Club Med to the chair lift at the bottom of the downhill course. He was on the hill for inspection three hours before race time. It was too early, in his opinion. He didn't need the whole morning to get ready. An hour would have been fine. AJ liked to take a few warmup runs, get into the starting gate, and punch it. But this was a Big Event, as grand and overdone as a royal wedding, so everybody was given lots of time to stand around. He took a run on the hill next to the course, then took the lift to the back side of the mountain and skied on the old downhill course, the site of his World Cup victory just two months before. Another athlete might have found some meaning, some inspiration, in that. Another athlete might have remembered how it had felt to win on the old course, and might have imagined how appropriate, how perfect, really, it would be to win on the Olympic course in the same season.

AJ didn't think those things. He just skied to the bottom and got on the lift.

He got to the start an hour early. Sylvanno Stoppani was already there. Stoppani, a former ski technician, was the European representative for Bula, an American company that marketed hilariously ugly hats and headbands for skiers. (Bula is a Fijian word meaning, roughly, "I wish you health, happiness, and prosperity, dude.") Bula, based in Durango, Colorado, wasn't the official clothing sponsor for any ski team, so it promoted itself by sending Stoppani to ski races to give things away. He was easy to spot: He was the tall, bearded guy wearing the multicolored cloth top hat with an imitation lamb's wool brim. (The hat looked like something the Cat in the Hat might have worn on a wild night out.) The American racers weren't supposed to wear Bula things in public—the ski team's official headwear sponsor was Conte de Florence—but they often did anyway. They liked the wacky, free-spirited Bula look. The day of the Olympic downhill, Stoppani showed AJ a bagful of hats and headbands, and invited him to come to his hotel later to take his pick of them.

Right on the Edge of Crazy

The television camera people followed AJ as he loosened up. He didn't pay any attention to them. Reporters had been hounding him all week; he was tired of them. "Vultures," he called them. AJ could tell from their questions that many of them didn't know anything about ski racing. After every training run, at least one reporter had asked him if he was disappointed that he had not come in first. God, that was infuriating. Every time he heard the question he felt like saying, "No, you idiot, I'm not." But he didn't say that. Instead, he took a deep breath and patiently explained that he didn't care where he placed in training runs; they were just for practice. The journalists made even more egregious mistakes in print. Recently he had seen a newspaper article that referred to Franz Heinzer as Mr. Second. That drove AJ crazy. Everybody knew that Heinzer's nickname, at least before he started winning all the time, was Franz the Fourth. In a way, AJ felt it was great to have all these people come to France to write stories about him. But in another way it was insulting. By deigning to appear only at the Olympics, the reporters seemed to be saying the rest of his career didn't matter. Who cared if he was first in Val d'Isère and second in Kitzbühel? The Olympics were a Big Deal; nothing else was.

AJ didn't buy that. In his opinion, the Olympics were a big deal mostly because the media said they were. Was this race really more important because M&M Mars had paid a lot of money to sponsor it and CBS had sent a thousand people to cover it? AJ didn't think so. At nineteen, he had gone to the 1988 Olympic downhill expecting it to be special, different from any other ski race. But he had seen that it wasn't any different. In Calgary, he had competed against the same guys he saw every week on the World Cup circuit. And he had seen that everything else—the jazzy, moving opening ceremonies and the dense thicket of journalists in the finish—was just decoration. Well, he felt the same way now. When he left the starting gate this morning, he would be competing against Franz Heinzer and Patrick Ortlieb and Marc Girardelli, the way he did every week. If the CBS camera people wanted to watch him stretch his legs beforehand, that was their business. He didn't care. He was thinking about the course now, about the line he would take. He knew the course so well now that it seemed he could envision every little bump and rut. That wasn't necessarily a good thing. AJ was tired of the Face de Bellevarde. He had skied it four times in three days, which was more times than he wanted to ski any downhill course. AJ generally got bored with a course after his third run, so he was past being sick of this one. Still, he wanted to do well, and felt he could. He stayed focused, going over the course in his mind one last time. When he got into the gate, he would be ready. He'd be psyched.

The race began on time at 12:15 P.M. Patrick Ortlieb, the six-foot four-inch Austrian, skied first. Ortlieb, twenty-four, the guy who had changed the position of a gate in Wengen, had a lot of fans in France. His father was a native of Strasbourg, France, who had moved to Austria, married a local woman, and opened a resort hotel. Patrick had grown up with dual citizenship in Austria and France. French ski officials, impressed with his skills, had once invited him to ski for his father's homeland, but Patrick had declined, saying he was Austrian through and through. As good as Ortlieb was, nobody expected him to win the gold medal in Albertville. He was a classic downhiller, a big, powerful, daring skier who did well at high speeds. But the turny, quirky Olympic course favored great technical racers, nimble little guys like Günter Mader, Marc Girardelli, and Markus Wasmeier, who had stolen off with Ortlieb's victory in Garmisch. This wasn't a downhiller's downhill. That was the talk, anyway. Well, Ortlieb apparently didn't hear any of the talk, because he popped out of the starting gate and skied a near-perfect race, finishing in 1:50.37, the fastest time of the week. Wasmeier, racer number two, finished a quarter of a second behind him. None of the next six racers—Hansjoerg Tauscher, Daniel Mahrer, Lasse Arnesen, Jan Einar Thorsen, Xavier Gigandet, and Brian Stemmle—came as close. Number nine, 1980 Olympic champion Leonhard Stock, lost control in the tower turn. He crashed through a gate, bounced off the fence, and sheared off another panel with his rib cage. Berni Huber and Helmut Höflehner, numbers ten and eleven, finished way back.

Franz Heinzer was racer number twelve. Like Ortlieb, Heinzer was a classic downhiller—big, sleek, fearless. But because of his brilliant performance so far that year, most people expected him to win a medal, and, having done poorly in Calgary, he desperately wanted one. Heinzer skied well, but not perfectly: When he threw his skis sideways in the finish and looked up at the scoreboard, Franz found he was . . . fourth! Franz the Fourth! Oh, he was pissed. Heinzer yanked his helmet off and flung it to the ground. *Shisdreck!* Brian Stemmle, the affable Canadian, was standing right next to Heinzer, chuckling at his frustration. Stemmle extended his helmet as if to say, "Want to spike mine, too?" Poor Franz. Patrick Ortlieb was still in first place.

AJ, racer number fifteen, knew nothing of Heinzer's fury. A few minutes before his starting time he stepped into his bindings and moved toward the shack. Gary Myers, the physical therapist, rubbed his legs. Meanwhile, Kristian Ghedina and Günther Mader, numbers thirteen and fourteen, blasted out of the starting shack, but neither managed to catch Ortlieb. AJ was next. If he could beat the Austrian, he had a good chance of hanging onto the gold medal. He cleared the fog from his goggles, ran in place, jiggled his shoulders, tapped his poles together three times. At 12:43 P.M. he leaned out of the start and tipped the timing wand. With a grunt he was gone.

He got a lot of air off the first jump, and took it in his usual way: knees together and tucked into his chest, index fingers pointing at the snow, poles trailing behind him like the tail of a comet. He made a mistake, a small one, in the high-speed left turn at the bottom of the first pitch: His upper body rotated to the left so that his shoulders turned uphill instead of downhill. A moment later, in the left turn before the tower corner, his weight shifted briefly so that his right ski, which should have been riding the snow, kicked out to the side in a sort of jazz dance step. Again, it was a minor mistake. Neither error concerned him much. You could make that sort of mistake and still win.

AJ skied the tower turn well, leaving plenty of space between himself and the fence. But then he made another mistake: In the end of the one-hundred-eighty-degree left turn, his upper body got twisted again, and again he lost some speed. Could he make up the time? In CBS's broadcast of the race that evening, commentator Andy Mill said, "He's got to ski perfectly in the most difficult sections of the course. I just don't think he's going to be able to do it."

AJ skied cleanly through the rocks. When he flew off the finish jump, his right hand got behind him for an instant; when he tried to bring it back, it spun in circles, a jet propeller blasting him forward. He landed cleanly and fell into his tuck, ducking his head almost between his knees. He tucked under the finish banner and he thought, OK, that was a solid run, I didn't make any major mistakes, it was a good effort, maybe I'll win. He zipped past his shouting parents, past a passel of flapping American flags, into the womb of the finish corral. He stood, spread his arms, and turned his long skis sideways, kicking up a cloud of snow into which he disappeared, the magician's final flourish.

On the side of the hill, near the big silver torch bearing the flickering Olympic flame, the scoreboard said: 1:51.98. 8. Eighth place.

Eighth? It was always a surprise to turn and see where you had finished: In a sport where the difference between winning and not winning was measured in hundredths of a second, no athlete could tell, as he wheezed beneath the banner, exactly where he had placed. Even when AJ felt he skied brilliantly, as he did in Val d'Isère and in the second race in Kitzbühel, he was never sure that the sensation would be matched by the result. The scoreboard always surprised you, no matter what it said. It flattered you, too, partly because it talked about you, only you. This time the scoreboard flattered and did not flatter him. Eighth? AJ felt the usual thrill of discovery, of finding out, followed by the moment of common disappointment that athletes, and other people, know: He wasn't first. He didn't win. It wasn't a miracle.

He stepped out of his skis and rested them against his shoulders so the cameras could read the brand name. He unzipped his turtleneck, took off his helmet. His head steamed. He took a moment to catch his breath and collect his thoughts. Eighth. It wasn't bad, really. It wasn't bad at all. He hadn't won, it wasn't a miracle, but he had skied well. He had taken chances. Some had worked out and some hadn't: That was how chances worked. Eighth was a good finish.

As he stood and thought about it, Franck Piccard of France, number twenty-three, finished a thrilling second, winning the silver medal. Piccard, who had won the super G gold medal in Calgary, did a little dance, and France went crazy. Meanwhile, Patrick Ortlieb began accepting congratulations on the gold medal. Nobody would beat him today.

AJ was in ninth place now. OK, fine, he thought. Eighth, ninth, what did it matter? He had still placed in the top ten, which was better than most knowledgeable people thought he would do. A year ago, no one had considered him a threat on the Face de Bellevarde. He was a glider, and this was not a glider's course. That had been the talk, anyway. So much for the talk. In case anyone doubted it after Val d'Isère and Kitzbühel, this would prove that he was a real skier, one of the best. Ninth: It was good. It wasn't a victory, but it was . . . well, it was about what he had expected. To win against this sort of competition you had to ski perfectly, but AJ didn't expect perfection. It wasn't realistic. He was too pragmatic to believe you could go out and ski a perfect run just because it was the Olympic downhill and CBS was covering it and his parents were wearing AJ Kitt Fan Club sweatshirts and America was sitting home, hoping for a Touching Story. The people at home cared only about the results, but AJ cared about something more than that. He was concerned mostly with the race itself—the way his edges held in the turns, how closely he followed the line, how well he maintained his tuck, the way his gut felt when he got air, the burning in his thighs in the finish schuss. The result was secondary. You did the best you could, and you got whatever you got. If he had finished first, he gladly would have accepted the gold medal and the endorsement deals and the guest spot on the Carson show. He hadn't finished first, but he had skied well and enjoyed himself. Everything had gone according to the program. I didn't lose, AJ thought. I just didn't win.

A moment after his run, Hank Kashiwa of CBS asked him to sum it up.

"It's a difficult course, real turny, and if you make a few mistakes and you're out of it. I'm pretty satisfied with my skiing," AJ said. And then, in deference to the folks watching at home, he evoked a subject he knew they were all thinking about—the 1994 Olympics in Lillehammer, Norway. The games were being held in two years instead of the usual four so the winter Olympics would no longer clash with the summer games.

"I'll get 'em in two years, I guess."

The Canadian racers finished the week as they had begun it: in pain. Brian Stemmle, his shoulder still sore, ended up twenty-third, and Felix Belczyk finished eighteenth, a letdown for someone of his talents. But at least he finished. Cary Mullen missed the second-to-last gate and was disqualified. And Roman Torn crashed in the rocks.

Nor did Marc Girardelli, the one-man team from Luxembourg, get the Olympic medal he had worked so hard for: He crashed halfway through the course, then squatted, put his head between his knees, and cursed his luck.

Girardelli was just skiing off the course when Tommy Moe, number twenty-one, zipped by. Tommy had been thinking about the race at these games for several years, and for good reason: This was a technical skier's course, and he was considered a fine technical skier. His ski company, Dynastar, had designed skis just for this course; his hero, Girardelli, was using the same kind of skis. Tommy, whose father and stepmother were watching in the finish, got nervous and made a few more mistakes than he would have liked. He ended up finishing twentieth. He felt he could have done better. And yet he was only twenty-one years old; he had a chance to ski in at least two more Olympic downhills. For Tommy, there would be other opportunities. He would put this one down to experience.

Reggie Crist, number twenty-four, had his skis on and was set to go when Tommy finished. He felt strange—not ill, just weird. He had awakened that morning with an odd feeling that would not go away. Nothing was the way it usually was. For one thing, Reggie usually didn't see so many people at the starting gate. Who were all these people? They couldn't all be press, could they? For another, his mother, father, and girlfriend weren't usually standing in the finish, wringing their hands and muttering, "Come on, Reg. Come on." But they were doing that now; Reggie thought his dad was more excited than he was. And several hundred million people around the world usually weren't watching on TV. Just that morning, Reggie had received another fax from his cousin. Scott said he had seen Reggie interviewed on CBS after the last training run, and wished him luck in the race. Reggie thought, Wow. People really are watching, aren't they? (As it turned out, America never saw him race: In preparing the tape of the downhill for broadcast that night, CBS edited out his run. The stingy network announced where he finished and that was it.) Even Reggie's new red downhill suit felt funny on him. All week long, he had tried to convince himself that this was just another race. But it wasn't, was it? The Olympic games really were different, weren't they? You could tell yourself it was just another race all you wanted, but every time you turned around something reminded you that you were wrong. This race was a Big Deal. At least it seemed that way to Reggie.

Now it was his turn to race. Reggie slid into the starting gate, listened for the beeping of the timing device, and pushed out. Gary Myers yelled, "Go go go go!" Reggie glided around the first gate, then skied straight toward the first big jump. He skied much straighter and faster toward the takeoff point than he had done in training. With a *fwoosh* he took flight. It was some flight. Reggie got so much air that he looked down and thought, Yow! Curtis Bacca, the Head ski technician, later told him, "I almost shit my pants when I saw how high you were." But Reggie wasn't scared up there, just surprised. And pleased. I really went for it, he told himself. For the first time all day, he felt good, as if things were going his way. And then he skied into the tower turn. As he had done in training on Friday, he skied too low in the turn. He thought, Well, this isn't where I want to be. No, it sure wasn't. Now he had to ski slightly uphill to avoid whacking the next gate. In training the day before, he had gained speed in that section. Today he lost speed. I'm not having my best run, he thought.

Reggie took a lot of chances after that, but every chance he took turned into a new mistake. When he tried to make up time by taking a straight line through a turn, he got thrown off balance and lost time instead. Nothing worked. By the time he skied through the rocks Reggie was thinking, It's not happening for me today. I'm fucked. It was true; he was fucked. Reggie hopped off the finish jump and tucked under the banner. He ended up twenty-eighth. As he stood and looked at the scoreboard, he wished he could take the lift back to the top and take the run over. Never mind that first run. He could do much better. That was the hell of it—he knew he could do better. But nothing could be done for Reggie now. He'd had his chance. After the race, his family was supportive. His dad congratulated him and said sincerely that he was proud, and his girlfriend hugged and kissed him. Reggie's mother, who had arrived just in time for the race, gave him a necklace bearing lots of little icons that were meant to bring him good luck and positive energy. So what if the race was over? It was just a ski race. As far as Diane Crist was concerned, it always helped to have good luck and positive energy.

For Reggie, the Olympics were over. He wouldn't be competing in the combined or the super G. He had been given one chance, one glorious chance, and he had . . . choked. He didn't sugarcoat the truth. I choked, he told himself. It was true. He had gotten so distracted by the hype and the pomp and the glamour that he sort of forgot to ski race. He couldn't believe it. Reggie had always considered himself a good big-event skier. In the junior ranks, and later at the American national championships, he had always skied up to his ability. He had just assumed he would do the same at the Olympics. Oh, it pissed him off to think that he hadn't. And yet . . . And yet it was part of Reggie's character to find something good in every experience, no matter how unhappy, and he managed to do that even now. He had choked, yes, but he didn't think he had failed. The knock against Reggie had always been that he didn't take risks, didn't lay it on the line. Well, he had laid it on the line at the Olympics. He had flown high enough off that first jump to scrape his purple downhill helmet on the blue shell of the sky. He had taken risks after that, too. They hadn't made him any faster, but at least he had taken them. Downhill racing had a way of revealing people's personalities. The sport had always shown Reggie to be a nice guy, and maybe a slightly timid guy too. But the Olympic downhill had changed him. In the Olympic downhill, Reggie had not been timid. Not particularly fast, but not timid.

Part of the fun of watching the Olympic downhill was seeing the racers who really had no business being in it. Of the fifty-six men who competed in the race that afternoon, a half dozen were rarely seen on the World Cup circuit. These were people who competed in the Olympics just for kicks, and so their countries would have a representative. Among them were Lotharchristian Munder of Brazil, Hubertus Von Hohenlohe of Mexico, Hee Choi Yong of Korea, and Emilian Focseneanu and Aurel Foiciuc of Romania. But by far the most beloved characters were Lamine Gueye and Alfonse Gomis of Senegal, Africa.

The two Senegalese, who taught skiing in nearby Tignes, France, didn't try to attack the Face de Bellevarde as much as just survive it. They skied down standing bolt upright, their arms thrown out wide as if they wanted to grab onto something and stop. They did not have to worry about getting hurt catching air because they usually didn't carry enough speed into the jumps to get any. It did not really matter how they skied; they were at the Olympics for laughs, mostly other people's. They signed autographs, gave interviews, and partied late into the night. One evening, Lamine Gueye poked his head into the room where the Americans were holding their team meeting. Someone asked him, "Where did you guys train?"

"For this?" he said.

"Yeah."

"The discos, man."

On race day, they proved it. Gomis, a small man who looked terrified every time he got into the starting gate, caught an edge in the first steep pitch, ten seconds into the course. His legs split apart, came together again, then split apart again. He got turned around backward, then fell. He tumbled at least two hundred yards, leaving behind a trail of equipment. When he finally stopped sliding he took an inventory of body parts and declared himself unhurt.

Gueye, the team captain, was no threat for a medal either. He skied like a man with no health insurance, finishing DFL, forty-fifth out of forty-five finishers, twenty-two and a half seconds behind Ortlieb. But hey, at least he finished. Some of the greatest racers in the world didn't.

About an hour before he was scheduled to race, Kyle Rasmussen met Curtis Bacca, the Head ski technician, at the start.

Kyle said, "You fired up?"

"Yeah, I'm fired up. Are you?"

"Yeah," the racer said. He added, "I'm going to go take a nap."

It was the only way he could think of to relax. Earlier that season, Kyle, a Los Angeles Raiders fan, had read Bo Jackson's autobiography, *Bo Knows Bo*. Jackson said he liked to go to sleep in the locker room for a few minutes before every football game. If it works for Bo, Kyle thought, why not for me? Besides, Kyle's aching back felt better when he lay down. He went into a building near the start and stretched out on a bench. He didn't fall asleep, but his heart stopped hammering and his breathing smoothed out. Some of the other racers saw him lying there and gave him funny looks.

Kyle had had quite a morning. His alarm clock had sounded before 7:00 A.M. He hadn't wanted to get up. His bed at Hotel La Becca was comfortable and warm, and his wife, Linda, was next to him, snoozing. Outside, the rising sun cast a quiet purple light on the mountains. Kyle had stayed still for a moment, relaxing, almost nodding off. And then he'd thought: Hey, today's the Olympic downhill. What am I doing in bed? He got up, dressed, kissed Linda goodbye, and headed for breakfast at Club Med.

During inspection he had thought, Geez, I'm not very nervous, considering this is the day of the Olympic downhill. Those words—this is the Olympic downhill—came to him again and again as he sideslipped the course. Kyle was not about to pretend this was just another race. It wasn't, and he figured he might as well be honest about it. And yet it didn't scare him, which was curious: He had always assumed this day would make him stiff with fear.

Kyle had finally gotten jittery after inspection. He took a few practice runs on the slope next to the downhill—the trail where he had trained for the super G the week before—and felt himself growing impatient. The morning seemed to go on forever. Once, Kyle rode the chair lift with Matt Grosjean, the American slalom and giant slalom skier.

"Well," Kyle said, "this is it. The Olympic downhill."

Grosjean could tell his teammate was nervous: Kyle kept yawning. It was the only way he could draw a deep breath.

"That's good," Grosjean told him. "Release that tension." Then he clapped Kyle on the back and said, "I got faith in you, man, even if you don't have faith in yourself." That was when Kyle had gone to the start to see Curtis Bacca and take his nap.

He rested for a few minutes, then went outside, stretched, and stepped into his bindings. It was time. Bacca wiped the bottoms of his skis. Kyle slid into the starting gate behind Paul Accola. The Swiss racer disappeared down the hill, and Kyle glided forward until his boots nearly touched the thin wand that would trigger the clock. He jammed his poles into the snow as if spearing a fish in a creek. He looked down the hill. Gary Myers, the physical therapist, stood next to him.

"Ten seconds," the starter said.

OK, Kyle thought. OK. OK.

Then he heard a voice in Myers's radio. Ueli Luthi's voice. "Accola's down."

So what? Kyle thought. One less guy to beat.

"Five seconds," the starter said. "Three, two, one . . ."

Kyle lunged forward . . . but he didn't go anywhere. He couldn't move. Somebody had him around the waist, and somebody else was shouting, "No! No! No! No!" Kyle thought, What the . . . ? He couldn't figure out what was happening. It took him a moment to get his senses. He looked around. Gary Myers and Curtis Bacca were bear-hugging him, holding him in the gate. Harald Schoenhaar, the official in charge of the start, was there with them, looking stricken.

"There's a hold!" Myers said. "Accola's down. There's a hold on the course."

Accola had whacked the net in the tower turn—the same red plastic fence Leonhard Stock had hit. He wasn't hurt, but the course workers needed some time to pick up his ski and replace a gate he had knocked down. Kyle would have to wait.

In the start, Myers and Bacca were worried about Kyle. He had been ready to blast off when they had aborted the mission. Wouldn't it freak him out? It had to at least rattle him some. And yet Kyle didn't seem upset. They kept asking him if he was all right, and he said, "Yeah, I'm fine." Indeed, he was more than fine. He was pleased. Kyle didn't say it, but as he stood there waiting to begin the most important downhill run of his life, he was thinking, This is great! With Accola out, TV will show my whole run! I'll get full coverage! Like Reggie, he was wrong: CBS showed only the bottom part of his run. But he had no way of knowing that then. He was thrilled. Now he would show people who he was.

He took off. He screamed off the steep first pitch and made a big mistake: He started his left turn way too late and ended up skiing out near the pine boughs. If the course had been a highway, he would have gone through the guardrail. Again he thought of Bo Jackson. Bo wrote that he woke up from his pregame nap only after he got tackled for the first time. That lousy turn awakened Kyle. He said to himself, Hey! Pay attention! This is the Olympic downhill! Get going!

He did, but it didn't feel good. God, he said to himself as he tucked toward the rock tunnel, you're not going very fast. But keep going. Keep going. He made a good turn through the rocks and sped down the last pitch. In the last, long right turn, he set the edge of his ski, lowered his shoulders, and thought, I hope I look good on TV. He really thought that. If he was going to ski in front of the whole world, he wanted to look sharp. He jetted off the finish jump and tucked toward the banner, his skis swimming across the snow.

Before the race Kyle had told himself, No matter what happens, be proud. You're an Olympian. When you get to the finish, be proud. His parents had come all the way from California to see him ski, and he intended to look proud no matter what. Now, as he skied under the banner and began his skid, he told himself, I didn't ski well, but OK, fine, I'm proud.

He turned and looked at the scoreboard.

It said: 15.

Hey! he thought. He pumped his right fist in the air. Gary Myers and Curtis Bacca, watching on TV from the top of the hill, went nuts, jumping around and high-fiving each other. Seeing this, some of the European coaches got alarmed because they thought Kyle had won.

Fifteenth! In the Olympic downhill! Kyle was still hyperventilating when Italy's Gianfranco Martin, racer number thirty, came down and moved him back to sixteenth place. But so what? He'd take it! It was his best downhill of the season by far. And what a day for it! He had beaten some of the best guys in the world. He had outrun Tommy and Reggie, too. AJ had finished only three-quarters of a second ahead of him. Kyle could live with that. Maybe he did have a wife and a kid and practically no hair and a bad back, but he could still ski. That'll show 'em, he thought. The team veteran, indeed! The end of my career, indeed! Maybe now he would get some publicity, too.

He made sure of it. After the race, Kyle lingered in the interview area much longer than usual. Instead of waiting for the reporters to approach him, he approached them. He talked to CBS and a Denver TV station and USA Today and anybody else he could find who spoke English. And he enjoyed it! In thirty minutes he probably exceeded his output of words for the previous week. After that he signed autographs for lots of French boys and girls and posed for pictures with giddy American tourists. His wife and parents were waiting for him near the chair lift, but that was all right; they could wait. This was Kyle's chance to be recognized, and he didn't know when the next opportunity might come.

The attention from his family was even more overwhelming. Kyle's wife and his mother just bubbled over. And Kyle could hardly believe the look of admiration he got from his father. Before the race, Clayton Rasmussen hadn't been able to stand still; he had paced around as if he were looking for something and had to find it in a hurry. Now, though, he was misty-eyed; Kyle wasn't sure he'd ever seen him like that. After lunch at Club Med, Kyle went to Linda's hotel room at La Becca and called his brothers in California. He woke them up. Greg, the one who had been so tough on him, said, "So you finally let 'em run, huh?" Thinking about it later, Kyle would say, "It kind of chokes you up inside, almost. You're almost shedding tears."

That night he thought about his cattle-rancher grandfather, Bill Airola, and tried to imagine what would happen the next time he saw him.

"Congratulations," Kyle supposed he would say. "You want to help me gather some cows tomorrow?"

Back in the United States, Bill Hudson was oblivious. The day of the 1992 Olympic downhill was supposed to be the greatest day of his life, the day he proved he was the fastest ski racer alive. Because of the time difference, the race was over by the time Bill got out of bed that morning in Utah. But he made no effort to find out who had won; he didn't call the ski team offices or turn on the TV to look for the results. He simply ate breakfast, got dressed, and went to the gym to work out. Meanwhile, in France, AJ was still describing his run for friends and family, and Patrick Ortlieb—Hudson's friend and colleague on the Head ski team— was still basking in victory. Later that day, someone mentioned to Bill that Patrick had won and AJ had placed ninth. "Hey, great," Bill managed to say.

But when CBS showed the race on TV that night, he did not watch. If he couldn't be there, he didn't care to see.

16

The Finish

After the downhill, everything else seemed anticlimactic. Such was the nature of downhill. Kyle skied well enough in the downhill part of the combined to have an outside chance at a medal, but he nearly fell in the first run of the slalom and that was that. AJ didn't finish the combined. He tweaked his leg going off the finish jump in the downhill, so he decided not to bother with the slalom. He had no chance at a medal. Why ski in pain just so he could finish eighteenth? In the super G, Silvain DaoLena's and Bill Egan's grand scheme for the French and American teams did not pay off: Kjetil Andre Aamodt of Norway won the gold, Luxembourg's Marc Girardelli the silver (he later got another silver in the giant slalom), and Norwegian Jan Einar Thorsen the bronze. Jeff Olson was thirteenth, which took some of the sting out of missing the downhill.

The downhillers competed in several more World Cup races after the Olympics, but to them the games still felt like an ending to the story. That was inevitable. Ever since their encouraging finishes in Val d'Isère and Val Gardena in December 1990, the downhillers had been looking forward to the Albertville Olympics as their chance at glory. The timing worked perfectly: They would spend the two seasons constantly improving and go to the Olympics at their competitive peak. Then they would show the world what they could really do. The games would be the culmination of all their work, the reward for their efforts and sacrifices.

And yet the two World Cup seasons leading to the Olympics hadn't turned out to be the steady schuss to greatness they'd hoped for. Instead, each season had developed its own distinct and memorable theme. The first season had been about loss. The trouble had been foreshadowed by Bill Hudson's concussion in Val d'Isère. Things had started to go wrong in earnest with a series of comical spills and foul-ups in Garmisch. After that, loss had become a sinister presence, a sullen figure who sent the athletes the wrong way off jumps and steered them toward treacherous holes in the snow. Failure had traveled everywhere with the downhillers after that hurtful week in Kitzbühel. It had ridden in the back of the team van, sneering and farting, and they had not been able to cope. Ultimately, their failure to cope with losing had become as debilitating as the losing itself. The downhillers had piled disaster upon disaster until finally they couldn't see over the top. Every one of them, even AJ, had finished the season wondering what had gone wrong.

The second World Cup season, the one right before the Olympics, had been different. It had been about victory, or maybe a more exact word is hope. AJ had been the only one who actually pocketed prize money, but the rest of the team had benefited too. The skiers traveled as a group for reasons other than convenience; they did it so they could watch and learn from each other. Well, they had learned something from AJ's success. After his win in Val d'Isère in 1991, they had quit thinking of themselves as losers, klutzes who crashed and knocked their heads against things. They had started believing in themselves a little bit.

But of course, downhill isn't really a team sport. Each guy was in it for himself, and each got something different out of it. What Todd Kelly got out of his first World Cup year was experience, which was what he needed most. He learned how to live for months in Europe, how to jump the camels in Val Gardena and how to ski the S-turns in Wengen. He spent the season with the also-rans; now, with his experience, he could pick up speed. Unfortunately, experience sometimes hurts. After the Olympics, the team competed in a World Cup race in Panorama, Canada. During one training run, the sun was hot and the snow slushy. When Todd started down the hill he thought, Man, we shouldn't be training today. But of course he pressed on. About a minute and twenty seconds into the run, he caught an edge and flew the wrong way off a jump, right at a net. Todd's last clear thought was: No problem. I'll land close to the net, make a sharp left turn, and everything will be fine.

He hit the net on the fly. He wound up in a heap, his skis and poles all over the place. After he figured out who and where he was, Todd looked down and saw that his right hand was hanging from his arm at a strange angle. It looked as if somebody had taken it off and reattached it the wrong way. The X-rays showed he had broken his wrist in fifteen places—shattered it, really. A few days later, a doctor rebuilt it with three steel pins. The surgery scar circled Todd's wrist like a bracelet, a permanent souvenir of his first year as a big-league downhiller.

AJ also had a profound learning experience in Panorama, proving you can never be too good to learn something by screwing up. On the last day of training, the unthinkable happened: He missed a gate near the bottom of the course. For AJ, it was a disaster. He felt it was essential to ski well the day before the race—to have the course "dialed in," as he put it. Missing gates was not part of the program. He went to sleep that night pissed off, and worried. The next morning, he got something new to worry about. When AJ arrived at the start, Rossignol ski representative Edi Waldburger, the man who prepared his skis, wasn't there, and neither were the skis. AJ couldn't believe it. Edi, a Swiss, was normally so dependable, so highly professional, that AJ and his teammates called him "Super Rep." AJ liked to boast that Edi had only made two mistakes in all the time he had known him, and neither one had made any difference. This was Edi's third mistake, and it was a doozy. It was also a test of AJ's concentration. Several racers left the starting gate, but still Edi did not show up. To hell with it, AJ said to himself. I'll race in my training skis. His training skis were too short for downhill (they were meant for super G), and they hadn't been properly waxed and sharpened. But what choice did he have? When AJ clicked them on, there was a buzz in the start. He could hear the murmur: Kitt's going to race in his super G skis. Can you believe it? About five minutes before he was supposed to race, Super Rep appeared, breathless. He had misunderstood when the race would start. Edi, always the professional, did not say he was sorry; he just did his job. Nor did AJ ask Edi where in hell he had been. He simply stepped into the skis and slid into the starting gate. In an instant he was gone.

At one time, AJ would have panicked in this situation. Just a year earlier, he had had problems getting to the start at Lake Louise; as a result, he had lost his concentration and crashed in the first turn. This time he kept his head. Stay focused, he told himself as he left the start. So what if you missed a gate yesterday? Forget Edi's mistake. Think about the turns. AJ made a few mistakes, but no serious ones. He skied fairly well through the turny section and finished fourth, not far behind the winner, Switzerland's William Besse. Now that was a thrill. Next to winning in Val d'Isère and almost winning in Kitzbühel, it was the biggest thrill of the season. "I really showed myself something that day," AJ said later. Right. He showed himself he could ad-lib a race and still perform well. AJ did even better the next day, finishing third. He finished the World Cup season third in the overall downhill standings, behind Franz Heinzer and Daniel Mahrer. That wasn't going to hurt his endorsement deals any.

While AJ kept finding new ways to improve, Tommy Moe just spun his wheels. His results in Panorama were mediocre at best. But that was only part of the problem; his real frustration went much deeper than that. After two difficult seasons, Tommy was pretty much the same racer he'd been when he started. Sure, he had skied well on occasion and he had gained useful experience. But he hadn't come close to reaching his goals of finishing in the top ten in a World Cup race or joining AJ in the first seed in downhill. He hadn't accomplished much at the Olympics either. When the 1992 season ended, Tommy was twenty-two years old, but in some ways he was still the same passive, tentative boy who had been known as little Tommy Moe. Tommy was a hilarious guy with a great attitude and tremendous athletic gifts. He was good enough to win; nobody doubted that. But so far, unlike AJ, he hadn't figured out how.

Jeff Olson's season had a happy ending. First, he had a couple of excellent results in World Cup super G races. Then he went to Aspen and notched his best World Cup downhill result of the year. Finally, he won the downhill at the U.S. Alpine Championships in Winter Park, Colorado. The course was ridiculously slow and flat—lots of inexperienced downhillers and even technical weenies skied it without difficulty—but Jeff didn't care; he was a winner again. He was also a little richer: His third national downhill title came with a $5,000 prize. "This pretty much washes the hard times away," he said after the race. God knows he had seen hard times. In the previous two seasons, Jeff had skied to hell and back. He had started out as a downhill star. Then he had spun around backward and ended up a complete basket case. Everybody had thought he was a goner. Finally, through sheer stubbornness and competitive desire, he had re-created himself as an excellent World Cup super G skier and a competent downhiller. Now he was a star again, or nearly a star, anyway. For Jeff, the lesson in all this was simple: Always ski facing downhill.

The downhillers and coaches went their separate ways after the nationals. Bill and Maggie Egan started building a home in Mammoth, California, Bill's favorite place in the world. Todd Kelly stayed home in Squaw Valley and recuperated from his hand injury; by early summer he felt well enough to go bungee jumping. Kyle Rasmussen returned to Angels Camp, California, where his grandfather congratulated him on a good season and then asked him to help him gather some cows. Jeff Olson spent the summer in Boston with an American woman he had met in France during the Olympics. Tommy Moe went home to Alaska to go kayaking, ride his mountain bike, and play tennis with his girlfriend, Megan Gerety. Reggie Crist attended the University of California in Santa Barbara, mostly because his girlfriend went to school there. Shortly after he arrived she decided to end the relationship; Reggie consoled himself by surfing and catching rays. He often spoke to Eric Keck, the huge Christian, who was also living in Southern California. Eric was attending Saddleback Community College, going to church, and working, for lack of a better job, as an exterminator. People occasionally asked him if he had any qualms about killing God's critters. "I can justify it scripturally," he would say. "God gave us dominion over the animals. They're meant to serve us. I'll step on an ant if it's my job. Or even if it's not my job." Eric's love of the Scripture had become so deep that he was considering becoming a pastor. He felt a need to plan for the future. He had married Beth Wacome, a pianist and singer, on New Year's Eve; now they were expecting their first child. The couple wanted as many children as God would give them.

If there was an opposite to Eric's pious, workaday life, AJ was living it. He spent the early part of the summer enjoying his money and celebrity. Shortly after the season ended, viewers of the cable sports network ESPN caught a glimpse of him at a tennis tournament near his grandparents' home in Florida; apparently he was famous enough now to get on TV just for watching sports. AJ declined an invitation to fly to Bangkok to be a judge in the Miss Universe pageant; he would have enjoyed

287

assessing all those women, but felt the trip would interrupt his training (AJ never quit working out, not even in the offseason). But he accepted an all-expenses-paid trip to a giant beach party in Myrtle Beach, South Carolina, where he served as resident mini-celebrity. If he continued to ski well, he could expect his life to be like this for a long time. McDonald's did not renew its headgear deal with him when the season ended, but his agent, Jon Franklin, was sure he could find another sponsor. A skier of AJ's caliber could expect to earn about five hundred thousand dollars a year in prize money and endorsements, according to Franklin.

AJ spent some time in his condominium in Boulder, Colorado, then rented it to a college professor and moved east. He bought a small lot on Rushford Lake, about an hour and a half from his parents' home in Rochester, and turned it into a waterskiing retreat for himself and his friends. He lived in an old mobile home and kept the phone number a secret. When he wasn't waterskiing, he lifted weights or rode one of his three motorcycles. He planned to replace the mobile home with a cottage at some point; the lake house would be his summer retreat. He still liked Boulder, and hoped to build a house in the foothills there someday. And of course he still dreamed of the buffalo ranch he would have when he retired from ski racing.

America's best downhiller didn't ski at all between mid-March and mid-June; it was the longest break he had taken in years. Then Bill Egan called and invited him to a brief training camp at Mt. Hood, Oregon. After spending so much time on water skis and on motorcycles, AJ wondered how it would feel to ski again. Three months was a long time. He had felt balanced and confident during the whole racing season; he wondered if he would still feel that way now. When he got to Mt. Hood and went cruising on his giant slalom skis, he knew nothing had changed. He skied gracefully, fluidly, as if he had never stopped. He enjoyed hearing the clatter of his skis and feeling the bite of the wind on his face. Waterskiing and motorcycling were fun, but nothing was more fun than this. Here, no engine pushed him and no boat pulled him; he was free. Great skiers move to a musical rhythm: four beats and a turn, four beats and a turn. AJ was an artist now, his skis riding like a bow over the string-like ripples in the ice. And yet skiing was never easy for him. The challenge was never-ending: You could ski all your life and never learn to do it perfectly. AJ liked that. He enjoyed learning about the sport, and about himself. That second thing was especially important. People play sports to see how they compare to others, sure, but that's only one of the reasons. They also do it to test themselves, to see what they alone are capable of doing. The important thing is not where you finish; it's who you are. When AJ was on skis, he was at his best—fast, confident, complete.

Bill Hudson lived with Kathrin Burkhart in Park City that summer. The year had ended disastrously: Both Reggie and Reggie's little brother Zach had beaten him in the nationals. He was so disgusted with himself at first that he considered announcing his retirement. Of all the downhillers, Bill was the only one whose career had actually gone backward. In 1990 he had been strong and sure; by 1992 he was frustrated and confused. But he didn't quit when the season was over, mainly because he knew he was too upset to make a decision like that right then. Instead, Bill began taking business courses at the University of Utah—"the U," as they call it in Salt Lake City. For the first time in months, he really enjoyed himself. In time, he began thinking about skiing again. All season, he had pretended that the crash in Kitzbühel had not affected his skiing, but of course it had. He could see that now. His body had recovered, but his mind never had. Well, maybe if he competed for one more season his mind would be all right. The more he thought about it, the more he knew he would like to go on ski racing. He was twenty-six years old now—not a kid, but not an old-timer either.

Early that summer he told Bill Egan he wanted to stay on the team. Hudson and Egan had a talk and patched up their friendship; they said they were sorry for the arguments they'd had during the season, and that was that. When the coaches met to choose the downhill team for the next season, Egan fought hard for Hudson and won.

"I've always thought that I would become the best," Hudson, as driven as ever, said that summer. "I've always thought that I had the talent and the motivation. I think it will be hard quitting if I don't become the best."

Every athlete's career ends in a sort of death. For Steve Porino, death did not come as a surprise. He went to the U.S. Alpine Championships knowing he had to ski well in the downhill to be invited back to the team for another season. But he did not, finishing in a tie for thirteenth. Instead of announcing his retirement right there, he went to Salt Lake

City and waited to see what the ski team would do. If the coaches did not want him back, they would have to tell him. They soon did. Bill Hudson's season had been bad, but Steve's had been worse; the team could not justify the expense of keeping him around. It hurt to hear those words; a punch in the stomach makes you feel sick even when you see it coming. Inevitably, Steve spent some time tallying up his losses. He had never competed in the Olympics or the Alpine World Championships. He had never won a World Cup race or even finished in the top fifteen. He had never won the American national downhill title. And—this one really hurt—he had not raced in Kitzbühel. Steve had carved his name in the side of the starting shack but had not skied out of it, had not earned a nasty scar as a result of a beautiful crash. He had served in the war but had not seen combat.

In a way, though, the end of his career came as a relief to Steve. He had grown weary of life on the road and even more so of not winning, and he was sure the coaches sensed that. It was time for him to begin the rest of his life, and the team's decision allowed him to do so. Steven "Jet Power" Porino was dead; long live Steve Porino. In September he would begin taking classes at the University of Utah. He was looking forward to being just another student, a regular guy. First, though, he wanted to have one last fling. Over the years, Steve had stashed away some of the money he had earned from his contracts with ski equipment companies. After the ski season, he and Kristina withdrew some cash and went on a long vacation. First they visited Taos, New Mexico, for a couple of weeks. Then they moved on to Lake Tahoe, California, and then to Maui. Hawaii's cool, sunny weather and fruity tropical drinks improved Steve's attitude even more: This was the vacation he had imagined the day he inspected the course at Kitzbühel, except he hadn't had to injure himself to take it.

In time, he stopped worrying about what he had lost as a ski racer, and started counting the things he had gained. For one, he had gotten to do exactly what he wanted to do for a long time. Most people, he knew, couldn't say that. Steve also felt he had gained a sense of adventure, a familiarity with risk. He had been a downhiller, and having been one he couldn't imagine himself ever taking the safe course through life. At the same time, he was mature enough to understand that every week would not culminate in some thrilling competition. "This is life, and there's not an award waiting at the end of every day," was how he put it. There were more gains, many more. He had met interesting people from all over the world. He had seen Europe (he hadn't liked it, but he'd seen it) and Scandinavia and South America. He had drunk beer in Germany and wine in France. He had ordered McDonald's hamburgers in several languages. Most of all he had skied downhill—not as fast as he had hoped, but still fast, scary-fast. He had absorbed the compression in Val d'Isère, zigzagged through the Aztec turns in Aspen, and skied through Hell in Garmisch.

And he had jumped the camels in Val Gardena. Now that was a memory. Like Todd and AJ and Jeff and the rest of his friends, Steve had first heard about the camels when he was a kid. And then he had gone and jumped them, had soared over them, his body in a ball and his skis floating on air. That was sweet, the sweetest thing of all. Yes, he had gotten something out of ski racing. In Val Gardena, Steve had gotten something rare and beautiful, something he would always keep.

Air.

Acknowledgments

When I called Bill Egan out of the blue in the fall of 1990 and told him I wanted to follow him and his athletes through the 1992 Olympics and record everything they said and did, he didn't hesitate at all. Sounds like a good idea to me, he said. He wanted exposure for his sport, and for his kids, that much. Ueli Luthi did too.

It could not have been easy to have me hanging around for the better part of two years, jotting things down and running my tape recorder, but Bill and Ueli handled it gracefully. In my first season with the team, Bill gave me a doctor's credential so I could get onto courses to watch training runs. "Here. You're a doctor," he said. In the second season, I was credentialed as a coach. At the Albertville games, Bill and Ueli got me a pass so I could go into the Olympic village to do interviews and attend team meetings. They helped me in so many ways I couldn't possibly list them all. Let me just say I could not have written this book without their support and cooperation.

The downhillers were equally unselfish. I'm grateful to AJ Kitt, Tommy Moe, Kyle Rasmussen, Reggie Crist, Jeff Olson, Todd Kelly, Eric Keck, and Steve Porino. Special thanks to Bill Hudson, who spent countless hours explaining the sport to me when I was first considering doing the book. I wish them all the best in whatever they do.

I was assisted by many others on the U.S. Ski Team. Maggie Egan was a great friend and researcher. The tireless Jim Tracy made my travel arrangements and kept track of the hotel bills so I could properly reim-

Acknowledgments

burse the team. He was also kind enough to share his room with me during the Olympics. Tim LaMarche was a fine drinking companion and roommate. Gary Myers did me a thousand favors. Dennis Agee, Curtis Bacca, Mike Decesaro, Edi Waldburger, Thor Kallerud, and Pat Savaria all helped in many ways. I'd also like to thank Tom Kelly, Jolene Aubel, Ron Goch, Lorri Sargeant, Keven Burnett, Brian Burnett, Steve "Lucky" Victorson, Gene "Topper" Hagerman, Deb LaMarche, Lester Keller, Horst Weber, Bruce Crane, David Kiefer, Courtney Brown, and Robert Higgins.

The following athletes sat for interviews or helped in other ways: Skip Merrick, Brett Grabowski, Zach Crist, Craig Thrasher, Bob Ormsby, Nate Bryan, Matt Grosjean, Jeremy Nobis, Kyle Wieche, Chris Puckett, Paul Casey Puckett, Joe Levins, and Megan Gerety. Also, many thanks to Ross and Nancy Kitt, Joe and Trilby Porino, Val Olson, Clayton and Ginger Rasmussen, Linda Rasmussen, Tom and Tyra Moe, Roger Crist, Diane Crist, and Sally Hudson.

Bruce Stoff, formerly of *Ski Racing* magazine, unselfishly offered help and advice when I was starting on the project. David Von Drehle, formerly of the *Miami Herald* and now of the *Washington Post*, introduced me to my agent, for which I can't thank him enough. And my friend Gary Pesso generously let me use his condo in Vail, Colorado, when I began doing research in November 1990.

I'd also like to acknowledge Rhonda Martyn, Joe Novello, Mark Schelde, Steve Melia, Mark Melia, Dan Shadoan, Andy Mill, John Sterling, Scott and Chris McPherson, Zane Dmytruk, Curtis Christian, Brad Roberts, Roman Torn, Dave Armstrong, Tim Murphy, Dominique and Beatrice Tempesta, Helmut Girardelli, Marc Girardelli, Dave Irwin, Bill Johnson, Jon Franklin, Caren Black, Madeline Haley, Danny Maddock, Gary Caskey, Sheree De La Hunt, Greg Bardin, Jeff Bardin, Mike Brown, Steve Pesso, Anna Joella Ankerlund, Florence Autret-Mouret, and the excellent press staff of America's Downhill in Aspen.

The *Miami Herald*, where I've worked for nine years, graciously gave me a leave of absence to travel with the skiers. Thanks to Dave Lawrence, Doug Clifton, Pete Weitzel, Susan Olds, Kenn Finkel, Liz Donovan, Gay Nemeti, Gene Miller, Bill Greer, Bill Rose, and especially Tom Shroder, who encouraged me from the start. My friend Christie Evans read an early draft and gave helpful advice. John Donnelly and Laura

Hambleton offered support, encouragement, and a place to stay during Hurricane Andrew. Curtis Morgan and Connie Ogle skied with me in Colorado and let me write in their kitchen when Andrew knocked out my power.

Henry Ferris is a marvelous editor and good friend. My agent, Esther Newberg, worked hard to make the project possible, and continued to be a great help throughout. I'm also grateful to Andrew Fabens and Amanda Beesley.

Finally, I'd like to thank my wife, Carol, and my son, Dyami, for their love and patience.

Miami, Florida
October 1992